VAIL LIBRARY
1 16 0002242703

D1042388

I'm Looking Through You

BY THE SAME AUTHOR

Remind Me to Murder You Later

The Planets

The Constellations

Getting In

She's Not There: A Life in Two Genders

I'm Looking Through You

GROWING UP HAUNTED

Jennifer Finney Boylan

Broadway Books, New York

PUBLISHED BY BROADWAY BOOKS

Published in the United States by Broadway Books, an imprint of The Doubleday Broadway Publishing Group, a division of Random House, Inc., New York.
www.broadwaybooks.com

BROADWAY BOOKS and its logo, a letter B bisected on the diagonal, are trademarks of Random House, Inc.

Parts of this book were first published, in much different form, in the *New York Times*.

Book design by Ralph Fowler / rlf design

Library of Congress Cataloging-in-Publication Data
Boylan, Jennifer Finney, 1958–
I'm looking through you : growing up haunted / Jennifer Finney Boylan. — 1st ed.
p. cm.
1. Boylan, Jennifer Finney, 1958—Childhood and youth. 2. Novelists, American—20th century—Biography. 3. Ghosts. I. Title.
PS3552.O914Z474 2008
813'.54—dc22

2007019199

ISBN: 978-0-7679-2174-9

PRINTED IN THE UNITED STATES OF AMERICA

10 9 8 7 6 5 4 3 2 1

First Edition

For my sister,

with love

The Coffin House, about 1925

So I'm wearing my footsteps into this floor
One day I won't live here anymore
Someone will wonder who lived here before
And went on their way

Something as simple as boys and girls
Gets tossed all around and then lost in the world
Something as hard as a prayer on your back
Can wait a long time for an answer

—Patty Griffin

Contents

Author's Note

Part I

Dirty Deeds 3
The Crystal Ball 19
Utopia 37
This Living Hand 52
You're Pathétique 70
I Got a Pretty Flower 81

Part II

Paranormal 107
The Monadology 118
Squeezebox 134
The Onion Patch 155
The Attic 169

Part III

All at One Point 181
Don We Now Our Gay Apparel 199
The Pearl 212
The Radiot 225
Reunion 239
Adagio 253

Acknowledgments 269

Author's Note

The events at the heart of this narrative took place a long time ago. While I have taken care to ensure accuracy whenever possible, in the end I cast my lot with Frank McCourt, who noted that a memoir is meant to be an impression of a life, and not a photograph. Since this is the story that I have chosen to tell and not necessarily the one that others would relate, given their druthers, all individuals appear in the story under pseudonyms; some have been obscured still further, in the hope of making them unrecognizable. The book contains no composite characters. The timeline has been expanded or contracted to suit the story's demands, and dialogue invented, in good faith, when memory failed. The story contains occasional elements of invention, in keeping with the facts of my life, not in order to shamelessly bamboozle the reader but in order to fill in gaps in the narrative, or to dramatize scenes that I did not witness firsthand.

The author may be contacted at JennyBoylan@aol.com, or through her publisher, Doubleday Broadway, a division of Random House, Inc.

I'm Looking Through You

PART I

Removing the tower, 1944

I'm serious, she said.
The only thing missing in this place is a dead body.

Dirty Deeds

I was in a biker bar. There were worse places. My colleagues, who had names like Lumpy and Gargoyle, thought no less of me simply because I was an English professor. *It's nothing to be ashamed of,* one dude suggested. *It's what's inside your heart that counts.*

The venue—the Astrid Hotel, in Astrid, Maine—was famous not only for the skankiness of its patrons but also for its ghost, an undead girl who walked its tattered hallways weeping in her pajamas. She'd drowned in the twenties, in the nearby Kennebec River. The girl was determined, supposedly, to find her father and her sister, who'd been guests of the hotel, back in the day. *Hey. Don't you know I can't swim?*

I had come to the Astrid to play with my friends in an R&B band, Blue Stranger, up on the hotel's grandiose stage, in what had once been a fancy ballroom. Now it had a cement floor, fiberglass tiles on the ceiling. On one wall was a rough-hewn mural of the north country. There were lumberjacks hoisting logs with skidders, fur trappers trudging through the woods on snowshoes. The Astrid Hotel itself was depicted on the mural as it once had been: a genteel mansion perched on a ridge overlooking Carrabec Falls.

It was on a rock at the bottom of the falls that they'd found the girl.

Over at the pool table, guys with tattoos and beards employed the ladies' bridge. There were mill workers and river guides, taxidermists and hippies. The bouncer chalked his cue. To his left and right were guys named Sleepy, Gangrene, Itchy, Monster, Weasel, and Happy.

The last song of the first set was "Somebody to Love," the Jefferson Airplane number. I was playing Farfisa organ through an old Leslie amplifier.

Your eyes, I say your eyes may look like his
But in your head baby I'm afraid you don't know where it is.

I liked this song all right. But sometimes, I don't know. It left me dispirited.

During the break, we all went up to the bar. The band's lead singer, my friend Shell, ordered me a drink.

I got out the book I was reading—*Pale Fire*, by Nabokov.

Shell looked over and sighed. "Hey. Professor Glasses. What now?"

I smiled. "It's a fake poem. And then there's commentary on the poem, written by somebody who doesn't exist."

She sighed. "Whatever."

"It's really interesting," I said.

When she wasn't leaping around the stage of the Astrid Hotel in spandex, Shell was the vice president of a savings bank. "You think?" she said.

I cleared my throat.

"Was he in Sherlock Holmes, the fellow whose
Tracks pointed back when he reversed his shoes?"

She smiled. "You really do live in your own little world, don't you?" she said fondly.

"That's so wrong?"

The bartender put two clear, fizzing drinks in front of us. There were what looked like prunes on the bottom. Shell handed me a glass.

"What's this?"

We clinked. "Fart in the Ocean," she said. "Tequila and Seven-Up."

"Served—with a prune?"

"Served," she said, "with a prune."

Why is it, I wondered, that women have to drink the undrinkable? In my day, I had seen my sisters order everything from a Pan Galactic Gargle Blaster (vodka, cider, cherry brandy, and Tia Maria) to a Warsaw Waffle (an unspeakable union of vodka and Maine maple syrup). Would it be so wrong if once in a while we had a nice pint of Guinness instead? But whenever I had a Guinness it was inevitable that one of my girlfriends would come up to me and say, *You know how many calories are in that, Jenny? As many as a steak dinner!* This, from someone who was drinking something called The Screaming Chocolate Monkey.

From the other end of the room a woman's voice rose in anger. "Leave me alone!" she shouted, then threw her margarita in the face of her good man. This dramatic imperative was greeted with applause and cheers by everyone except for the fellow whose face was now covered with triple sec.

Shell looked at me and smiled. "Brandy and Boyd LeMieux," she said wistfully. "They're the perfect couple—she's an ex-model, he's an ex-Marine."

Brandy stood up and headed toward the bar where Shell and I were sitting. She was an attractive woman, in a dilapidated sort of way. "You want a cigarette?" she asked.

"I don't smoke."

Brandy laughed. "Right," she said.

"Jenny here's an English professor," said Shell.

Brandy LeMieux laughed like this was funny. "Yeah," she said. "And I'm an astronaut." She picked up Shell's drink, downed it in a single gulp. Didn't eat the prune, though. She looked at my book.

"What's that? Any good?"

"It's Nabokov," I said. "You like Nabokov?"

Her mouth dropped open, as if I were one of the Beatles. *"Whoa,"* she said. "You really *are* an English teacher. Aren't you!"

"I guess."

Shell patted my shoulder. "Well," she said. "I'll let you two chat. Then she headed over toward the place where Boyd was sitting, staring sadly into Brandy's empty margarita glass.

Brandy and I watched as Shell sat down next to him. I could imagine the counsel she was offering. *Don't worry, Boyd! There are plenty of other fish in the ditch!*

"What a nerd," Brandy said. "My husband. I can't believe I ever married him." She looked at me. "You married?"

One of the awkward hallmarks of my life is the way relatively simple questions command complex answers, the kind that require a PowerPoint presentation and several *Oprah* shows to do them justice. I am more than a little hopeful, in most situations, to be seen as human. But there are plenty of times I don't want to go into the details. Especially when I'm sitting next to a woman who's just downed a drink with a prune in it.

"You're wearing a wedding ring," Brandy said, trying to help.

"It's a long story," I said.

Brandy raised her empty glass and clinked it against mine.

"You go, girl," she said.

"*You* go." We were friends now.

"You're really pretty, did you know that?"

"I don't *think* so," I said.

"Will you buy me another drink?"

"Sure," I said. The bartender cut another Fart in the Ocean.

"Boyd wants to put me in a time machine," said Brandy.

"Hate that," I said.

"He can't see me where I am. Only where I was."

"Where are you?" I said.

She reached out and squeezed my hand. "I'm here with you, Jenny."

"My son wants to be a time traveler," I said. "When he grows up."

"Well, the hell. Maybe he can use Boyd's machine, after he's done with it."

The topic of superpowers, including time travel, was a frequent one in our house. There were times when it seemed like it was all we ever talked about, Grace and me, and our middle school–age children, Paddy and Luke. I maintained that the only two superpowers worth having were super-strength and super-speed. Ten-year-old Paddy, for his part, advocated the power of virtual reality, the power of time travel, and something else he called super-stickiness, which might be the thing that enables Spider-Man to climb walls, or might be something else entirely. In any case, Paddy said that super-strength and super-speed were mutually exclusive. "If you have super-strength," he maintained, "it slows *down* your super-speed."

I knew well enough to let Paddy have his way in these discussions, even though I didn't exactly understand what the power of virtual reality was, not that it hadn't been explained to me again and again. "It's the power to turn your imagination into reality," Paddy said, exasperated that such an explanation was even necessary.

I'm not saying the power of virtual reality isn't a good thing. Honestly I'm not. But I've been in lots of situations in which super-speed would have been extremely useful.

Boyd got up from his table and started heading toward us. "Shit," said Brandy. "Here we go again."

She took me by the hand. "Come on, follow me." We walked out into the foyer, then into the ladies room. Brandy leaned against the wall, next to the paper towel dispenser and grinned at me. "So what do you think?"

"About what?"

Brandy rolled her eyes. "Duh, Jenny," she said.

I appeared to have agreed to something that had not been put into words.

"Look at you," she said. "You're trembling like a leaf!"

"I am not."

"The fuck you're not. Come on. It's really okay."

She pulled me into the handicap stall. Then she drew toward me and put her arms around my back and hugged me. Her body was soft and warm, and her head fell against my shoulder. I was a lot taller than Brandy.

"It's really okay," she whispered, and then she raised her head and kissed me on the lips. Then she kissed me again. I felt her breasts pressing against mine. "Nngg, Jenny," she said. "Nnnngg."

I pulled back. Incredibly, my first concern in this skanky situation was making sure I didn't hurt Brandy's feelings.

"Listen," I said. "You're sweet, but you know, like—"

"Please," said Brandy achingly. "It's my birthday."

And I thought, *It's her birthday?*

"You don't understand," I said. "I'm married."

Brandy didn't understand what this had to do with anything. "So?" she said. "I'm married, too!"

I heard the voice of Jimmy Stewart in the back of my head: *This is a very unusual situation!*

"I should go," I said.

"Wait," she said. On the wall behind her were phone numbers, profanities, names of men and women enclosed with hearts. Her eyes filled with tears. I didn't want to wait for her, was in fact more than eager to get out of this particular situation. But I couldn't leave.

"What?"

Tears rolled down her cheeks. "Nobody knows me," she said.

"Brandy," I said. "I'm sure that's not true."

"It's like having a dog. Like a Saint Bernard."

"What is?"

"The secrets," she whispered. "Everywhere I go, they have to go, too."

"What secrets?" I said.

She laughed to herself. "*What* secrets," she said, as if it was the most obvious thing in the world, what her secrets were.

"Have you thought about talking to someone?" I said.

"Jenny?" She looked at me as if I were on drugs. "I'm talking to *you*."

"I mean, you know. A professional."

"You mean like a shrink?" she said, stunned by the suggestion. "Oh, I've talked to plenty of shrinks, believe me."

"Listen, Brandy. I don't know you. I'm just an English teacher."

"But that's what I need," she said. "An English teacher."

I tried to think of what could possibly be so wrong with her that the only thing that could help her was an English teacher. Nothing came to mind.

"What's wrong?" I said.

It seemed to take her a long time to put it into words, as if she were trying to find the courage to say something she had never spoken out loud before in her life. "I don't want to be who I am," she said finally, in a hoarse, desperate voice.

Amazingly, I understood what this felt like. I'd had this feeling lots of times, when I was younger. "Okay," I said. "So who do you want to be?"

"I want to be someone—" she said. "Who writes poems."

The words hung in the air between us. I blew some air through my cheeks, and felt bad for her. There'd been a lot of progress in the field of psychology over the years, but so far as I knew there was still no cure for poetry. I don't know. Ritalin, maybe.

"Have you . . . ," I said. "You know. *Tried* to write poems?"

"No," she said. The tears spilled over her lashes again and rolled down her face. "Because I don't know how. Because I'm not the kind of person who writes them."

"Maybe you could change. You could be that kind of person. If you wrote some. Why don't you try?"

She stopped crying and looked at me suspiciously. "My poems would suck," she said with an air of clairvoyance.

"Probably at first. Then you'll write some more, maybe you'll get better."

"You think?" she said.

I nodded cautiously.

"And then—" she said. "I'll be somebody else?"

I wasn't sure what to tell her. To be honest I was less interested in helping Brandy than I was in getting out of the ladies room. At the same time, I didn't want to lie to her. It seemed likely to me that she was clinging to a false hope, the idea that writing poems would make her into somebody else. What seemed more likely was that, when all was said and done, she'd still be herself, except that now she'd own a rhyming dictionary.

But what the hell. I didn't know Brandy's future any more than I knew my own. Encouraging her seemed just as likely to be an act of kindness as of cruelty.

"Why don't you write," I said, "and see who you are afterward?"

Brandy took this in. "Okay," she said hopefully. "Okay." She looked at me hungrily. "And then—if I wrote a poem good enough—maybe you'd reconsider?"

"Reconsider?"

"You know," she said, softly brushing her fingertips against my shoulder. "Maybe we could be girlfriends, you and me? And if I ask you to kiss me, next time you won't act like I have leprosy and junk?"

I sighed. I don't underestimate the power of literature. But that would have to be one hell of a poem.

"Good luck," I said, by way of answer, and then left the stall. She didn't follow me. Out in the bar, I could hear the sound of Big Head Chester tuning his guitar. "You coming?"

"I'll be along," said Brandy. "I'm going to start working on my poem right *now*!"

"Good for you," I said, and washed my hands at the sink. "That's great."

"Hey Jenny," she said. "Do you ever wish you were a man?"

"A man?" I said, stunned. I looked at myself in the mirror. "Not really."

"I do," said her voice, from the stall. "Sometimes."

I dried my hands with brown paper towels.

"What do you think it'd be like?" said Brandy.

I told her the truth. "I don't know, Brandy," I said. "Kind of like being a woman," I said. "Only less so."

I returned to the foyer of the old hotel with my head spinning. On the walls around me were framed photographs of John Wayne, Jesus Christ, and Elvis. It reminded me of something, but I wasn't quite sure what. Out in the ballroom Big Head Chester was noodling around with the opening riff of "Paint It Black," the Stones tune. I heard the crack of the cue ball as a guy named Freebird made the break over on the pool table. The nine ball fell into the side pocket.

I'd gone on many travels in the last few years, voyages that had taken me halfway around the world, to Chile, and Venice, and the Turks and Caicos. But it's fair to say I had never felt quite so far away from home as I did at that moment, at the bottom of the worn-out stairs of the Astrid Hotel. Looking around at my hairy companions, my ears still ringing from the volume of the band, the memory of Brandy's lips on my neck, I thought of the phrase my sister and I used to call at the end of a round of hide-and-seek: *Olly olly oxen free.*

That was when I saw her, frozen at the top of the stairs: a young girl, about eight years old. She was dressed in odd clothing, a Victorian nightie. Her blond hair fell to her shoulders. Her head was cocked to one side, as if she'd just been asked a question.

"Hey," I said.

The girl didn't move. I couldn't be sure she'd even heard me. "Are you okay?" I said.

Then she turned her back, drifted up to the top step, and dissolved into the door.

For a moment I stood there, looking toward the upper stories of the Astrid Hotel. Then I climbed the stairs, one hand trailing along the rickety banister. I had a pretty good sense that I ought not to be following this girl, wherever she was leading. I followed her anyway.

When I opened the fire door, I found myself at the end of a beat-up corridor. It didn't look as if anyone had stayed in the upper rooms of the Astrid Hotel for a long time. One empty room followed another, the doors wide open, bare mattresses on the floor, water stains on the ceiling.

"Hello?" I said again, more softly this time, and as I said it, I felt the hairs on my arm all stand on end.

I walked to the end of the hallway and looked out the window. Standing there, I realized what it was that seemed so familiar about the Astrid Hotel. It reminded me more than a little of the house I'd grown up in, back in Pennsylvania. On the walls there were holes where gas lamps once had been. The wallpaper was peeling.

From where I stood I could see the waterfall in the Kennebec River, could see the place where the little girl had drowned. There was a path from there to here. In the parking lot below, Brandy was fighting with Boyd, who looked to me as if he was now auditioning for the soon-to-be-available role of Brandy's ex-husband.

Jeez, I thought. I'm surrounded by Exes. The place was lousy with them. There was Brandy, for one, the ex-model. Her husband, Boyd, the ex-Marine, was another.

As for me, I was an ex-man, which is different from being one of the X-Men, although over time I've found it's less different than I'd hoped.

The world is full of Exes, of Priors and Formers, people who can never quite live in the present. Sam Kinison (the ex-comedian) used to do a very funny bit about all the former astronauts who'd become alcoholics, men who'd returned triumphantly from the moon only to find themselves unable to proceed with life post-splashdown. *Pardon me!* he'd scream. *I was only on another planet!*

Or, as the songwriter Ray LaMontagne sings, *You see, I been to hell and back so many times I must admit you kind of bore me.*

Over the years I'd seen plenty of people who had more serious cases of the Exes than I did, and most of them weren't transsexuals, either. People like Art Garfunkel, or Danny Bonaduce, or Michael Dukakis—just to pick three kind of at random—are seen as vaguely comic figures, people who are so completely defined by what they Used To Be that we are unwilling, even irritated, by the prospect of seeing them As They Are Now.

How is it, I wondered, that some people manage to integrate their lives, and live in the moment, while others become stuck, become Exes, haunting their own lives like ghosts? How do we learn to Be Here Now (in the words of Ram Dass, the former Richard Alpert)? How do we let go of the past, when its joys and injustices are such a large part of making us whoever it is we've become?

Maybe, I thought, you do it by writing poems, by trying to tell your ridiculous and incomprehensible story. Who knows? It was possible that Brandy, a consumer of prune cocktails, was better equipped at unraveling the mystery of life than I was.

There was an echo from a distant room, the remote whisper of a human voice.

I thought about going over to visit our brand-new haunted house for the first time with my family, on a summer day in 1972.

Just like that girl—the one who'd vanished over the edge of Carrabec Falls—I'd lost my father and my sister, too.

Hello? I said, looking down the long, empty hall. *Is anybody there?*

I see the girls walk by *dressed in their summer clothes. I have to turn my head until my darkness goes.*

Lydia and my father were in the front seats of the VW. The windows were down. It was the *Exile on Main St.* summer, and the Stones were everywhere. My father, who had briefly been a classical musician, looked over at my fifteen-year-old sister with wonder and disappointment.

"I suppose you like this kind of music now," he said witheringly.

"You could suppose I like a *lot* of things," said Lydia, and punched in the cigarette lighter. Her long blond hair flapped around the car.

"Whoa-*ho*," said my father, and changed the station to WFLN, the classical station. They were playing "Comes a Train of Little Ladies," from *The Mikado*. A chorus of girls was singing: *Is it but a world of trouble, sadness set to song? . . . How we wonder, what on earth the world can be!*

"Bo-ring," Lydia observed.

"I like it," I said, looking out the window.

"Whoa!" said my sister. "The creature speaks!"

"Your brother's not a creature."

My sister turned around in her bucket seat and gave me a good hard look to see whether or not this was true. I was a curiously androgynous thirteen-year-old, with a shirt that bore an image of a cartoon moose. Beneath the moose was the phrase I ACT DIFFERENT BECAUSE I AM DIFFERENT, written in goofy 1970s paisley letters.

Are its palaces and pleasures fantasies that fade? sang the chorus. *And the glory of its treasures, shadow of a Shade?*

"This is the street," said my father, as we drove past big houses with lawns and wrought-iron fences. At first glance Philadelphia's Main Line didn't seem like a neighborhood where our family would fare very well, what with our secondhand cars and gelatinous dog and large cast of deranged relatives, some of whose voices still bore the unmistakable accent of the Old Country.

We pulled into the driveway.

"No. Wait," said my sister. "You're kidding."

Before us was an enormous, collapsing Victorian mansion. It had been painted white at some point, but now green moss or mold was flourishing on its stone walls. The house was three stories tall, with crazy dormer windows and a gabled roof and several crooked chimneys and a pair of bayonet-sharp lightning rods.

As I stared up at its curious peaked roof, I saw a curtain move softly in an upper-story window.

"Welcome home," said my father, and turned off the radio.

"I don't believe it," said my sister.

"Believe it," said my father.

We walked up a stone staircase. My father put his key in the lock, and the back door swung open. For a second we paused on the threshold: my father, my sister, and I. Then Dad walked inside. Lydia and I lingered a moment longer, uncertain.

"It's like the Munsters' house," said my sister. She meant, in a bad way.

"What?"

"You know that show, *The Munsters*?"

"I *love* that show," I said.

"I know you do," my sister said thoughtfully. "It's sad, really." She didn't look sad.

In the yard was a twisted apple tree. As I watched, one of its apples fell onto the ground with a *thunk*. There were dozens of apples on the ground, slowly rotting. There was a sweet smell in the air, like cider.

When I turned around, my sister wasn't there anymore. Wherever my father had gone, Lydia had followed him there.

"Hello?" I said, and walked into the Coffin House to find my father and my sister.

There are times when I feel as if I've spent the rest of my life searching for them.

"Hey," said a voice. "Are you all right?"

I looked up, and there was Shell, standing in the hallway of the Astrid Hotel.

"I'm okay," I said.

"Liar," she said.

"Hey listen, Shell," I said. "When you look at me, who do you see?"

She looked confused. "What are you talking about? You're my girlfriend. Jenny the Giant. Professor Glasses. Who else would I see?"

"You don't see James? You don't see the person I was?"

"Of course not." She looked concerned. "Why are you talking like this?"

"I don't want to be an Ex," I said. "I don't want to be Art Garfunkel."

Shell came over and stood by my side. "I've known you a long time," she said. "Sure, sometimes when we're together, you remind me of stuff we did ten years ago. I mean, there are some jokes I think I've heard you tell, oh, about a hundred ninety thousand times. That doesn't make you—what did you say? Art Garfunkel? Whatever that means."

Through the window in front of us we could see the rushing waters of the falls.

"Did you ever hear the story—that this place is haunted?" I said. "That there's some little girl who walks the halls, looking for her family?"

"Jenny," said Shell, rubbing my shoulder. "You're not her, either."

I nodded. "I saw her."

Shell looked suspicious. "What? Where?"

"I saw her on the stairs. She looked at me."

In the gorge below us, mist from the falls rose into the winter night.

"Jenny Boylan," said Shell. "Are we going to stand here having some sort of fuckin' dark interlude, or are we going to play some rock and roll!"

It was a good question. I considered my options.

"Let's rock," I said.

As we walked down the stairs, I could hear the rest of the band starting a tune without us. The grating chords of AC/DC shook the old mansion. Shell's husband Nick was singing: *Dirty deeds, done dirt cheap! Dirty deeds, and they're done dirt cheap!*

Shell sighed. AC/DC wasn't her favorite. "I suppose our band plays this kind of music now," she said, as we reached the bottom of the staircase.

"You could suppose a lot of things," I said.

When I walked into the Coffin House for the first time, I'd found myself in a rickety pantry with a set of crazy shelves nailed into some pine paneling. Just beyond this was a decaying kitchen in which there appeared to have been a recent fire. Next to the refrigerator were the stairs to the cellar. I thought I heard voices.

"Hello?" I walked down into the damp basement. There was a smell in the cellar of mold, and old cans of paint, and oil from the furnace. There was sheet music glued at jaunty angles on the walls, including the score for "Roll Out the Barrel." The lyrics suggested that, if its guidelines were carefully observed, one might *have a barrel of fun*.

The basement was huge, like a catacomb. A layer of dust covered everything. Ahead of me was a dim light, cast through a small window with bars on it.

A pegboard was on one wall, black painted shadows showing the position of tools that were not there: a hammer, a saw, a pair of wrenches.

On the other side of the room was a dark chamber, with a sign on the wall. The sign read: BILL HUNT, LABORATORY. My parents had bought the house from the Hunts. They'd lived there twenty-three years.

I walked toward Bill Hunt's laboratory. There was a set of shelves on the wall, some stains on the floor where, presumably, the mad scientist had dropped his beaker after drinking the potion that made him normal.

I wouldn't have minded some of that potion my own self.

A strange blue mist moved across the cellar, paused by the laboratory, and hovered there in midair, considering me. It wasn't human exactly, but you could see where its head would be. Then it faded into the wall.

"Jim?" called my father. "Are you down there?"

I headed back to the foot of the stairs. My father and sister were standing at the top, two shadows surrounded by light. I looked in the direction where the ghost had been, but it was gone now. Had I seen it at all?

"What are you doing?" said my sister.

"Looking for you," I said.

I climbed the stairs back to the kitchen. I picked up the keys to the house, which my father had left upon the countertop.

"So we're definitely moving here?" I said. "It's final?"

My father looked at me curiously. "Don't worry," he said. "Pretty soon it'll feel like you belong here."

I looked around the burned-out kitchen and tried to imagine the future. For a moment I considered the years ahead: the party my parents would throw for me when I turned sweet sixteen, with its champagne fountain and cheesy accordion band; my girlfriends and me on a Saturday night cooking up a big dinner for everybody in the kitchen, with pork chops and coleslaw and baked beans; even, distantly visible like a ship on the horizon, the day of my wedding. I stood on the front porch and threw my bouquet toward my bridesmaids. My father wiped the tears from his eyes, his little Jenny all grown up at last.

"Earth to Mr. Moose," said Liddie.

I was still holding the keys in my right hand. I reached up to turn on the lights in the kitchen, and the key to the house made contact with some exposed wires in the wall.

There was a forking blue flash, like an arc of Sith lightning, as current surged through the circuit, across the key, and through my body. I heard a sizzling buzz as the shock raged through me.

Everything went dead, and then there was a sound like someone banging a copper pot with a metal spoon, a few inches from my ear. As I hit the floor, I thought, *Whoa. That thing that just went* klunk? *That was you, girlfriend! They've shot you full of juice!*

Then I was rising into the air. I didn't know where I was going. I wondered if I was part of the blue mist now. The dangling cobwebs trailed across my cheek. Our lives went by: my sister heading to an Alice Cooper concert in 1974; my father softly weeping when the dog died in 1982; my children running down the stairs in their bathing suits in 1999; my mother and I here alone on the night of an ice storm in the twenty-first century. She called out to me in the night: *Jenny, help me. Jenny, please help.*

Lydia was rubbing my shoulder. "Hey. Mr. Moose. Say something." Her eyes shone. "Please?"

"I'm all right," I said. I was lying on the floor. "I got a shock."

My father and sister held me in their arms, encircling me. There we were, all together.

"My boy," Dad said, and his voice broke. He looked away for a second, then looked back. "For a moment I thought we'd lost you."

The Crystal Ball

"Greetings from the mysterious East," said my grandmother, swaying a little. She was wearing a Japanese kimono and a turban. She sat down at a card table, upon which was an inverted goldfish bowl. That was going to be the crystal ball.

"I am Madame Casbah!" she suggested. "Seer of the unseen!"

The neighborhood children were all sitting cross-legged on the living room floor: the two O'Connor girls, from Tennessee, and the three McCabe sisters: Woojee, Ronco, and Kay-kay. There were boxes all around us. It was my last birthday at our old house, in the farm town of Newtown Square. Within six weeks, my family would all be headed toward Somerset, and the Main Line, and the house with the sentient fog.

Madame Casbah looked into the crystal ball. "The spirits are among us. Speaking! Let's see if they know anything."

We all sat there quietly for a moment. We didn't hear any spirits.

"There is a girl among us," she said. "Who is making a journey. A girl who is very special."

For a moment, of course, I assumed she was talking about me. I *was* making a journey, as it turned out. We all were.

"Her name is—Liiiiiii-dia."

My sister and I both hung our heads in embarrassment.

"What's that, spirits? The year ahead brings what?"

The mystic closed her eyes and swayed for a moment. If you didn't know better, you'd have thought she was swaying because the spirits were speaking.

"Changes," Madame Casbah said ruefully. "Chaaaaanges."

We all giggled nervously.

"I see what the year to come holds for this girl," said Madame Casbah. "Do you want to know?"

The girls nodded yes. We wanted to know.

"I see—" said Madame Casbah. "A *man*."

We all screamed.

"Gammie," said Lydia, mortified.

"A man," said Gammie. She reached into her kimono for a package of Kents, got comfortable. "Now when a man appears, there's one thing you need to find out about him." She lit her cigarette with a silver butane lighter. "Does he have a lot of—*money*."

We laughed, but not as hard. "That is what you need to find out," she said. "Because there is one thing, that is the most important thing in the world. Do you know what that thing is?"

She looked around the room expectantly.

"MONEY," she bellowed, and slapped her hand on the card table, hard. The fishbowl rolled over, and Gammie reached out and grabbed it moments before it rolled off the edge and shattered on the floor. She took another long drag from her cigarette, exhaled. "That is the most important thing. In a man." She took another drag, held it in. We watched, breathlessly, as she retained the smoke. Then she blew it all out. And she said again, loudly, "MONEY!"

We all laughed, although it would have been hard to say at what.

"Let me tell you about my*self*," said Madame Casbah, sucking on her Kent. "I like *men*. And I like men—who like money!"

She paused to make sure we understood, before she ventured onward to her conclusion.

"And men, who like money—*LIKE ME!*"

My sister's cat crept into the room and curled up on my lap. Its name was ba-BOING!

"Now how do you think," my grandmother continued, "you get men with money to like you?" She looked around at the room.

"It's not by cooking. Don't let anyone ever tell you that it matters if you can cook or not, because it doesn't. Your *servants* will cook! You know what's more important than knowing how to cook? *Hiring good servants!*"

She smoked her Kent. "And another thing," she said. "It's fine if you're good in bed, but that's not the most important thing either. You know why? They all end up with whores anyway! You know all this, don't you, girls? Men *always* have whores!"

We looked at one another. I kind of wished someone was getting this all down on paper. It was important information.

"So then. What does a man really want, more than anything?" She leaned forward. "HE WANTS TO BE CONTROLLED. He might"—here she paused to hack mightily into her fist—"he might *say* he doesn't want to be controlled, but he *does*. And how do you control a man, so that you can spend his money?"

We were all silent now, the girls and me. We had no idea how this was going to turn out.

"You give him a little pizzazz!" said Gammie. "That's the secret! *Pizzazz!*" She sucked on her Kent, blew the smoke out among us. "PIZZAZZ!" she shouted again.

"Now what is pizzazz?" Madame Casbah asked. "Where do you find it? Is it something you can buy in the store?"

She looked at us as if we were all assholes.

"You can't buy it in the store!" Madame Casbah shouted. "THAT'S NOT WHERE PIZZAZZ COMES FROM! Do you want to know where you find it? Where you can find—PIZZAZZ?"

We nodded our heads, reluctantly. At this point we had to know, even though we all sensed that it was knowledge we'd have been happier without.

She pointed to her heart. "In here," she said. "In your *bosom*."

Some of the girls laughed, since the word *bosom* itself was surrounded with more than a little voltage. Madame Casbah looked at us with suspicion.

"Your bosom, I say!" she said. "That is where pizzazz comes from. YOUR BOSOM!"

"Who wants cake and ice cream?" said my mother, appearing from the kitchen. We were all thinking the same thing: Where have you been? Don't you know what's been going on out here?

"I'm not done telling fortunes," Gammie said. She looked around. "Who wants her fortune told?"

The O'Connor sisters and Woojee and Kay-kay and Ronco were unified by a single thought: *Sweet weeping Jesus, please let her tell someone else's fortune*. Gammie looked from face to face. All the girls looked downward, afraid to meet her eyes. Then her gaze fell upon me.

"You, Jimmy," she said. "Let's ask the spirits for *your* future."

"No, please," I said. "Don't."

"What's the matter?" she said. "Are you scared?"

In point of fact, I *was* scared, and not only by the possible contents of Madame Casbah's fishbowl. In the weeks leading up to the move, I often lay awake at night, thinking of the sentient mist I'd seen in the basement of the new house. It was bad enough that I'd seen it hovering down there in the cellar. But what was worse was my certainty that somehow, in its own foglike nether-brain, it was aware of my presence as well, and considered me a kind of kindred spirit.

It would probably not have eased my mind if I'd known that I was not alone in my fear of the translucent. According to a CBS News poll taken in October 2005, 48 percent of Americans believe in ghosts, and nearly a quarter claim to have either seen or felt their presence. Other polls show that younger Americans are more likely to believe than older ones, and that, surprisingly, the more education one has, the more likely one's belief in the supernatural.

In any case, you don't have to believe in ghosts to believe that people, or houses, or even certain pieces of music can be haunted. I have a friend who survived a bout with cancer more than ten years ago. "But every day," he says, "I think about it, like it's some dark demon, still lying in wait for me. Like that thing with the wings in the 'Night on Bald Mountain' part of *Fantasia*. That's what it's like to be a cancer survivor. You always think that thing is chasing you." Does he believe in ghosts? "Of course not," he said. "Don't be ridiculous."

I have another friend, a scientist, who claims to be a realist in all things. But don't even think of playing James Taylor's "Fire and Rain" on the stereo in her presence. "I'm sorry," she'll say, as she hits the off button. "But if we listen to this song, I'm going to have to get in the car and go poison my ex-husband."

Generally, I don't put on that song if she's around.

In my youth, as now, I was a skeptic, knowing full well how often people believe not what is true, but what is convenient. When it comes to the truly supernatural, I suppose I'm not unlike Ebenezer Scrooge, when he has it out with Jacob Marley.

> *"What evidence would you have of my reality, beyond that of your senses?" [asks Marley.]*
>
> *"I don't know," said Scrooge.*
>
> *"Why do you doubt your senses?"*
>
> *"Because," said Scrooge, "a little thing affects them. A slight disorder of the stomach makes them cheats. You may be an undigested bit of beef, a blot of mustard, a crumb of cheese, a fragment of an underdone potato. There's more of gravy than of grave about you, whatever you are!"*

Or, in the more succinct words of Chico Marx: "Who are you going to believe, me or your own eyes?"

Anyway, as far as the *danse macabre* was concerned, by the time I was thirteen, my card was already full. In addition to the undead, for instance, I was terrorized by a paint-by-numbers portrait of a German shepherd that hung in my bedroom. My fear of the painting was so severe that on one occasion I got out of bed, took a fork from the kitchen, and scratched out its eyes. My mother, who had painted the picture herself, discovered what I had done the next day, and said, "But why, Jimmy? Why?" I didn't know what to tell her.

I also feared an advertising jingle for tanning butter whose lyrics were *Bain de Soleil for the Saint-Tropez tan.* I feared another one for Windsong perfume, which went like this: *I can't seem to forget you, your Windsong stays on my, Windsong stays on my, Windsong stays on my mind.*

I feared the illusion produced when two mirrors were held face to face, creating an endless regression of mirror faces, a tunnel to a place I surely did not wish to visit.

I feared a book entitled *Mysteries of King Tutankhamen's Tomb*, which contained a photograph of the boy king, his corpse all shriveled up like a twice-baked potato. On his chest was a bouquet of flowers which the author claimed "still bore the two-thousand-year-old scent of long-dried tears."

Above all, I feared that I was crazy as a loon.

This is not a book about being transgendered, per se, and I'm all too aware that the whole subject will strike more than a few readers as annoying, for which I can only say I am truly very sorry. I feel that way sometimes, too.

It's probably worth mentioning—just in case this still needs to be said—that the thing I felt didn't have much to do with being gay or lesbian; it was, even then, not about who I wanted to go to bed *with*, but who I wanted to go to bed *as*. Nor was it about clothes, particularly; my condition had more to do with spirit than spandex.

Nor did it have anything to do with the various cultural constraints of masculinity or femininity, by which I mean to say I felt no particular desire, for instance, to play with dolls. I know a lot of grown women who found Barbie irritating when they were little. That didn't make them boys, either.

There are all sorts of theories about why transsexual people feel the things they feel and interested readers can pursue those theories, if that sounds like a good time to you. Some researchers think it's neurological, having something to do with brain structure. Others think it has something to do with an event that happens when the developing fetus is about six weeks old in utero. Yet another faction feels it's about rejecting a whole binary system of gender, and embracing something both messier and more elusive. Who knows?

I do have to say that I don't find *gender theory* especially helpful, in terms of explaining the thing I felt. I resent, to no small degree, the idea that a theory should even be necessary. To be honest, just about the only theory I trust is *story*, and I'm hoping that, before all is said and done, the tale I am trying to tell can stand in for the theory. In the meantime, I am sustained by a saying of my mother's: "It is impossible to hate anyone whose story you know."

Back then I knew very little for certain about whatever it was that afflicted me, but I did know this much: that in order to survive, I'd have to become something like a ghost myself, and keep the nature of my true self hidden. And so I haunted that young body of mine just as the spirits haunted the Coffin House, as a hopeful, wraithlike presence otherwise invisible to the naked eye—like helium, or J. D. Salinger, or the G-spot.

My one chance, I thought, was that someday someone might fall in love with me, and that the alchemy of passion would transform me into a human like other humans. Maybe, I thought, if I was funny enough, or clever enough, or inventive enough to be desired, I might yet leave my translucent self behind and at last turn into something solid.

Lydia, for her part, had fears of her own. My blond-haired, red-cheeked sister was always beautiful, but she was especially beautiful on a horse, cantering around a ring, hurtling over fences. If it was cold, Checkmate's breath would issue from his nostrils in great steaming clouds. When she competed in shows, the grandstand would be silent as she raced past. Then, after her round, people in the grandstand would cheer and holler as Lydia took a victory lap, tipping her velvet hard hat to the crowd.

We had a whole room full of Lydia's trophies, walls of blue ribbons, long streamers marked GRAND CHAMPION.

But Lydia liked being alone with the horse more than showing. There was nothing quite so sweet as those moments at the end of the day when she'd brush him or braid his mane or tail. Checkmate's barn smelled like leather and fresh hay. Spiderwebs hung down in a great profusion from overhead, and in one corner was a hornets' nest the size of a soccer ball.

One afternoon, a year or so before our move, she'd fed Checkmate a carrot, and rubbed his soft nose and patted him on the withers. Until that second, everything had been silent. Then he made a sound she hadn't heard before, and all at once he snapped his head back and broke his tether and ran, his eyes wild with a sudden, unexplainable panic. He galloped down a dirt path and out into the road, where a woman in a Volkswagen was, just at that moment, coming up over the hill.

There was a tremendous crash. My sister rushed down the dirt path to see what had happened.

She was still holding the currycomb in one hand.

Lydia stayed home from school for a few days, mostly looking out the window of our house in Newtown Square. Every once in a while she said, in a small voice that did not sound like her own, "Why didn't they protect me? Why didn't they stop it?"

I wasn't sure who she meant by *they*. My parents, I guessed. But it was hard to know for sure.

Eventually she got out of bed and went back to school. She'd been changed by her loss, though, as any child might be. She'd had that great love, with that beautiful creature, and then all at once, for no apparent reason, she'd lost him. And that, I think, is what she feared most—that the unnamed force that had taken the horse from her was still at large in the world. As Truman Capote wrote, in a somewhat different context, *Of what were they afraid? It might come back.*

By the time of our move she didn't ride anymore. Hundreds of ribbons, blue for first place, red for second, yellow for third, and so on, were packed into boxes, along with her trophies. On the outside of the box, my sister wrote, in Magic Marker, *Checkmate. To store in attic.*

As my father had signed the papers at the real estate agent's office, I'd read through the deeds of the Coffin House, dating back to the time before the place was built. The oldest one was dated 1740. It had been written with quill and ink, on parchment.

The deed signed by Lemuel Coffin specified a number of provisions pertaining to what could or could not be built upon the property. For instance: *on these grounds at no time hereafter shall be erected any hotel, tavern, drinking saloon, blacksmith shop, carpenter's shop, wheelwright shop, steam mill, tannery, slaughterhouse, skin dressing establishment, friggery, livery stable, glue factory, soap factory, candle factory, starch factory, or other building for offensive uses, purposes, or occupations.*

It was a long list of prohibitions, and I was aware that the phrase "offensive uses, purposes, or occupations" covered a lot of ground. Using the strictest possible interpretation of the deed, there was some question whether or not we'd even be allowed to have my grandmother over, a woman whose antics, sometimes, were right up there with *starch factory*.

On the day that my father had first taken my sister and me over to the house, he'd spent no small amount of time making sure that I had not been killed by the jolt of electricity. "I'm okay, really," I kept saying. "I just got a shock."

"If you got electrocuted," he said, "I would be so disappointed."

"Speak for yourself," said my sister.

Dad took us on a tour of the first floor. There was a dining room with a fireplace and a rec room with zebra-skin-patterned paneling. Chandeliers made from wagon wheels hung from a ceiling with exposed rafters. There was a bar in the corner. Down a few flagstone steps was a fireplace, and above this, built into the wall, a fish tank. There weren't any fish in it. It looked kind of like a swingin' bachelor pad from the sixties, just before the bachelor was mysteriously stabbed.

Then he took us into the living room. Its walls were painted black.

"The piano goes here," he said, pointing to an alcove. I could tell by his expression he was already imagining the future. I would be seated at the piano, torturing Mozart, while he sat in a wing chair by the fireplace smoking L&M Kings. At some point during my performance, he'd announce, "All right. Now play it backward," and I'd have to do what he said. It was my father's theory that playing music backward, or in seven-eight, or in ragtime built character.

Another one of his character-building exercises was to halt us in the middle of a family argument and force each of us, upon his command, to advocate the exact *opposite* of what we'd been arguing so far. "If you can't see both sides of the issue," he'd say, "you don't have a case."

My sister entered the room, and my father put his arm around her. He didn't put his arm around me so much, for which you could hardly blame him. Things were different with boys.

"Jeez," Lydia said. "Where's the coffin?"

"Coffin?" I said.

"I'm serious," she said. "The only thing missing in this place is a dead body."

"Let's go upstairs," my father said. "You can choose your rooms."

My feet creaked on the old steps. The second floor looked even darker than the first. My sister lingered at the bottom of the stairs.

"Black walls," she said. "Am I surprised?"

"I think it's kind of cool," I said.

"Hmm," my sister noted. She looked at my shirt, with its moose, and the suggestion I ACT DIFFERENT BECAUSE I AM DIFFERENT. "But then, of course, there's a reason you think it's cool, Mr. Moose."

"What's that?" I said.

"You're a fag," she observed.

"I guess," I said.

"Come on, kids!" called my father.

We walked up the groaning stairs. At the top of the landing was a huge oak window with a sill so deep that two people could sit on it and make out. Just to the right of this beautiful window was a small, crooked staircase that led back down to the kitchen. There was a closed door at the head of the stairs. I opened it and found a dark, wood-lined room. It was strangely cold, considering that it was summer in Pennsylvania.

Something in there said: *Get out.*

I thought it over. Getting out suited me fine.

I walked out of the back office and up two more steps to the second floor. I found Lydia in a large chamber with many windows, two closets, and a set of drawers built into one wall. "This is my room," she announced.

"Wow," I said. "It's great."

"Get out," she said. It was the second time, within minutes, that I had received this same suggestion.

Directly across the hall from my sister, my father stood in another formal bedroom, with wall-to-wall green shag carpeting and a walk-in closet. Apparently, he'd found his room, too.

That left one other option on the second floor. I opened a door to find a room with blue wall-to-wall carpeting and white walls. A girl's bedroom.

My father came up behind me. "Is this—*my* room?" I asked. I wasn't sure.

"Actually," my father said, "we thought you'd want to be up on the third floor. That's where the Hunt boys lived."

I walked back out into the hallway and stood at the bottom of a long stairway that led up into the darkness. "But you're all down here," I said.

"I bet you'll like it up there," my father said. "You'll have the third floor all to yourself!"

I walked slowly up the stairs, which creaked even more violently than those to the second floor. I stopped halfway up and looked back down. My father and my sister were watching me ascend, as if I were Amelia Earhart climbing the stairs to the Lockheed Electra. For a moment I thought they were going to wave good-bye.

There were four rooms in my new kingdom, plus a bathroom. The first one on the left—which in time would be called the Brown

Study, even though it was neither brown nor a study—had stained amber wallpaper with streaks and shadows. Years later, when I first read Charlotte Perkins Gilman's deranged narrative "The Yellow Wallpaper," I knew that she was describing something I had seen.

There was a small door in the wall of the Brown Study that led to a space with no floorboards. It looked like a passageway, but I could not imagine where it led. I saw the bricks of a chimney at the back.

By the window were two floorboards that seemed to be of a different kind of wood than the others. I reached down to touch them and found that the boards moved. There, in a secret hidey-hole, were two copies of *National Geographic* magazine from the late 1950s. The magazines fell open to pages of naked girls from Samoa.

Okay, I thought, and stood. Not this one.

The other room on that side of the hall was small and spare, the kind you'd see in a bed-and-breakfast in Amish country. The ceiling slanted at crazy angles. There was a crack in one wall. In time this chamber would be known as the Gammie Room, after my grandmother, the one-woman starch factory.

No, I thought. Not this one either.

A door at the far end of the hallway opened on what we would later call the Monkey Bathroom. It had bright red walls spattered with wild white drops. There was a red shag rug on the floor. There was a strange smell in here, the legacy of the Hunt boys' chimpanzee, whose name (we learned later) had been Jesus.

I looked in the large circular mirror that stood above the sink. There before me was a feminine creature with chopstick arms and legs. My glasses were covered with a blurring film, so that in some ways it appeared as if I were looking out at the world from an aquarium.

I didn't like looking in mirrors so much.

The bedroom on the other side of the hall was all torn up, as if someone had drunk a fifth of Jameson and gone nuts with a crowbar. Big sheets of torn wallpaper hung down from the ceiling, and the floorboards were warped and discolored. There was a dead radiator in one corner. A bare lightbulb hung down from a wire.

In time this would be called the Haunted Room.

That left the first room on the right at the top of the stairs. I opened the door to see a built-in desk on one wall, some pine paneling. There was paper on two of the walls, covered with party horns and confetti and the sheet music for "There Is a Tavern in the Town." I'd heard this song performed once on *Sing Along with Mitch*, a television show where a big band leader with a goatee waved his baton around and invited viewers to follow the bouncing ball.

It was strange how dark the room was. Its windows didn't seem to let in much light. The ceiling, like the one in the room across the hall, slanted at crazy angles.

The lyrics on the walls of my new bedroom read:

O, dig my grave both wide and deep, wide and deep,
Put tombstones at my head and feet, head and feet,
And on my breast you carve a turtle dove
To signify I died of love.

I heard the sound of an apple hitting the ground outside. I looked out the window and realized that I was in the room I had seen from the driveway, the one in which I had seen the tattered curtains move.

I felt a creeping voltage in the air, and the hairs on the back of my neck stood up. The room grew cold, as if a window had been opened in December.

And then something passed through me. I'd been speared by an icicle, stabbed by something I could not see.

"Ahh," I said.

I spun around. The room was empty.

From across the hall came a soft rhythmic sound, something brushing against the floor. I recognized it, after a moment, as the sound of a broom sweeping.

I got up and opened the door—I didn't remember having closed it—and walked out into the hall. There I was, on the third floor of the old, creaky house, its rooms and hallways empty and dark.

Once again, an undulating blue mist, like the Northern Lights, drifted from the haunted room, floated across the hallway, and vanished into the wall.

On the first of August, drunken, laughing madmen backed a moving van down the driveway of our house in Newtown Square and then fell, one after the other, out of the cab, like a troupe of circus clowns. My mother had gotten the name of Thorssteinsson Van Lines from someone out at the barn. Their specialty was moving livestock, and who knows? If we'd had a mess of pigs to load onto their truck, instead of the boxes of our family's meager possessions, maybe things would have turned out different.

Instead, the Icelanders fell onto the driveway, then stood up and said something in their incomprehensible language and laughed and fell over again and then stood up. Mr. Thorssteinsson, the foreman, approached my father and then said the following words: "Ve are movers! And now! Ve vould like some tasty *chicken*!"

The other men stumbled into the house and fell over and laughed, then stood up. Two of them went to the piano and, without any hesitation, flipped it over on its side and started taking its legs off with a monkey wrench.

"Be careful," said my father. "My own father gave me that piano!"

"Oh, Dick," said my mother. "I'm sure they'll be careful." She was getting her purse so she could drive to Kentucky Fried Chicken and buy the Scandinavians a bucket of the Colonel's Traditional Recipe.

The movers thought my parents were very, very funny.

"Jimmy," said my grandmother. "Lydia." She nodded toward the door. "Get in the car." Apparently all of this was too much even for Gammie to stand, which was a fair measure of how much trouble we were in. A few minutes later, my grandmother was firing up the engine of her black 1956 Dodge Seneca. Lydia and I sat in the back of the car, while Gammie sat up front with her devoted friend,

Hilda Watson, a tiny woman from North Yorkshire whose hearing aids were only intermittently functional. On the far side of my sister was my poor aunt Nora, a professional seamstress who constantly complained of being chilly. Sitting in direct sunlight didn't help her either. The closer to the sun she got, the more violently she shivered.

In Aunt Nora's lap was a sock puppet stuffed with fluff, in the shape of a cat. This was one of Nora's original creations, something called a kittygirl. She made these the way other people's aunts knit sweaters. My sister had a whole box full of kittygirls and, incredibly, even one or two kittyboys. The kittyboys always looked a little restless to me, though. It was clear enough that a kittyboy was rarely satisfied with his lot in life.

Once, I'd shamefully asked my aunt if she would sew me a *puppygirl*. She just looked at me as if I were crazy. "A *puppygirl*!" she said, disgusted. "There's no such thing!"

I turned around in my seat and watched as we pulled out of the driveway and our little house faded away.

It wasn't a long drive from Newtown Square to Somerset, but the distance from Pennsylvania farm country to the affluent suburbs of the Main Line is perhaps not measured best in miles. As we drove down Darby Paoli Road, we passed the estates of the gentry, the rolling fields filled with quarter horses and springhouses and duck ponds. A lot of the mansions had cutesy names, like Bagatelle, or The Gewgaw, or Xana-deux.

"You know what the problem with kids today is?" my grandmother said all at once.

"What?" I asked.

"They don't eat enough dirt!"

My sister and I looked at each other.

"Dirt?" asked Lydia.

"I said *dirt*," said Gammie. "When I was a girl, we ate dirt all the time! Now, nobody does!"

"Why would you eat dirt?" I asked. "Is it good for you?"

Gammie looked amazed by my stupidity. "Of course it's not good for you!" she shouted. "It's DIRT!"

"Whoop? Whoop whoop?" said Hilda Watson. This sound, a kind of startled interjection, was the sound Hilda made when she suspected that a response was required of her, even if she did not necessarily know what had been asked.

"Can you turn up the heat?" said Aunt Nora, sewing on a kittygirl's eye. "It's freezing in here."

"Did they eat *dirt* over there in Yorkshire?" my grandmother shouted.

Hilda, who had begun her life in a tiny village in England, near the border with Lancashire, looked astonished. "We had pudding on some occasions," she said, her dignity intact.

"I'M NOT TALKING ABOUT PUDDING," shouted my grandmother. The Dodge had a strange device that has since gone completely out of fashion—the stick shift on the steering column—and Gammie kicked us up into overdrive as the car sped through Bryn Mawr. "I'm talking about dirt!"

"Oh dear," said Aunt Nora. "I'm so, so, so cold!"

"I know what you're talking about," said Hilda to my grandmother. "I don't wish to discuss it."

My grandmother shook her head. "You're a ton of fun, Hilda."

"I'm so, so, so *cold*!"

"There's no reason to be rude," Hilda observed.

"You think this is rude?" said Gammie. "You wait."

That night, I lay on my back in my new room. The window was open, and from outside came the sounds of the Pennsylvania night in summer—crickets and cicadas, the far-off whistle of a train. The humidity was intense, so thick and oily you could practically make a hoagie out of it.

On the floor slept my dog, Sausage, a sad, rubbery Dalmatian from whose eyes seeped an inexplicable brown goo.

I said my prayers before closing my eyes. *"Please, God. Don't let anything bad happen to me in here. Okay?"* At the time, it was my theory that I might petition the Lord with prayer.

Petition the Lord with prayer!

Afterward, I lay there with my eyes shut and waited for sleep to take me away. But sleep did not come.

There was a creak out in the hallway. After a moment it was followed by another. Sausage lifted her head, then growled. The creaks continued, softly, one after the other, the footsteps coming closer and closer to my door. Sausage growled again. I opened my eyes.

Slowly, the door to my room creaked open, a little bit at first, then all the way.

I pulled the covers over my head and shut my eyes. Once again I petitioned the Lord with prayer. *Please make it go away. I won't ask to be a girl anymore if you'll just make it go away.*

There was a long pause. Sausage growled once again, more softly this time.

Then the door creaked closed. The footsteps padded down the hall.

Was it a scene such as this that Madame Casbah had foreseen, several weeks earlier, as she gazed into her crystal ball? A furrow had creased her brow as she considered my future. "I see—" she'd said, and squinted, as if the crystal had gone dark. "I see—"

The girls and I all sat there in anguish. What was it she saw? Was it too horrible to describe?

At that moment, my sister's cat, ba-BOING!, jumped out of my lap. Sausage hurtled after it. The cat ran beneath the card table, beneath Madame Casbah's chair, and into the kitchen. Sausage pursued ba-BOING! beneath the card table and out the door. As she did so, she banged the legs of the table, and the crystal ball overturned, rolled toward the table's edge, and fell to the floor, where, with a tremendous crash, it shattered into a hundred pieces.

"Well," said Madame Casbah, looking at the smashed crystal. "That does it." She reached up, took the turban off her head, and placed it on the card table, next to her pack of cigarettes.

It was clear that Gammie was now done telling fortunes, which was just as well. She'd already been stumped trying to come up with one for me.

I didn't hold that against her, though. For the longest time I couldn't come up with one for me either.

Utopia

Along with our new house came a new school, Haverford, an all-boys' private institution in the heart of the Main Line. The headmaster, Mr. Flinch, was a sour six-foot-six man who'd had polio as a child and now limped around the deteriorating Victorian haunted house which served as the Upper School building, barking at the boys and pointing out that we didn't have enough *gumption*.

The faculty at the Haverford School was a strange collection of dedicated scholars, nineteenth-century gentlemen, and arm-flailing halfwits. Among the latter was my homeroom teacher, Mr. Varmin, known behind his back as Chilly Willy. He stood at the front of the room, saying *Settle down, settle down*, over and over again, although it was not clear whether he was speaking to us, or whispering, desperately, to himself.

Then there was Chopper, who taught World Literature. One day, we were sitting in his classroom discussing Utopia. "You think it's possible?" he growled. He was a gnarly, bald, red-faced man whom we all suspected had a heart of gold, even if he spent most of his time yelling at us. "Mr. Carver?"

I had expected to feel out of place in this school, but in no time at all the whole deranged institution began to feel like home. In part this was because my fellow students were an even stranger collection than the faculty: nerds, boy millionaires, hippies, and orangutans-to-be. Mr. Carver, for instance, was a thin, nervous child with a nose like a sharpened pencil. "Muh, maybe an anti-Tuh-Topia?" he said. "Muh, maybe that's muh, more like it?"

"A *what*?"

"The opposite of a yuh, yuh, yuh, yuh, Utopia—"

"Name an example. From the reading."

Mr. Carver was shaking. I hoped he wasn't going to go to the bathroom in his pants again. When he felt truly cornered by Chopper, this was his "nuclear option."

"*Nineteen Eighty-fuh-Four*," Mr. Carver said. "That's an example of a nuh, non-Topia. And that's luh, less than tuh, twelve years away."

"Fewer," yelled Chopper.

"Um," said Mr. Carver.

" 'Fewer' is amount. 'Less' is degree."

"The thing is," suggested a guy named Otto, whose father had invented color television, "if Utopia is a perfect society, then it can't possibly exist, because each person's idea of Utopia is different." He looked pleased with himself. "Isn't that right, sir?"

Chopper thought it over. Then he said, *"Shaddap."*

Otto looked discouraged.

Against one wall of Chopper's classroom was a cello in a hard case. Once a year, at Christmas, he played the cello with the school orchestra. Strangely, when Chopper played the cello, his grumpy old face transformed into that of a cherub.

"Mr. Gordon?" said Chopper. "Your thoughts."

Gordo looked distracted. His father was the weatherman on the local CBS station. "I don't know, sir."

"You have no thoughts?" said Chopper.

"No sir," said Gordo. "Not right now."

"Out."

"What? I—uh—"

"Out!"

Gordo got his books and left the room.

"Anybody else here who doesn't have any thoughts?"

We all kept silent.

"Which of the texts best represents Utopia?" Chopper growled. "*1984? Brave New World? The Communist Manifesto?* Paine's *Common Sense*?" He looked at my friend Zero. "Mr. Zodner?"

"Well," said Zero. "I think Utopia lays somewhere in between."

"*Lies* between," yelled Chopper, slapping his hand on the desk. "Lay, transitive. Lie, intransitive. Correct?"

"Yes, sir," said Zero.

"If you don't know the difference between 'lie' and 'lay'? You may as well give up now. Drink *poison*."

"Sir?" asked Mr. Wedgwood. He was a happy-go-lucky, goofy guy. Nothing bothered Wedgwood.

"Whaat?"

"I was just wondering—when was the yo-yo invented?"

"Out."

"No, sir—I'm asking for a reason—"

"OUT!"

"See, the reason I need to know—"

Chopper pointed toward the door. "OOOOUUT!" he shouted.

Wedgwood got his things and left. We had already lost two of our classmates, and we still had a half hour to go. It didn't look good. Sometimes Chopper threw all of us out the door at once, and sometimes he threw us out one at a time. One at a time was a lot worse.

"What about you, Mr. Boylan?"

My heart pounded in my breast. "What about me, sir?"

"Utopia," he said. "Possible? On Earth?"

"Well," I said. "Maybe Utopia is in our own minds."

"That," Chopper observed, "doesn't mean anything."

"I mean, perhaps if we're ever going to be happy, we ought to look inside ourselves. Instead of to the world."

Chopper growled. "What do you see, Mr. Boylan?" he said. "When you look inside yourself?"

I blushed. Chopper was getting personal. "I don't know," I said.

"You don't know your own soul?" said Chopper.

I didn't know what to tell him. This was the worst, when Chopper reached into you and started pulling your guts out.

"I know it," I said. "I just don't have words for it."

It was very, very quiet in World Literature now. Chopper was turning redder, which was something I did not even know was possible. "Mr. Boylan," he said. "You *find* words for it." He looked at each of our terrified faces. "Each of you find the words to describe the things you feel. The things you know. You find those words as if your life depends on it."

Chopper slapped his hand down on the desk. *"As if your life depends on it!"* he shouted.

He looked over at my friend Doober. "Mr. Duberstein," he said. "Your thoughts."

"Well," said Doober. "Maybe there's, like, some other universe? Parallel to this one, except it's backward? Like, when they're sad, they laugh, and when they're angry they cry? It's like, when radio waves go out in space and then bounce back at us? And you can pick up on your radio, some announcer talking from, like, fifty years ago, except that it's actually *really happening* in, like, some other dimension?"

Chopper pointed to the door. *"Out,"* he said.

My sister came up the stairs. I heard her coming. It took about five seconds to unhook the bra I'd swiped out of a hamper and whisk it into one of the hidden panels in my room. The socks the bra had been stuffed with fell onto the floor. It was one of the nice things about the old house—the abundance of hidey-holes and secret panels that swung back into the walls. I closed the panel, then pulled my shirt on.

"Jimmy," Lydia said, knocking on my door. "Open up."

I was just about to slide back the deadbolt when I realized I was still wearing earrings. So I reached up, snapped them off, and stuffed them into my pockets.

Then I swung open the door.

"Hey," I said. Lydia sat down on a red swivel chair in the middle of my room, the same one I'd been sitting in a moment before, reading Thomas Mann's *Tonio Kröger* in German while wearing Playtex products.

"What are you doing?"

"Nothing," I said.

"Cool," said my sister.

"Just this German." On the floor by my bed were two rolled-up balls of socks.

Sausage raised her head from the floor, looked at my sister, and groaned. *Her again*, the dog suggested.

"What do you think the story is on that dog?" Lydia asked.

"I don't know," I said. "She has a thyroid condition."

"Your dog is retarded," said my sister.

"I guess."

"It's sad, really. You and that dog. I don't know which one to feel sorrier for."

"You don't have to feel sorry for me," I said.

"But I do," she said.

Lydia lit up a cigarette, blew the smoke toward me. I coughed.

"So," I said.

"So what," said my sister.

"Are you up here for any particular reason?"

She looked at me curiously, raised an eyebrow. "What's with your ears?"

Lydia had noticed the red marks left on my earlobes by my clip-ons. She didn't wear clip-ons since she'd gotten her ears pierced. I wouldn't get mine pierced, of course, for another thirty years.

"Nothing."

She thought this over. "Have it your way," she said. My sister went over to my Sears stereo and put *Jesus Christ Superstar* on the turntable.

She skipped right over the overture and started in with Judas's song "Heaven on Their Minds."

She handed me her cigarette. It was a Tareyton, the brand whose smokers were often featured on TV with black eyes, happily boasting that *they'd rather fight than switch*. Which is more than we could say about some people.

" 'My mind is clearer now,' " Lydia said, singing along with Judas. " 'At last, all too well, I can see, where we all soon will be.' "

Next door, on the other side of the leaking swimming pool, lived the Labrador family. They had a son about my age named Benny. I'd met him the morning after we moved into the Coffin House, when he and a bunch of other guys had shown up and asked me to join their football game.

"I don't know," I said. "I'm not really into sports."

They stood around awkwardly for a few moments, then left. I felt bad about being rude to my new neighbor, but it was the truth. I'd already taken to skipping sports at Haverford, an apostasy for which I'd already been reprimanded, twice, by the limping Mr. Flinch.

One afternoon in the late fall, as I was sitting out by the pool, a Frisbee came over the fence that separated our house from the Labradors'. Benny appeared a moment later. He was a good-looking guy with big lips. "How's it going," he said as I handed him his Frisbee.

"Good," I said.

"You guys all moved in now, I guess."

"Pretty much."

He looked at our house. "It's spooky in there, isn't it?"

I shrugged. "Kind of," I said. What I was thinking, actually, was, It's spooky out here, too.

Then he said a curious thing. "You guys find that hidden staircase?"

I looked at Benny Labrador. If there was a hidden staircase, it was a little embarrassing for us not to know about it.

"There's a hidden staircase?"

Benny nodded. "Supposed to be. The Hunts were always looking for it."

"Did they find it?"

"I don't know," he said.

"Where was it supposed to be?"

"Started on the second floor, behind that study. Went up to the tower."

"What tower?"

Now he really thought I was stupid. "They didn't tell you about the tower? There used to be this huge tower on the front of the house. But the people who lived there before the Hunts took it off."

"Why would they take the tower off?"

"I don't know," said Benny. "I heard somebody got killed up there."

"Who got killed?"

"Some kid," said Benny.

The train lurched a little as we crushed the girl beneath our wheels. Then we stopped in the Bryn Mawr station. On the other side of my window a crowd gathered, their faces blanched in horror. I asked the girl sitting next to me what was happening.

She had one of those amazing top-drawer Main Line accents. "I'm everly sure I would not know," she said.

"I think we ran someone over," I said.

She looked at me as if I were insane. "You're a hoot," she said.

It took a while to separate the coaches. It was impossible to remove the body while it was trapped under the wheels, and since the girl was dead, there was no alternative but to uncouple the cars and pull us back, thus making it necessary, in fact, to run over her a second time, this time in reverse.

When the car came to a halt again, everyone in our coach remained silent for a moment. Then the man in front of me stood up and walked to the front of the car and looked out the window. His expression when he turned back to take his seat told us all that we needed to know.

For a moment we all sat there, thinking. Then another man stood to look. Soon there was a line going down the middle of the old, decaying train car, men waiting for their chance to look out the window at what lay below.

I got up and took my place in line. No one said anything. When the boy in front of me left the window, I stepped forward, put one hand against the glass, and looked down.

There on the rails was the mangled body of a girl my age. She was wearing blue jeans and a work shirt. She had waist-length blond hair. She'd been run over right at the neck on the one rail, and at the abdomen on the other. Her dark blood was everywhere. A pair of glasses lay broken several feet away from her head. She looked a lot like I would have, I thought, if I'd been (1) a girl and (2) dead.

I walked back down the aisle to my seat. The girl who'd been next to me had gotten up while I was gawking and changed seats, as if my presence was the only thing that could possibly make the entire affair more dreadful. She'd shifted across the aisle and now had buried her nose in a copy of *Dubliners*, by James Joyce. We'd read some of those stories in Mr. Prescott's class, Literature and Death—"Araby" and "The Dead," along with Tolstoy's "The Death of Ivan Illych," and Mann's *Death in Venice*.

To me, Mr. Prescott seemed depressed sometimes.

Gazing up into the darkness I saw myself as a creature driven and derided by vanity; and my eyes burned with anguish and anger.

That night there was a story about the tragedy on Action News. The girl had been standing at the station without a coat, watching the trains come and go, mulling over her options. The stationmaster said she "seemed despondent."

Finally the train I'd been on had come into sight, and she'd made up her mind.

I wondered if, like Anna Karenina, she had had just enough time to think, before the train crushed her, *Wait, wait. I've made a terrible mistake.*

That night, as I translated *Tonio Kröger* in the room with the wallpaper that read *O dig my grave both wide and deep*, I heard a sound I had not heard before, coming from the room on the other side of my bedroom wall. By now I was used to the sound of disembodied footsteps, was used to the doors on the third floor opening and closing by themselves. I was getting used to a lot of things.

This time, though, what I heard was the sound of someone softly weeping.

I went out to the hallway and listened.

The weeping stopped. Slowly I pushed open the door of the Haunted Room. The chamber, with its torn-up wallpaper and the stains on the ceiling, was being used for storage. It was full of garment bags hanging in the closet, old boxes on the floor.

"Lydia?" I said.

She was sitting in the dark.

"Lydia?" I said again. "Is that you?"

"Leave me alone."

"Hey," I said. "It's okay."

"I said, leave me alone," she said again. "I mean it."

I stood there for a moment, not sure what to do. But then I figured if she wanted to be left alone, I'd leave her alone. I went back into my room and locked the door and returned to the never-ending translation of *Tonio Kröger* for my German class.

A moment later I heard her walk back out into the hallway and down the stairs.

I crept out into the hall again, opened the door of the Haunted Room. There, in the place where Lydia had been sitting, lay the box of her horse show ribbons with its cover removed. There was another open box containing her old bridle and a currycomb. On the side of the box were the words: *Checkmate. To store in attic.*

I wasn't sure what this occasion called for, but decided to see whether ice cream would make a difference. I went downstairs to the burned-out kitchen and got out the blender. Into this I placed two scoops of vanilla, a cup of milk, and some Hershey's chocolate syrup. I let the blender churn everything around for a while, then poured the shake into a tall glass we'd gotten for free at an Esso station.

I put a straw in it, then walked back upstairs and knocked on Lydia's door.

"Leave me alone."

"I made you a milk shake," I said.

There was a long pause, then she opened the door. Her face was all red. I handed her the shake.

I went over to a chest near her bay window. It was covered with kittygirls. We sat there for a while, my sister and me, not saying anything. She had Tom Rush on her stereo.

Good-bye to this house and all its memories
Little sister remember try to look ahead

Lydia drank her chocolate shake. "This is good," she said.

The ghost first looked me in the eyes on a night in November. I woke up at about two in the morning in my bedroom with its wallpaper bearing the images of sheet music and party horns. I wasn't sure why I'd woken. Raindrops ticked against my windowpane. Steam hissed from the old radiator in the corner.

Sausage raised her head and growled.

I got up. Slowly, tentatively, I opened my door and peeked into the hallway. There was nothing there.

Above my head was the trapdoor to the attic. The hair on Sausage's back was standing straight up.

The door to the bathroom where Jesus had lived was open. I saw my own reflection as I drew near.

Just as I reached out to touch the doorknob, I saw that there was someone behind me in the mirror, an older woman with long blond hair, wearing a white garment like a nightgown. Her eyes were a pair of small red stars. She seemed surprised to see me, and raised one hand to her mouth, as if I were the ghost, as if I were the one floating, translucently, in the mirror.

I spun around. The hall was empty.

The dog turned toward the top of the stairs, her tail still standing out straight. She growled again.

On the street outside I heard the *shush* of tires as a car rushed along the wet pavement. Thunder rumbled in the distance; the storm swept through.

I stayed where I was for a moment, frozen, my heart pounding. Who was this woman? I wondered. What did she want? She'd worn a curious, regretful expression, as if she wanted to warn me that something terrible was just about to happen to our family but, being translucent, was powerless to stop it.

One afternoon at Haverford I walked into the music teacher's room to find the captain of the wrestling team, Gus Niemeyer, wearing a bra stuffed with socks. "Boylan," he said.

"What are you doing?" I said.

"I'm in the operetta," he said. He pulled an ornate Japanese kimono over his head. "I'm Katisha."

The school was putting on Gilbert and Sullivan's *The Mikado* that spring, and in a bit of what might be called nontraditional casting, Mr. Prescott had cast Gus Niemeyer as the villainess in the musical. Usually the Upper School productions relied on the girls at Haverford's sister schools to fill the female roles in its plays. Not this time, though.

Mr. Parcival, the music teacher, walked into the room. "Ah. Niemeyer," he said. "I see you're all ready." He sat down at the piano. Mr. Parcival was the founder of the Delaware Valley Accordion Quintet. He had a goatee.

"Boylan," said Gus Niemeyer. "Do you want something?"

"Me?" I said. "Want something? What would I want?"

"Beats me," said Gus. Then he sang in his bra like the sea.

On a morning in February I walked home through the snow, lugging my Haverford School briefcase with me, a popsicle stick in my mouth. When I came through the door, I saw from the coats that everyone else was already home. I found my family sitting around the fireplace in the black living room. There wasn't a fire.

"Jimmy," said my father. "Come in. Sit down."

My sister's face was covered with tears.

"What's going on?" I said. I assumed the worst, that my parents had opened one of the hidden panels where I kept my makeup and my clothes. They'd finally discovered the terrible truth: that when no one was looking, their child was nipping off to Transylvania.

"There's something we have to talk about," said my mother. She was sitting with her hands folded in a wing chair, like a china doll.

"What is it?" I asked, sitting down.

"Your father has cancer," my mother said.

I looked at my father, who was calmly smoking an L&M. "Cancer?"

He nodded placidly.

"Melanoma," said my mother.

My sister's face told me most of what I needed to know. "He's got this mole," said Mom, "that has turned a funny color, you see. The doctors are going to take off the mole and test it. If the cancer's spread, he'll have to have radiation, or chemotherapy, or both."

"Will that stop it?" I said.

No one said anything.

"Dad? Are you going to be okay?"

My father laconically smoked his cigarette. We all sat there waiting for his response. He blew a smoke ring in the air. It drifted toward the portrait of his father above the mantelpiece. James Owen Boylan, my grandfather, was suspended on the wall, frozen in his wire-rimmed glasses and his suit coat. He'd died in 1940, when his boy was only twelve.

My father gazed distantly at the man in the painting. "Hope so," he said.

I lingered after class. "Mr. Jameson?" I said.

Chopper was erasing the board. *"Whaat?"* he said.

"Do you think there's life after death?"

He stood there motionless for a moment, holding his eraser. A vein on his temple throbbed. *"Whaat?"* he said, more loudly this time.

"Life after death," I said. "Do you think there is such a thing?"

"Out," he said, shaking his head. Clearly I'd asked a question which was nearly as stupid as Wedgwood's query regarding the yo-yo.

"No, sir," I said. "Please."

Chopper opened his mouth, but then he paused. "Well, what's your opinion, Mr. Boylan?"

"I don't know."

"I made you read the Bible. I made you read the Koran. And you don't know?"

"I'm just not sure."

"Is this something you need to know this afternoon?"

I considered the question. "Maybe."

"What's up?"

I didn't want to tell him. "My father has cancer," I said, quietly.

Chopper's jaw moved up and down, as if he were chewing something. "What kind?" he asked.

"Melanoma."

Chopper nodded, as if he knew what this was. "And so you're asking *me* if there's heaven. Is that it?"

"Yes sir."

Chopper's classroom was a rich, wood-paneled room with a fireplace. There was an American flag next to the fireplace, busts of Shakespeare and Homer on the deep window ledges. Chopper looked at the top of his wooden desk, which was covered with the themes we'd written about Utopia. Mine was one of them.

"Of *course* there's heaven," he grumbled. "How could there not be heaven?"

"Yes, but sir."

"Whaat?"

"How do you *know*?"

At that moment, the door swung open. Mr. Flinch, the headmaster, poked his head in the door. He gave me his evil eye. I knew what this was about, too. I'd skipped sports again, which at Haverford was like skipping communion.

"Boylan," said Mr. Flinch. "My office. Now."

Chopper looked at the headmaster with contempt. "I'm talking to the boy, Thatcher," he said.

"I want him," said Mr. Flinch. "In my office. He's skipped athletics, six days running. That cannot be tolerated."

"He's got his reasons," said Chopper.

"I'll be the judge of that."

"Oh shaddap," said Chopper.

"What?"

He pointed to the door. "Out," he said. I thought he meant me. But he didn't.

"Out," Chopper said again.

"I will *not* be rebuffed," said Mr. Flinch.

"Out!"

The headmaster blinked in amazement. Then, slowly, like a beaten dog, he slunk out of the room.

Apparently Chopper was the only person who had more gumption than Mr. Flinch.

I stood there, amazed by the miracle. Chopper looked at me with fiery eyes.

"You think you can write about what's going on at home? You think you could tell a story about it?"

"I don't know."

"You're a horrible writer," he said. "But you're not as horrible as the others. You write about the things you feel. I'll count that as sports."

"You'll count it as—"

"Do you have a hearing problem, Mr. Boylan?" said Chopper. "I said I'd count it as sports!"

It was another miracle. In a single moment, I'd gone from death row to freedom.

"Thank you, sir," I said. He pointed at the door. I headed out.

Just before I left the room, however, Chopper looked at me and made what passed in his case for a smile. "You see, Mr. Boylan," he growled. "I *told* you there's heaven."

This Living Hand

If, as Aristotle said, character is fate, then so, I would argue, is architecture. Surely whoever it is we become is the result, in part, of the houses in which we live. I know that my character was formed by growing up in a haunted house, in the same way that the character of my friend Gordo, the son of the TV weatherman—just to pick one other example—was fundamentally shaped by sharing a room in his parents' colonial with his younger brother, Tim, a tiny boy with flaming red hair who could, unexpectedly, sing like Luciano Pavarotti.

In the wake of my father's treatment for cancer, Dad and I set about stripping the wallpaper in my bedroom and painting the walls light blue. This was typical of my father, who could truly discern no significant difference between home renovations and psychotherapy.

We had WFLN on the radio as we began the job.

"What's this music?" I asked my dad.

"Aaron Copland," he said. "Third Symphony." Dick Boylan smiled. "He used that melody twice," he said. "He took it out later and used it in the *Fanfare for the Common Man*."

"I like it," I said.

"You think?" said my father, slicing through the sheet music with a wallpaper stripping tool. "Some people feel it's overly sentimental."

Actually, the overabundant sentimentality of the music—or of anything, really—was what I liked best. I'd found this in my own work as well, as I sat down to write the story of my family's suffering for Chopper. *We live inside a cloud of tears*, I wrote. *A cloud of laughing tears that cry. They laugh a cloud that is not real. Because they has to die.*

I had to pause, now and again, to remember one of the fundamental aspects of my prose: Hey! This is counting as *sports*!

I'd been working on my story for Chopper for a month or so, and while I was glad to have a chance to record my astonishing thoughts (which unexpectedly rose into iambic pentameter, Irish ballads, and, now and again, science fiction), the process of writing wasn't bringing me any closer to the question that had launched me on this work in the first place, namely, the issue of heaven. I assumed that there was a secret to the universe, known full well by at least a few of the adults in my life, but they wouldn't say what it was. I suspected that my father, in particular, knew the secret to the universe, on account of his brush with death. But whatever knowledge my father now possessed, he wasn't going to just come out with it. As was always the case, the truth had to come out slowly, through riddles, and music, and silence.

My father had left the hospital with part of his back sliced off and a section of his thigh grafted onto the place where the mole had been. The doctors claimed they'd "got it all," that Dick Boylan would be back to his old self soon enough.

But they didn't know everything.

He stripped off another swath of damp paper, then stood for a moment looking at the exposed bare plaster. "Hey," he said. "What do you make of this?"

There on the plaster, at shoulder level, was a line written in fancy cursive script.

In this room in the year 1923 lived Dorothy Cummin, who was not of sound mind, and drowned.

I looked at the creepy words for a beat, then went back to work. A moment later, I found a number of drawings on the plaster walls that lay beneath the paper. They'd been done in pencil, at about knee level, as if the person who'd made them was either very small or had been sitting on the floor. There was a cruel-looking man with a top hat and an animal with four legs and wings and a mouth full of sharp teeth. There were some wavy lines that might have been the ocean. A sun and moon. Rain falling from a large black cloud.

My father sliced off a few more sheets of wallpaper. The plaster was covered with drawings, all done in the same juvenile hand, none of them more than two or three feet off the floor.

Next to the closet we found a face with an open mouth, long hair, and eyes filled with tears. It looked a little like the translucent woman I had seen in the mirror.

My father got out his pack of L&Ms. He stood there by the sad, knowing face of the girl on the wall for a while, smoking, and did not say a word.

"Mr. Moose," said my sister, knocking on my door. "Open up. It's me."

"Just a second," I said.

Through the door, she could hear the sounds of struggle. Clearly I was up to something.

Lydia knocked again. "C'mon, c'mon," she said. "What are you doing in there?"

"Nothing." A moment later the door swung open. My face was all red.

My sister looked suspiciously around my bedroom. "What the fuck?" she said.

"Sorry," I said, blushing deeply. "I was exercising."

My sister nodded. "Exercising," she said. It seemed about as stupid a thing for me to be doing as anything else, but then this was only because the possibility that I was *actually being someone else while she wasn't looking* hadn't occurred to her.

"So," she said. "You psyched for this party tonight, out at Ashley's?"

I did not really know Ashley Pennypacker, the debutante. I knew her parents lived in a castle, a place with its own gatehouse. The only thing missing was a moat and some serfs.

"I'm psyched," I said.

Lydia went over to my stereo, and put *Jesus Christ Superstar* on the turntable again. This time she went for Pilate's song. *I dreamed, I met a Galilean. A most amazing man! He had that look you very rarely find. The haunting, hunted kind.*

When we performed *Jesus Christ Superstar*, the part of Pilate usually fell to me. Because she was older, my sister always got to be Judas. We didn't have a regular Jesus, which meant that the part of the Messiah frequently had to be played by the dog.

"What are you wearing?"

"Me?" I said. "These jeans?"

My sister sat down in my red swivel chair and lit up a Newport. "I don't mean right *now*. I mean later."

"Oh. Well, I don't know. Dad said he had a tuxedo. Somewhere."

"Tuxedo's good," she said. She picked up a book, one of the Chronicles of Narnia. "You're reading this?"

"The Last Battle," I said. I was a big fan of C. S. Lewis. It was reassuring, the way Aslan kept rescuing everybody.

Lydia looked around my room. "We should leave here around eight," she said. "We'll pick up Nelson on the way over."

Nelson was her current boyfriend, a big guy with a beard. He was the captain of something called Episcopal Wrestling. Sometimes Nelson picked me up and spun me around over his head, then slammed me down on the floor and pinned one of my arms behind my back. My sister said this was a sign of affection, but I wasn't so sure.

"Doesn't the party start at seven?"

"Of course it starts at seven. That's why you get there at nine. Don't you know anything?"

As it turned out, I *didn't* know anything.

"What is a debutante party, anyway?" I said. "What's the point?"

"Ashley is being presented to society," my sister explained.

"What does that mean?" I said. "Society? I mean, isn't it, you know, bullshit?"

"Of course it's bullshit," my sister said. "Everyone knows that."

"So—why are we going to this party again?"

"Because," Lydia said, blowing smoke out my window. "We're showing the culture what bullshit it is."

"How are we doing that?"

"By imitating its phony rituals."

"We're imitating its rituals? Is that what we're doing?"

"Exactly," said Lydia. "All those stuck-up people won't be able to tell us apart from people like themselves."

"But doesn't that make us as bad as they are?"

"No," said Lydia. "That means we start to turn the whole culture inside out."

"Wow," I said. The evening was more complicated than I thought. Not only was I going to have to wear a tuxedo, I was going to have to wear one ironically.

"You know, no one's making you go," Lydia pointed out. "I asked Ashley to invite you as a favor."

"I want to go," I said.

"Don't worry, Mr. Moose," she said. "You just hang out, drink some punch, dance to the band."

"All right," I said. "Okay. Okay."

She looked at me closely. I wondered, not for the last time, whether or not she had an inkling of my secret identity. Sometimes I wanted to scream it out at her. *Hey. I'm really your little sister. You know that, right?*

"You seem flipped out," she said.

I shrugged. "I don't know these people," I said. "What if they're mean to me?"

"It's okay, Jim," she said. "When worst comes to worst, remember the golden rule."

"What's that?"

She smiled. "Just be yourself."

. . .

A couple of hours later I was sitting in the backseat of our Volkswagen, as Nelson drove us toward Ashley's house, which was actually a compound called Clockwork Hollow Farm. On the radio Joni Mitchell was singing a song called "Little Green." My sister and I sang along.

"What the fuck is this song about, anyway?" said Nelson.

My sister sighed. "What do you think?" she asked, as if it were obvious.

"Beats me," said Nelson.

"It's about her baby."

"Joni Mitchell doesn't have any baby," said Nelson.

"The person in the song has one," said my sister. "Her stupid boyfriend got her pregnant."

"Joni Mitchell isn't the person in the song?" said Nelson.

We drove down a hill, at the bottom of which Darby Creek flowed directly across the road. This was something called the Old Gulph Ford.

"Lift your feet, Liddie," said Nelson. As we crossed the ford, several inches of creek water slowly rose into the car through the rusted-out holes in the VW's floor. When we reached the other side, the water drained out through the same holes.

"Just a little green," my sister sang. It was her favorite song.

"I'm just saying," continued Nelson. "Why is she pissing and moaning? She's got options. Right?"

"Options?" said my sister. "Is that what you call it?"

"Just because she's got options, that doesn't make her happy," I said.

"What? She'd be happier if she *didn't* have any options?"

"She gives up the baby!" my sister shouted. "Jesus! While Mr. Natural heads out to California and sends her *poems*? She gives up her *baby*!"

"Sometimes there aren't any good choices," I noted.

"Christ," said Nelson. "Sometimes women act like they're happier when they're miserable."

"Yeah, well, who is it that makes us miserable?" I said, looking out the window. At the bottom of the ridge to our right I could see the rushing waters of the creek. Then I realized my slip. I cleared my throat. "I mean *them*. Makes *them* miserable."

Nelson shook his head. "Ya got me," he said.

"Can we talk about something else, please?" said Lydia, turning off the radio.

"Anything you want," said Nelson.

We pulled into the driveway. Clockwork Hollow Farm was an immense preserve, with cornfields and a gatehouse and a barn full of quarter horses and a meadow full of long sweet grass and a small hill, atop which sat a mansion many times larger than the Coffin House, and which I could tell even at this distance contained no leaking ceilings, warped floorboards, or secret laboratories. It was older than our house, too. Not far from the house, overlooking the whole affair, was a giant observation tower with an enormous clock. As we parked the Volkswagen in a field full of Mercedeses and Lincolns, a deep bell up in the tower rang out, once.

"Don't ask for whom the fuckin' bell tolls, F.G.," said Nelson, straightening his cummerbund.

F.G. was his nickname for me, an ingenious cryptogram for *fag*.

He picked me up and held me over his head, spun me around a couple times, and slammed me down into the sweet grass. "It fuckin' tolls for thee!"

"Don't call me that," I said.

"For god's sake, Jim," said my sister. "Don't be such a crybaby."

"Sorry."

We walked into Clockwork Hollow Mansion. The place was lousy with penguins. There were waiters with trays of canapés and men in waistcoats carrying platters of champagne flutes. There were antique couches and Oriental carpets and statues of philosophers and sylphs. The doors to the outside stood open, and through them I could see a large white tent, in which there was an eight-piece big band, a dance floor, and a buffet table that was manned by dudes in starched white hats.

This was all something of a shock to me, since in Newtown Square the wildest parties I'd been to involved snoozing on the floor in a sleeping bag after making your own sundaes with Bosco chocolate syrup.

I turned to my sister to say *Whoa*, but my sister wasn't there anymore. So I leaned against a pole in the tent and watched the band. A guy at the microphone allowed as how he had the "Rockin' Pneumonia and the Boogie-Woogie Flu."

I laughed. A girl next to me looked at me with curiosity.

"Is something risible?" she said. "Do share."

"This guy," I said, indicating our man. "He's so bad he's good."

She raised an eyebrow. "You're contradicting yourself. How can he be both bad and good?"

"No, I'm saying he's so bad that it's kind of in a category all his own."

She thought this over. "Is he bad?" she said.

I nodded. "Yeah," I said. "He stinks."

"Ah, that explains it," she said. "You see, I wouldn't know. I have no way of telling."

I looked at her. She was wearing a white dress like my sister's. She had shoulder-length blond hair, high cheekbones. "Well, you can take my word for it," I said. "He's terrible."

She nodded grimly.

"Pretty weird scene," I said. "Don't you think?"

"How so?" she said. "Has something come off kilter?"

"You know," I said. "All these characters. The guys in the chef's hats. That clock tower. It's kind of freaky, don't you think?"

She nodded, as if we were in agreement. "It's divine," she said.

The girl seemed strangely familiar to me, which was odd because I was certain I had never met her before.

"What do you think goes on in that clock tower?" I said.

"Goes on?" she said. "Goes on how?"

"I mean, what's it doing there? Don't they have watches?"

"Who's this we're discussing?" said the girl. "And please. Don't mumble."

"I'm saying it looks creepy. Like the kind of place where you'd lose your mind and commit hara-kiri."

"Are you unhappy?" asked the girl.

"Me?" I said. "No, I'm just saying."

"I'm so relieved."

I realized, with a shock, that the girl I was talking to was the same one I'd sat next to on the train the day we'd crushed the despondent stranger beneath our wheels on the Paoli local.

"Tuesday," said a dashing young man, inexplicably, as he arrived on the scene.

"Dicky-Duck," said the girl.

He stretched his arm toward me. "Rich Swarthmore," he said, as if I were a guy just like himself. He was following the ancient code of the Main Line, which is: *There are no such things as strangers. Only snobs we haven't met yet.*

"James Quackenbush," I said. "Call me Quacky." One of the amazing things about the Main Line is that you could say something like *Call me Quacky* to people, and they would.

"Tuesday Ballinger," said the girl.

"We've met before," I noted.

"Have we?" said Tuesday.

"Yeah, we ran over somebody one time. With a train?"

The girl looked at me curiously. "You're a hoot," she said.

"I guess."

"Dicky? Let's dance."

The young man nodded. "Good to meet you, Quacky."

Good-bye, Tuesday, I thought, as they walked onto the dance floor beneath the white tent, where the assembled delegates were tying a yellow ribbon 'round the old oak tree.

Tuesday fell into Dicky's arms, and they slowly spun around to the music, hopelessly in love. It struck me that the song probably wasn't half so horrible if you were listening to it while somebody held you in their arms. But I couldn't say for sure. When it came to matters of the heart, as Tuesday had observed, *I wouldn't know. I had no way of telling.*

• • •

Later, up in the gruesome clock tower, I observed girls in formal dresses doing Jell-O shots by the enormous, rotating gears. Dudes in tuxedos put one end of a hose in their mouths, the other end attached to a giant funnel into which their brethren poured brew dog after brew dog.

The apex of the tower was reached by a set of endless circular stairs that went around and around the tower's pitch-dark innards until at last one arrived at the clockworks. The clock face was made of translucent white glass, allowing the soft light that illuminated the tower room to shine through. The hands of the clock were connected through a series of gears and pulleys to an electrical mechanism, a sequence of relays and fuses, and a tangle of thick wires. It was a very good place to smoke pot, apparently, or to have beer poured into your gullet through a funnel. I liked hanging out up there, watching my peers laughing themselves silly inside the timepiece's extravagant brains.

Through the walls of the tower we could hear the sound of the band, the voices of the partygoers out in the tent. There were horses nattering in the barn and the rush of water in a creek. Voices called out and echoed in the night.

I sat by the enormous gears, watching the antics of my betters for some time, until at last one of the partygoers recognized me. This was a guy named Funus. Like my sister's paramour, Nelson, he was a parishioner from the Episcopal Wrestling Squad.

"Hey, I know you!" he said. "You're Lydia Boylan's brother."

"That's me," I said.

"I heard," he observed, "you're a fag."

Everybody looked at me. There were about a dozen people up there in the tower, and each one stopped what he or she was doing and turned to the matter at hand. Fortunately, I had a response to this, a creepy poem by Keats that I had memorized for an occasion just such as this.

This living hand [I explained] *now warm and capable*
Of earnest grasping, would, if it were cold

And in the icy silence of the tomb,
So haunt thy days and chill thy dreaming nights
That thou wouldst wish thine own heart dry of blood!

Funus thought this over, took a swig from his Michelob. "*What?*"

"'*See here it is,*'" I said, and stretched out my hand. "'*I hold it towards you.*'"

"You *are* a fag," said Funus. "Aren't you?"

"Funus," said a lovely woman with big black eyes. "Stop."

"I call 'em the way I see 'em," said Funus. He turned to his associates. "Am I right?"

His compatriots nodded somberly. I was a fag all right.

I stood up. "You'll excuse me," I said, and left the clockworks. Behind me, I heard the voices of Funus and his friends raised in hilarity and celebration.

It was dark in the stairwell. The staircase hugged the walls.

"Hey," said a voice. I looked over, but I could not see anyone.

"Hey," I said. "Who's there?"

"It's only me," a girl's voice said, as if this answered my question.

"Well," I said. "That's a relief."

I sat down on the top step. "How long," she said, after a while, "do you think it would take, if you jumped off the edge of the railing? Before you hit the ground, I mean."

I thought it over. "Maybe ten, fifteen seconds," I said. "It's farther than it looks. This tower is like three or four stories tall. Maybe five."

"Do you think it'd be interesting? Or would it all be too scary? The falling."

"Scary, I'd think."

She sighed. "Yeah. It's a shame it'd be that way, though, you know? It'd be nice if you could enjoy it, the flying. Like you were a mockingbird, or an owl."

"Maybe," I said, and thought, Like a mockingbird? Or an owl? Who was it I was talking to? Mrs. Edgar Allan Poe?

"Don't worry, I'm not jumping," she said. "I was just thinking."

"I know."

"I can barely see you," she said. "It's so dark." From behind us came the sound of Funus and his tower guard, their voices once more raised in celebration. The invisible woman reached out with one hand and felt my face. Her hand dropped down to my bow tie. "Oh," she said. "You're a boy."

"Yeah," I said. "I'm a boy all right."

"I thought so at first," she said. "But then your voice is so—"

"I know," I said. "It's a problem."

"It's a nice voice," she said.

I reached out and felt her face. My hands touched her long, silky hair. "And you're a girl."

"Yeah." She reached out and touched my face again, ran her finger along my long pointy nose, brushed her palm across my cheek. I slid closer to her. She smelled like white flowers.

"What if it didn't hurt?" she said. "You could do it then."

"I don't know," I said. "It seems so stupid. You'd miss out on everything."

She thought about this. "I'm going to miss out on everything anyway."

"What do you mean?"

"Someday. I got neutropenia. You know what that is?"

I knew what it was. There was a girl at my sister's school named Faith Bartelsby who had it. Earlier in the year, I'd gone with a bunch of my sister's friends to donate our white blood cells for her. We'd all lain there in our chairs at the Bryn Mawr hospital as the doctors took a pint of blood from each of us. Then they took the blood and spun it around a centrifuge until they got all our white blood cells. After that, we got all our own blood back. It had been an odd experience to go through, especially when our own blood was fed back into our arms through big red tubes. It was warm, the blood.

"You're Faith Bartelsby, aren't you?"

"Yeah."

"I gave you some white blood cells. Last fall."

"Oh," she said. For some reason this didn't cheer her up. "Thanks."

It took some of the mystery out of it, knowing who she was.

"Does it hurt?" I said. "Having that? Neutro—?"

"Neutropenia," she said. "Yeah, it hurts. It comes and goes though. Right now I'm okay."

"Well, good," I said. "So you're not going off the edge of the stairs then."

"Not tonight," she said.

I gathered from this that she was looking on the bright side, which was what I usually tried to do. But then she started to cry.

"It's okay," I told her, even though it wasn't.

"I just want to be like everybody else," she said.

"Tell me about it." I wiped the tears from her cheek with my thumb. From outside we heard the band playing. "(I Can't Get No) Satisfaction."

"Are you sick, too?" she said.

"Kind of," I said.

"What do you have?"

I thought about it. If I was ever going to tell anybody, now might be the time. She didn't even know my name. To her I was just a shadow.

"I can't tell you," I said.

"Oh," said Faith. "Okay." She stood up. "I should go."

"I don't suppose you want to—" I didn't finish the sentence. I already knew the answer. Whatever it was we had been doing, it was now nearly over.

Faith leaned forward and kissed me on the neck. It was soft. The clock tower rang the hour: eleven o'clock. We were nearly deafened by the thunderous gonging of the bells in our brains.

"See ya," Faith said, and went down the stairs. I listened to her footsteps recede, circling around and around that old tower, until at last I heard the door at the bottom open and close. There was a quick flash of light from outside, and the girl's moving shadow flittered against the stone wall. Then she was gone.

I waited for a while, my hand on the railing, before following her. It was a long way down. It probably would take you ten or fifteen seconds before you hit the bottom, if you jumped.

Before that, though, you'd be flying in the air, like a mockingbird, or an owl.

At twelve-thirty that night, I was sitting at the keyboard of a concert grand piano, an instrument the size of a yacht. At one point it had apparently belonged to Charles de Gaulle, although how it had gotten from Paris to Clockwork Hollow was beyond me. The harp cover was up, too, supported by the long stick, so the whole instrument rang like a bell. To make the scene even more theatrical, the piano was placed at the bottom of a huge circular staircase that swooned upward into the heart of the mansion.

I sat on the piano bench, playing the McCoy Tyner version of "My Favorite Things," while a large crowd of fabulous swells gathered around me, drinking champagne. To my surprise, playing the piano, which had always been a fundamentally private activity, turned out to be a social grace, something that made up for the fact that I had a grandmother who danced on top of barstools and that I lived in a haunted house with a cat named ba-BOING!

I played for a long time, going through the strange amalgam of jazz standards, rock and roll tunes, and lounge music that constituted my core repertoire. I did "Sugar Blues," with a bass line that showed off my left hand's grotesque reach, a spread that enabled me to play walking tenths. After "Sugar Blues" I did "Bye Bye Blackbird," a song I liked not least because my hero, James Thurber, had had his massive brain hemorrhage while drunkenly singing it at a party.

At one point, Tuesday Ballinger came in from outside and placed a long-stemmed glass of Chablis on the piano next to the music stand. She winked at me as she set it down, and with that wink I understood that—against all odds—I'd broken into society.

I drank the glass of wine. Another one magically appeared. My playing started getting a little sloppy. I forged onward through "Moonlight Cocktail" and "Well You Needn't" and "China Cat Sunflower." I kept on drinking. I'd been drunk before, but not at this stratosphere. The crowd of people watching me slowly grew. It was an amazing spectacle, me at the keys of the endless piano, the circular stairs swirling around us. At one point I actually felt the entire house slowly spinning around me like a top. On the steps of the whirling staircase stood couples drinking cocktails in their tuxedos and their strapless ball gowns.

Somewhere around one A.M., I decided, What the hell—I might as well sing. Until this evening, I'd been embarrassed by my singing voice, which was decidedly feminine in pitch; when I sang my voice came out two-thirds Emmylou Harris and one-third Rochester from the *Jack Benny Program*. But I had my audience in the palm of my hand. I was vast! I contained multitudes!

So I sang one.

Just a little green
Like the color when the spring is b—

At that moment, however, my hands left the keys as I unexpectedly rose into the air. For a moment I thought I'd levitated into the air, buoyed upward by the antigravitational forces inherent in my stoned soul picnic.

But then I realized that the reason I was suspended in space was that Nelson was holding me aloft. "Hey!" he said. "What did I tell you! This kid's a fag!"

Then he slammed me down onto the Oriental rug. As I hit the floor, everybody laughed, the men as well as the women. People held their sides in hilarity. The folks on the stairwell had to clutch on to the banister of the whirling, rotating stairs.

I didn't blame them for laughing. It was pretty funny, if you thought about it.

"Are you a fag, or what?" inquired Nelson.

"I guess," I said, getting back up and sitting down on the piano bench. Amazingly, I started in on "Goodbye Pork Pie Hat."

"Keep playing, F.G.!" said Nelson. "Don't quit now! You're the life of the party!" He could hardly believe me.

"Don't call him that," my sister snapped.

"What?" said Nelson.

"His name," my sister said, "is Jim."

"I thought he was Quacky," said Tuesday Ballinger.

There was a stunned silence.

Lydia marched over to the piano bench and grabbed me by the hand. "Come on," she said. "We're leaving."

"Aw," said Nelson. "We're all just having fun."

"You're cruel," said Lydia.

"It's all right," I said.

My sister went up to her date. Her face was red. "Nelson Bushmill," she said. "You're a bastard." She smacked him. It made a fresh, cheerful sound, her hand against his cheek.

"Aw, hey," said Nelson. "We're just kidding around. Don't get so emotional." He put his big arm around my back. "We're friends, F.G. and me. Aren't we friends?"

She smacked him again, harder. This time she'd hurt him. He pulled his hand back.

"Go on, try it," said Lydia. "I'd like to see it."

"Fuck you," said Nelson. "Fuck the both of ya."

Lydia bowed her head to the room, which by now seemed to consist exclusively of Episcopalian wrestlers. All the other ladies and gentlemen had scattered. "Good night, everyone."

Then she turned. For a moment I stood there, looking at the room full of stunned, large men. Then my sister grabbed my hand and marched me outside.

"I don't think they meant any harm—" I said, incredibly, since of course harm was exactly what they'd meant.

"Don't. Say. Anything," Lydia suggested.

We walked through the Pennypackers' meadow toward the car. Up in the tower, I could see shadows of people moving behind the enormous, luminous dial of the timepiece.

I sat down in the VW, and my sister fired up the engine. Moments later, we were headed down the long driveway and out into the quiet street.

My sister turned on the radio. Cher was singing "Half-Breed."

"You don't even see yourself, do you?" said Lydia. "You don't have any idea."

"About what?" I said.

But my sister didn't answer. We drove back to Somerset through a beautiful night full of twinkling stars. On the way home, we passed through the ford in Gulph Mills and the waters of the creek again rose, then drained through, the rusted-out holes in the Volkswagen's floor. We listened to the AM radio. "We're an American Band." "Smoke on the Water." "The Monster Mash." "Space Oddity."

We left the car in the driveway of the Coffin House and headed inside. As we reached the bottom of the third-floor stairs, I gave my sister a hug. She squeezed me.

"Good night, Jim," she said. It was the first time I remembered her using my actual name. Usually, as far as Lydia was concerned, I was Mr. Moose.

"Good night."

She stood there for a moment, and watched me ascend the steps back to my other universe.

I reached my room, got out a negligee from a secret panel, and got in bed and said my prayers. *Forgive Funus, Lord. Forgive Nelson. They can't help it if they're stupid.*

And God bless Faith Bartelsby. Maybe I could see her again sometime. If it is Thy will. In a room with some lights on in it. Amen.

But Faith Bartelsby would die just a few months later. One morning, while eating my breakfast, I saw her obituary in the *Philadelphia Inquirer.*

"Oh no," I said. My mother, who was frying bacon at the time, looked over at me with concern.

"What's wrong?" she asked.

"This girl who died," I said.

There was a photograph of Faith next to her obituary. She'd been a sweet, beautiful girl. Maybe I shouldn't have been surprised by this, but I was. I'd never seen her face before. She had freckles.

"Oh dear," my mother said. "Was she a friend?"

I remembered the smell of her hair, the feeling of her lips against my neck. Her voice in the dark, softly saying, *It's only me.*

"No," I said. "Not really."

You're Pathétique

Skip Frasier, the piano tuner, was a tall, reedy man with a mustache. He arrived at the Coffin House one afternoon while the rest of my family was out, his wife, Dottie, in tow. Dottie had a one-year-old baby she called Pine Top. She sat down in front of the painting of my grandfather, put Pine Top on the floor. He crawled toward me.

Skip took the cover off the piano, threaded the felts between the strings, then banged a tuning fork against his knee. Pine Top grabbed my finger and stuck it in his mouth. He made a happy sound, the baby.

"Hey," said Dottie. "He likes you!"

"Can I pick him up?" I said.

"Sure," said Dottie, with a sigh of relief. Pine Top gurgled in my arms. "That's so weird. Usually he *hates* people."

"Can I get some *quiet*, Dottie?" said Skip, banging the tuning fork against his knee once more, then holding it to his ear.

I picked up Pine Top, carried him over to the piano. Little Pine Top smelled like powder and baby breath and sleep. He pointed at his father.

"A," said Pine Top. Skip held up the tuning fork.

"That's right," said Skip. "That's A."

"Wow," I said. "That's amazing he can tell the notes."

Skip shrugged. "A's the only note he knows."

"I'm getting my guitar," Dottie announced, and walked across the living room through the grand archway with the keystone, back outside to Skip's Volkswagen bus.

"You been playing this instrument too hard," said Skip. "You been getting a buzz out of it?"

I thought about this. I wasn't sure what the answer was.

"Yeah," I said. "I get a buzz out of it sometimes."

"Look," said Skip. "There's a crack in the soundboard."

"A crack?" I said.

"That's going to mess up the sound, man," said Skip, who was now working his way up the scale with the tuning wrench.

"Can you fix it?"

"Replace the soundboard?" He looked grave. "For a piano? That's like open-heart surgery."

"It's serious, then."

"It's serious." He looked sad. Pine Top reached up, grabbed my glasses, and threw them on the floor.

"Some of the ivories are split, too," said Skip, looking at the keys. "It's like you been playing with a screwdriver."

"I should be more careful," I said, picking up my glasses. "Sometimes when I play I forget. It's like I go into this trance."

Dottie came back in with a guitar. She sat down by the cold fireplace and started strumming something.

"You have to be gentle," Skip said. "If you want people to listen to you, you know what you do? Speak softly."

"A," said Pine Top.

"I don't get it," I said.

"You play at top volume all the time, everybody's just going to want to run and hide. But if you bring your voice way down—like this—everybody has to lean forward, pay attention, try to figure it out. That's called *dynamics*."

"I never thought of that."

"Yeah well," said Skip. "That's why your soundboard's cracked."

Dottie was now singing something; I couldn't make out the words.

"Can I show the baby the house?" I said.

"You show him whatever you want," said Skip.

I carried the baby throughout the house, showed him the family room with the zebra-striped paneling and the wagon wheel chandeliers. I took him into the kitchen and let him pull one of the plastic bricks off the wall. He laughed.

I loved having the baby in my arms, although partly it made me sad, too. I would never be anyone's mom. Pine Top was as close as I would get.

We went up the back stairs and into my mother's study. I put him down on the floor and let him crawl around for a while. Pine Top loved books. He reached for volume after volume, knocked them off the shelves, ripped off the covers and stuck the paper in his mouth. From downstairs came the sound of Skip Frasier banging on the higher strings, bending the notes back into tune.

There was a big, heavy *klunk*. I looked over at Pine Top. He had gotten hold of the family Bible, a huge, oversized volume about the size of a cinder block. The book fell open to a color plate of Moses parting the Red Sea.

"That's the Bible," I explained.

"A," said Pine Top. He grabbed the page in front of him and pulled.

The Scriptures tore in half.

"No," I said. "No!"

Pine Top kept on pulling on the fine, tissuelike paper of the Bible, until the page came right out in his hand. He raised it to his mouth.

My heart beat quickly. I took the page out of the baby's mouth, put it back in the Bible, closed the thick book, and returned it to the shelf. Pine Top looked at me and started to cry.

"Oh, it's okay," I said, holding the baby to my breast again, although of course what I had wasn't exactly a breast. "Bible had to go bye-bye."

And Pine Top wept.

"It's okay," I said, rocking him back and forth. "There are other books."

Pine Top didn't want any of the other books, though: He didn't care about the autographed copy of *Victory in My Hands* that Harold Russell had signed with his prosthetic hooks, wasn't interested in all the first editions of Somerset Maugham, didn't want to look at the *Guide to Palm Reading*, either. What he wanted was the Bible.

Dottie didn't come up the stairs for him, even though Pine Top was now beside himself with woe. She just kept singing her far-off song. I picked up the inconsolable child and walked around the house with him. My shoulder was wet with his tears.

We went to the window on the second-floor landing, the place where, in years to come, I would sit and make out with people in hopes of becoming more likable. A bird flew past.

I carried Pine Top into the pink sewing room, a room that had once been a nursery. It didn't cheer him up, though.

Finally I sat down on the bottom stair of the staircase that led up to the third floor, and I sang to the child.

Just a little green
Like the crocuses when the spring is born.

When Dottie finally came up the stairs, she found the baby asleep in my arms. "Wow," she said. "You're really good with kids."

"He's a sweetie pie," I said.

"You're better with him than I am," she said. "I don't know what the hell he wants half the time."

"We could trade," I said, laughing.

Dottie was still holding her guitar. From downstairs, Skip called out to her. "C'mon, Dottie. We gotta go."

Pine Top opened his eyes and smiled at me.

Dottie gave me a strange, piercing look.

"Here," she said, and handed me her guitar. I gave her back her baby. He began to cry.

Now I was holding her guitar, which was a brown-bodied acoustic. On the neck was written the name of the manufacturer: Stella.

"You keep it," Dottie said softly.

"Your guitar?" I said. "No way."

"Yeah," she said. "My gift."

She said this all so softly I almost doubted I'd heard her right. "But I don't know how to play guitar," I said.

Dottie shrugged. "Me neither."

"C'mon," Skip shouted from downstairs. "We're leaving!"

"I have to go," she said.

"You're really giving me your guitar?"

She nodded. "Maybe it will help you," she said.

"Help? I don't need help," I said.

She gave me a look that said, You think? Then she walked down the creaking steps, through the front hallway, and out into the waiting microbus.

I stood at the top of the stairs and listened as the Volkswagen departed. I strummed the open strings of the guitar—a dissonant chord. It rang in Stella's insides.

"Poor baby," I said. I wouldn't see him again.

There didn't seem to be much question that Pine Top was now doomed. It was bad enough having Skip and Dottie as parents—but now he had a far greater curse. He'd torn the pages of the Holy Bible. No matter what happened to him from now on, he would never be able to untear it. He would carry the burden of what he had done the rest of his days.

I sat down on the stairs and tried to play the blues on the Stella. But I didn't know how.

Twenty years later, in a bar in Ohio, Pine Top Frasier stabbed a man through the heart. They caught him, though. Gave him the death penalty.

Later his sentence was commuted to life without parole.

For a while I was thinking I should go to the prison and talk to him. Who else would go see him? I wondered. Not Dottie. I thought I should ask him if he remembered me carrying him around the Coffin House, if he recalled the taste of the Scriptures in his mouth.

But I had a pretty good sense how it would go. A guard would say, *Pine Top, there's some chick here to see you,* and he'd come into the interview room wearing his orange jumpsuit, and I'd be sitting there on the other side of the glass. He'd sit down on his chair and pick up the phone and say, *Who the hell are you?* or *What do you want from me?* and I wouldn't really have a very good answer.

It had been a long time since I'd held him in my arms.

Things on the third floor got nuttier. I had a red swivel chair that occasionally would spin around by itself, usually while I was working on the never-ending translation of *Tonio Kröger*. Other times, I'd come up the stairs and find my desk chair balanced precariously on top of my desk.

One afternoon I was practicing a speech for Ancient History. I was wearing a bra while I did this, although it was my intention to take off the bra before giving the actual speech. It was easier to rehearse this way, though. When I looked like myself I felt less nervous.

I was one of a group of seven boys assigned by Mr. Gripps to discuss the Wonders of the Ancient World. To my surprise, I'd wound up with the Hanging Gardens of Babylon. I didn't know anything about them.

We'd been assigned our wonders at random.

"The Hanging Gardens," I said, in my Walter Cronkite voice, "were built by Nebuchadnezzar to cheer up his wife, who was depressed. She came from a land of mountains and rivers and green fields, but after her marriage was stuck in Babylon, which was not all it was cracked up to be. Nebuchadnezzar decided to make her happy by building a fake mountain for her and then covering it with plants that flowed. The Hanging Gardens were a Wonder of the Ancient World. Except that no one knows if they really existed. Were they an actual wonder? Or something somebody just made up a big story about? Now it is a mystery. But it is interesting to believe them if you can."

Then, as now, I was, in equal measures, hopeful and inarticulate.

The door to my room creaked open. I stood there in my bra looking over at the child who did not exist. My red swivel chair slowly revolved.

I shuddered. "*Quit* it," I said.

From the piano downstairs came the sudden, crashing notes of the *Pathétique* Sonata. I stood there for a moment, feeling the goose bumps on my arm, as the song unwound.

I took off my bra and stuffed it back in the secret panel. Then I walked downstairs, my heart pounding.

At the bottom of the stairs, I paused. I couldn't quite see the piano through the archway to my right. The music stopped.

"Who's there?" said a man's voice, thin and tired.

"It's me." I stepped forward.

My father was sitting on the piano bench, smoking a cigarette. "I didn't know anybody was home," he said.

"Neither did I," I said. I still wasn't sure if he was real. My father never played piano anymore. And here he was playing Beethoven?

He took a long drag on his cigarette, blew the smoke out into the room. "Sorry about the noise," he said.

"It's fine," I said. "You ought to play more often, Dad."

"Now, now," he said sadly. "The torch has passed."

"But you're good," I said. "Why don't you play?"

"Ah, well," he said. "There's no pleasure for me in murdering things of beauty."

This was a major difference between my father and me. Murdering things of beauty was my stock in trade.

"It sounds better since Skip Frasier tuned it," I said. "Doesn't it?"

"You bet," said my father.

He got up and went over to the couch. I could tell from his manner that he was embarrassed I'd heard him playing. I wanted to tell him there was nothing to be ashamed about, especially if you compared it to practicing a speech about the Hanging Gardens of Babylon while wearing a bra you kept hidden in a secret panel. But I kept this observation to myself. There were some wonders people could do without.

Dad sat down with a copy of the *Evening Bulletin*, a paper that would fold eight years later, in 1982. My father, too, would cease publication pretty soon, but we didn't know that then.

He looked up from his paper at the oil painting of my grandfather.

"You know what's funny," said Dad. "I never look at that picture, of my father. Sometimes I forget it's him."

"What was he like?"

"I don't know," he said in a distant voice. "He died when I was twelve, you know. The same year he gave me that piano. I got the piano for my birthday in June. He was dead by the fall."

"Don't you remember anything about him?"

My father thought for a long time. Then he said, "He always wore white in the summers. A linen suit. And he smoked a pipe." He stared once more at his father's face, having a private conversation.

"I'm sorry you lost him," I said.

"Hm?" My father's eyes fell from one James Boylan to the other. "What's that?"

"I said I'm sorry you lost him. Your dad."

He nodded. "You bet." His voice broke. We lingered there, the three of us, for a long moment, grandfather and father and son.

"I guess I should finish my homework," I said.

"Good show," my father said.

"I'm doing an oral report," I said. "For Mr. Gripps."

"On what?"

"The Hanging Gardens of Babylon."

"Ah," my father said, in his distant, wistful voice. "The ancient world."

I'd told him I was leaving but I didn't leave. We didn't have many moments like this. I sat down at the Cable-Nelson.

"So Dad. You feel okay?"

"You bet."

"Seriously. Now that they took off, you know . . . that mole. Do you feel like yourself again?"

My father didn't respond right away. "I do and I don't," he said softly. "The graft they gave me, putting part of my leg on my back. I'm all rearranged."

"But you're cured, though, right? That cancer. It's not coming back. Is it?"

He sat there for a long time, the smoke from his cigarette curling toward the ceiling. He was silent for so long I wondered if he'd forgotten my question.

"You'll take care of them?" he said. "When I'm gone."

"Who?"

"Your sister. Your mother. They'll need you to be the strong one."

"Me?" I said. "What are you talking about? You said you were okay now."

"That's right," he said.

"So you don't need me to be taking care of anyone. The doctors said they got it all."

"But just in case. It'd be your job. To look out for them, if you had to."

I played a couple of random notes on the keyboard, high in the upper octaves.

"You will, won't you?" said my father. "Tell me you will."

"What?"

"Look *out* for them," he said urgently. *"Be the man."*

"You said I wouldn't *have* to," I said. He was starting to annoy me now. "You said you'd be *fine*."

He took a long drag of his cigarette, held the smoke in his lungs. Then he blew it all out again.

"Why don't you play something?" he said.

"What?" I said. I didn't want to play him anything, if he was going to talk crazy.

"How about Schumann's 'Träumerei'? From the *Scenes from Childhood*?"

"Fine," I said.

"Only," he said, "play it in ragtime."

"Fine," I said, and gave it to him. Ragtime. Like that made any sense.

He sat there in his chair, staring into the fireplace, as I played "Träumerei" like a mentally challenged Jelly Roll Morton.

In German the word means *dreaming*.

Halfway through the song, I found tears welling up in my eyes, and they spilled over my lashes and ran down my face. I hated that he could see them, but I couldn't wipe the tears off while I was playing.

Slowly he got out of his chair and came over to the piano, sat down next to me on the bench. Then he put his hand on the side of my face.

"Now, now," he said kindly. "That's enough of that."

As I was writing this book, it occurred to me to go and find the old Boylan family Bible, to seek out the page that baby Pine Top had torn. I knew it was a right-hand page and that the tear had gone all the way across the thin paper.

My partner, Grace, who was making chicken curry in our kitchen at the time, pointed out to me that any torn right-hand page would also be a torn left-hand page on the opposite side. She's smart that way.

And so I started with the New Testament, which is where I remembered the tear taking place. I started with Revelation and worked my way backward. And yet, I got all the way to St. Matthew, and found all the pages unharmed. Had I imagined all this? Remembered some story that had never even taken place?

My son Luke, twelve years old, sat down next to me on the couch and asked what I was doing. I told him I was looking for a page that had been torn in the Bible, thirty-three years earlier.

"Maybe," Luke suggested, "the page healed itself. Maybe God joined the pages together again and undid the tear."

"Maybe," I said, but I wasn't so sure. It seemed odd that God would go to all the trouble of healing a tear in a page but let the human who had torn it wind up on death row.

I started in on the Old Testament, again flipping my way backward, from Ezra toward Genesis.

I'd almost begun to suspect that Luke was right, that the Bible had healed itself, when I found the page. It wasn't in the New Testament, and it wasn't a huge tear. It was a small thing, really, a little corner missing from a page in Exodus. You'd hardly even notice it.

I wondered how many other memories I had of things that had never happened, how many tears I'd cried over stories I had all wrong.

The rip had taken several words out of two verses at the end of Exodus 1; this is when the Hebrew midwives refuse to carry out the orders of Pharaoh:

> *21 And it came to pass, because the midwives feared God, that he made them houses.*
>
> *22 And Pharaoh charged all his people, saying, Every son that is born ye shall cast into the river, and every daughter ye shall save alive.*

I Got a Pretty Flower

Wedgwood—the boy whom Chopper had banished from his classroom for inquiring about the provenance of the yo-yo—lived out on a farm in Nether Providence, not far from an old Quaker graveyard. Wedgwood, a sweet, likable guy, spent his summers digging graves in the cemetery. He said it was the best job in the world. As for the occasion when he fell through the earth and wound up waist deep in an old rotted coffin containing the bones of a nineteenth-century member of the Society of Friends, even that didn't dampen his spirits. "Okay, so maybe it was like being sucked down into a hellhole," Wedgwood observed. "But then I climbed back out again. I was fine!"

Wedgwood's mother and father headed off for a month in Bimini that summer, and in the absence of his trusting, loving parents, Wedgwood decided it would be clever if he devoted himself, in the meantime, to boiling hashish on his kitchen stove. I don't know where he got the recipe. The procedure seemed to be: (1) take two pounds homegrown marijuana; (2) boil for twelve hours; (3) add resins; (4) simmer on low for five days, or until hallucinogenic; (5) serve 'n' eat!

I didn't really know Wedgwood all that well, but by 1973 I'd made enough progress on a little Vox Continental organ to be a peripheral member of a rock band, The Comfortable Chair, that was playing at the party where the narcotics were being boiled. My friend Doober was the drummer. Membership in the band didn't entail much actual performance. On a typical night, we'd all show up, plug in our instruments, and blow into microphones, saying "Check! One! Two! Check!" Then we'd spend a couple of hours trying to tune. While all this went on, girls sat in easy chairs, smoking cigarettes, looking on in wonder.

The hash sizzled on low on the stove for a couple of days until, at last, it turned into a viscous gray glue. Then the glue hardened into a kind of jagged slime. Wedgwood chipped away at it with a screwdriver, put some in a pipe, and passed it around. It created a sensation in our lungs similar to that created by the inhalation of industrial waste. This impression was offset, though, by the psychological effect the slime created, which was to make us inarticulate, frightened, and suicidal.

Everybody wanted to try some.

I slept and woke, ate scrambled eggs—compliments of the Wedgwoods' chickens—played "Turn On Your Love Light" for three or four hours, smoked some of the industrial waste, felt like I wanted to kill myself, went back to sleep. When I woke up I was hungry again. Then I had more scrambled eggs. In the next room, the band was playing "Turn On Your Love Light." Doober came over with a pipe full of industrial waste. "Want some?" he said.

"Okay."

Doober lit up. I watched as he turned blue, then green, then choked and hacked, his hand moving to his throat in the universal sign language for *I'm suffocating*.

One of Doober's signatures was the unexpected quotation of lines originally spoken by the Cowardly Lion. At this moment, for instance, as he recovered from having smoked the horrible poison, he said, "Read my medal. Courage! Ain't it the truth?"

Then he handed the pipe to me. "It's harsh," he said.

Next thing you knew, I was up a tree. A spider from Mexico slid down a glowing silver thread. I could see the Quaker graveyard from this altitude, where the dead people were. My tongue had veins in it.

From the house came the sounds of "Turn On Your Love Light."

Then I was out in a cornfield, lying on my back in the middle of the night. A girl came out and lay down next to me. It was Sarah Towers, a friend of Doober's. She had chestnut brown hair, very large eyes, and merry cheekbones like the Wizard of Oz. I'd seen her on stage at a couple of the plays put on at Haverford's sister school, Shipley. The last time I'd seen her, she'd played the part of somebody's Russian uncle in a play by Chekhov. They'd given her a long black beard, about which I was ambivalent. It wasn't her best look.

"James," she said.

"Hey," I said.

"What are you doing?"

"Looking at the stars. Northern Crown."

She lay down next to me. I showed it to her, the small, twinkling half circle of stars, just to the left of the Herdsman. It was my favorite constellation. We lay there for a while looking up at it.

"You're so different like this, James," she said.

"Different from what?" I said.

"Usually you're so wound up. Like a top."

"I am?" I said. "I don't know. Maybe I'm nervous."

"What are you nervous about?"

"I don't know." I felt bad, lying to her.

"Are you nervous now?" she said.

"Not so much," I said.

Actually, as she reached out and touched my hair, I was *very* nervous, because Sarah Towers was just about the most fabulous creature I could imagine. Sarah was smart, tough, and funny, and yet she wore her vulnerability right out in the open. I admired that, wished I could learn to pull off that trick myself, instead of having to bury it beneath a wall of hilarity and speed.

I turned over on my side and looked at her. She was far more interesting than any stars.

Our lips met. We kissed softly beneath the stars in the cornfield between the Wedgwoods' and the graveyard. Sarah drew small circles on my arm with her finger as we kissed and kissed again. I didn't want to be a girl so much at that moment. I still hoped, in my ridiculous, buoyant fashion, that love would cure me of whatever it was that I had.

I don't think this is such a stupid theory, by the way, even if it turns out not to be true. The world is full of false hopes, plenty of them dumber than the idea of being transformed by love.

From another universe we heard the sounds of the band back in the house. I could picture Doober leaning forward into the mike as he sang.

Without a warning, you broke my heart
Taken it baby, torn it apart
And you left me standing, in the dark crying.

Later, Doober wandered out into the field and saw the two of us lying next to each other in the dark. "Hey Sarah," he said. "I guess you met James."

"I'm trying," she said, and looked at me with those twinkling eyes.

"You guys want some of this?" He torched up a bowl of the industrial waste, sucked it down into his lungs, and coughed and hacked like he was going to hock up his own heart and hold it up for us to look at.

Then he fell over.

"No thanks," said Sarah, putting her arm around my back again. "We're good."

A few days later I walked down to the railroad tracks and sat down on a hill with the guitar that Dottie had given me. I could see a station to my left, about a half mile to the west. To my right was a large overpass with signal lights on it. A couple of kids had been electrocuted on it the summer before. The high-voltage wires hummed softly in the summer heat.

I played a couple of chords on the Stella. I wanted to be Lightnin' Hopkins, or Leadbelly. The only problem, of course, was that there weren't a lot of traditional blues tunes for transsexuals. The closest I could come was "I Got a Pretty Flower."

Now I got a pretty flower, way back in my flower yard.
Now I got a pretty flower, way back in my flower yard.
I got a fence built around it, whoo Lord, to keep all these mens out.

A long freight train rumbled toward me from the east. I kept singing.

To be honest, I hadn't made much progress with the Stella. I couldn't get my long spindly fingers—which came in so handy with the piano—to make any sense of the neck. I never would figure out instruments with frets; over the years, I've owned a banjo, a mandolin, and an electric bass, and I was as clueless with each of them in turn as I was with the acoustic.

As the freight train lumbered past I kept on singing. The passing train roared, drowning out the sound of my voice. I liked looking at the names painted on the sides of the boxcars as they passed, and thinking about all the places they'd come from. SOUTHERN SERVES THE SOUTH. BANGOR AND AROOSTOOK. CHESSIE SYSTEM. A freight car passed with its doors wide open, and I thought about my uncle Sean, a man who spent most of his life riding the rails in boxcars just like this.

From the opposite direction came a passenger train—the local Penn Central heading in to Philly. As it rushed past, I saw, for a split second, the surprised face of Sarah Towers looking out one of the windows.

Sarah headed east, and the last car of the freight train headed west. Soon enough the only sounds were the humming of the voltage in the electric lines, and my bad guitar. I thought of Sarah: her smart, amused eyes; her soft moonlit kisses. *What are you so nervous about, James?* Those circles she drew with one finger on my arm.

You got the same kind of flower I got. Why do you want to bother mine?
You got the same kind of flower I got. Why do you want to bother mine?
Now you tend to yours and treat 'em just right. Hoo Lord, they will be just as fine.

That night I sat with Lydia up in the Brown Study. She'd been fighting with my mother; I'd come home to hear them yelling. My mother had gone into her room and kept the door closed for a while.

Through the window came the sounds of an approaching train. We sat there in the Brown Study with the big window open, listening to the night.

"Do you ever want to just go down to the tracks?" I said. "And jump on a boxcar? Go wherever it would take you?"

Lydia wrinkled her nose. "What are you now," she said. "Mr. Bojangles?"

I glowered at her. "Fine."

"I heard you're going out with Sarah Towers," she said. "Is that right?"

"I don't know," I said.

"How could you not know?"

"We're just hanging out."

My sister picked a pack of Tareytons off the couch, lit one up. "She's nice," she said. "What are you going to do with her?"

"Do? What do you mean, 'do'?"

"Well," said Lydia. "You haven't exactly dated a lot before."

"I'll figure it out," I said.

"You think?" She blew a smoke ring toward the ceiling. "Just treat her nice, Jimmy. Okay? Make her feel like she's important."

"She is important," I said.

"So," said Lydia. "What's the problem?"

"Who said there was a problem?"

"Fine," said Lydia.

I sighed. "I don't know. Sometimes I feel like I'm all wrong, like she'd have to be crazy to want to hang out with me."

"Don't worry, little brother," said Lydia. "Everybody feels like that."

Sarah Towers came over to my house. We sat in my room and listened to Bob Dylan on the record player. *And only if my own true love was waitin'. And I could hear her heart a-softly poundin'.* We made out on the bed, with all our clothes on. At one point we fell off of the bed, together, making a sound like *klunk*. Then we rolled around on the floor.

A little later I took her down to the kitchen and made her a sandwich. Ham and Velveeta on rye bread, toasted in the toaster oven. Fake bricks fell off the wall.

"Wow," said Sarah in a dreamy, far-off voice. "This is a *really* good sandwich."

"Well," I said modestly. "I'm good with cheese."

I lay on the floor of my mother's office, the odd little room at the top of the back stairs, looking at the photos in *Aku-Aku*. The book had been autographed by the author, Thor Heyerdahl, who was pictured on the cover looking up with an astonished expression at one of the giant statues on Easter Island. There were other pictures in the book as well: women in grass skirts doing the hula, guys in caves surrounded by skulls.

"Mom, I want to go here someday," I said.

She looked at me. Something crossed her mind. "Jim," she said. "Don't you want to get your hair cut?"

"Not really," I said.

"Maybe just a trim?"

What I really wanted was to ask her how to do a French braid. "I'm okay."

"Really?" she said.

"Sure, Mom," I said. "I'm fine."

"Well, good," she said.

The old study creaked, as if we were in a wooden boat.

I stared at the pictures of the statues on Easter Island, at the women in their flowered leis, the men covered with tattoos.

"What book are you reading?"

"*Aku-Aku*," I said. I showed her the cover. "It's about Easter Island?"

"Oh, Thor Heyerdahl," she said. "The Norwegian explorer! I met him!"

"I know," I said. "He signed your book."

"Such a nice man," my mother said, sighing. I looked at the cover. He didn't look nice. "Do you like his hair?" my mother asked.

"It's fine for him," I said.

My mother sighed. "Why do you want to go to Easter Island, darling?"

I shrugged. "I don't know," I said. "Because it's so strange, I guess. And because it's so far away."

Incredibly, I did wind up on Easter Island some thirty-two years later, after I became female. On that occasion, I watched the sun rise from the rim of a volcano with a gorgeous Rapa Nui native named Senga, a man with waist-length black hair whose back was covered with tattoos. Senga looked at my wedding ring and asked if I was married. "I do not have a husband," I said, thinking quickly. "Got rid of the man. Kept the ring." Senga smiled, then gave me the thumbs-up sign.

"Mom?" I said. "Do you ever feel scared in this house?" On one of the bookshelves was the big family Bible, one of its pages now torn by baby Pine Top. She didn't know about that, either.

"Scared?" she said. "Why, no. I have your father, and your sister, and you."

"I mean of, I don't know. Ghosts?"

"Ghosts?" said my mother. "There are no such things as ghosts."

It seems strange to me now that I'd never raised the issue of the house's haunting with any of the other members of my family. At the time, though, I was convinced that the ghosts were simply one more thing I needed to keep hidden, an aberration that needed, at all costs, to remain classified. If word got out about the creaking footsteps and the floating mist and the old woman in the mirror, who knows what else might be disclosed? It would start with zombies—all this truth-telling—but it wouldn't end there.

"You're sure?" I said. "That there's no such thing as ghosts?"

"Well, there's the Holy Ghost, of course," said Mom. "But we call that the Holy Spirit."

"So you believe in spirits?"

"Well, of course," said Mom. "Everyone should believe in spirits."

"What are spirits?"

"Well, that's not for us to say, is it?" She looked at me lovingly. " 'For now we see through a glass, darkly; then we will see face to face. Now I know in part; then I will know fully, even as I am fully known.'"

Then she sat down on the floor with me and softly brushed my long blond hair.

A week or so later Lydia came up the stairs with two of her friends. I'd been reading Melville for Mr. Thresher's class on literature of the sea. Lydia knocked on the door. I slid up the batpole.

"Hey," said Lydia as I swung the door open. "This is Tammy and Lexi."

"Hey," I said.

"They want to hear your imitations."

"Okay," I said.

The girls came into my room and looked around at the strange slanting ceilings, at the books all over the floor.

"So who do you want to hear?"

"Who can you do?"

"He can do anybody," Lydia said.

"Nixon? President Nixon?"

"I am not a crook."

"Elvis Presley?"

"Wella wella wella wella—"

"Marlon Brando?"

"Stella!"

"Martin Luther King?"

"I have a dream."

"Bob Dylan?"

"Jeez, I can't find my knees."

"Whoa," said Lexi. "Can you do her? Can you do Lydia?"

"Sorry," I said. "I don't do women." I felt a little self-conscious saying this, since of course this was not, technically speaking, true. Years later, I would think of this moment, when I was imitated—with eerie accuracy—by Will Forte in a *Saturday Night Live* sketch. My friends were afraid, at first, that my feelings might be hurt because I had been portrayed in that sketch by a man. *"But that's all right,"* I cleverly said. *"A man played me for years."*

"Well, you should," said Lexi. "You'd make a good chick." She looked at the others. "Don't you think he'd make a great chick?" Her eyes widened as she got an idea. "You should let us turn you into a chick. Shave your legs, do your makeup and shit. What do you think? You want to do it?"

"I don't think so," I said. It was what I imagined a well-adjusted person would say. "It sounds pretty weird to me."

"Yeah," said Lydia. "And you're old Mr. Normal."

"Maybe we could just style your hair," said Lexi, unwilling to let go of the idea. "Do you have any hot rollers?"

"I don't think so," I said again.

"My mom's got some," said my sister.

"I don't want you to put my hair in curlers!" I said. They were starting to annoy me now, these girls. Anyway, my hair didn't look good with hot rollers. I'd already tried.

"Can't we just do your makeup?" said Lexi. "Give you some lashes? Then we could sit around, the four of us, and pretend we're all sisters."

I looked at Lydia, who did not seem to think there was anything particularly odd about this conversation. "He's already got a sister," she noted, truthfully enough.

"Let's do something else," said Tammy, who, strangely, was uninterested in turning her friend's brother into a woman. "Do you have any cards? We could play Old Maid."

"Bo-ring," said Lydia.

Then Lexi got another idea. "Let's have a séance."

"A séance?" said Tammy nervously.

"Yeah. Try to contact dead people. Ask 'em what the deal is." She looked at the other girls. "You wanna?"

"I don't know," I said cautiously. I wasn't sure I wanted to know what the deal was.

"Oh Jim," said my sister. "Come on. Don't be such a crybaby."

"Okay, fine," I said, exhausted. "You want to contact dead people, let's contact dead people."

"Okay," said Lexi. "We all sit in a circle, and join hands, like this."

We did as she suggested.

"Now we sit in silence, reach out to the other dimension."

"What dimension is this?" asked Tammy.

"The dimension *beyond*," said Lexi. She crushed out her cigarette in an ashtray.

Everything was silent in the big house.

"Spirits," she said. "Are you there?"

Nothing.

"We should turn the lights out," said my sister.

"No," said Tammy. "Please?"

"It's fine," said Lydia, getting up and flicking the switch. Now we were all sitting in the dark.

"You know who we should try to contact is Mary Jo Kopechne."

"Who?"

"The girl who died in Ted Kennedy's car. I bet she'd have stuff she wants to get off her chest."

"But—we don't know Mary Jo Kopechne!" said Tammy, getting upset.

"You'd rather contact somebody you know?"

"I don't *know* any dead people," Tammy said.

"How about that girl?" said my sister. "Faith Bartelsby? The one who died of that blood disease?"

"We're not doing her," I said angrily.

"Did you know her?" asked Tammy. "I knew her."

"I gave her some white blood cells," said Lexi.

"*Everybody* gave her white blood cells," said my sister, annoyed. "Died anyway."

"Let's just leave her alone," I said.

"This is really freaking me out," said Tammy.

"Everybody be quiet," said Lexi. We sat there holding hands, the three girls and me. Light slanted into the room through the transom.

"Mary Jo Kopechne," said Lexi. "Come forward to us. Rise from your watery grave."

Nothing happened. We sat there in the quiet.

After a while, Lexi spoke again. "Mary Jo Kopechne," she said. "Come to us. We ask to open a bridge, between this world and yours."

"Um," whispered my sister. "Maybe we shouldn't talk about a bridge."

Tammy laughed nervously.

"Ssshhh."

"Come forward," said Lexi in a very commanding, supernatural voice. I suspected she'd done this before. "A channel is open between your world and this room. Come to us, and tell us of your soul."

We sat there for a long time. And then I began to feel something. It was the same sensation I occasionally got in the house, as if something was drifting toward us.

I had a pretty good feeling it wasn't Mary Jo Kopechne.

The others felt it, too. We couldn't see anything. Lexi gasped.

A voice said something. We couldn't make out the words. Whatever it was, she sounded dead when she said it.

I felt dizzy. "What was that?" Tammy said. "What was that?"

The voice came again. It sounded like it was coming from underwater. I thought of the words that my father and I had found written on the walls of this chamber: *In this room in the year 1923 lived Dorothy Cummin, who was not of sound mind, and drowned.*

Help us, whispered the voice. *Help us*.

Lexi screamed, and my sister got to her feet and turned on the lights.

"She touched me!" said Lexi. "I felt her hand on my back!"

"That was him," said my sister, a suspicious smile on her face.

"I didn't touch her," I said.

"I mean the voice. You did the voice."

"I couldn't understand it," said Tammy. "Did you?"

"She said 'help us,' " said Lexi. She was pretty upset, considering that all of this was her idea.

"This is all bogus," said my sister. "Come on, let's get out of here. You want to go skinny-dipping out in the pool?"

The girls rose and headed down the stairs. I went with them. My sister paused on the landing and gave me a look.

"Not *you*," she said, as if I were nuts.

I stayed at the top of the stairs and watched them all recede. A moment later I could hear them outside, walking out to the leaking pool. "That was him," my sister said. "That voice was *him*."

But it wasn't me.

My father's career slowly flowered. Even now there are people around who would gladly explain to you the way my father changed the face of trust banking, how he masterminded the merger of Provident and Pittsburgh National Banks and created a megalith called PNC Bank.

But I'm not one of them. To me, he was always my father, the brilliant, slightly shy man who loved his family, and his dog, and the sound of the piano.

Often he disappeared for days at a time, as his career took him to New York or London. He'd come home from these junkets with a weary expression, then sit down with a glass of bourbon and a cigarette. The dog would come over and rest her face on his thigh, and he'd stroke her ears. "Good Sausage," he'd say.

Sometimes the cat would come over, too, and then the international financier would have to say, with all the dignity he could muster, "Ba-BOING!"

Because of his travels that year, he missed my piano recital. I think he was more upset than I was about it. He was all excited about the piece I was playing, Strauss's *The Blue Danube*. It didn't mean all that much to me. The best thing I could say about it was that it made me think of *2001: A Space Odyssey*, which took place halfway to Saturn. *I'm sorry, Dave. This conversation can serve no further purpose.*

"You break a leg," he said as he stood by the door with his London Fog raincoat and his suitcase.

"I'll try."

He looked self-conscious, as if he wanted to say something but didn't know what. "I'll listen at noon on Saturday, wherever I am."

"It's okay, Dad," I said.

He nodded, then moved toward me. There was an odd moment. Then he extended his hand, and I shook it.

"Okay, old man," he said. "You remember what we talked about?"

"What?"

"The other night? When you surprised me? Playing the *Pathétique*?"

I remembered.

"You said you'd look out for them," said Dad.

Oh for God's sake, I thought. *This* again.

"You're getting older now, Jim," he said. "Sometimes you'll have to be the man of the house. When I'm not around."

"Me?" I said.

"Sure, you," said my father. He lowered his voice. "The key to looking out for people," he said, "is not to let them know you're doing it."

"Okay," I said. Once I got finished washing out my panty hose in the sink there was no reason I couldn't be the house's man, as long as I kept it secret. Who knew? It was possible that I had talents so deeply hidden even I didn't know about them. "I'll try."

He patted me on the shoulder and then headed out, with his briefcase and his trench coat, leaving me in charge.

By the time he got back, our house would be unrecognizable.

On Sunday, the phone rang. It was Sarah Towers. We hadn't talked for a while.

"Hey James," she said. She drew out the long *A* sound. I loved to hear her say it.

"Hey."

She paused for a moment. "Where you been?"

"Oh, I don't know," I said. "I've been busy."

"Really?" said Sarah. "With what?"

"Nothing," I said. "I had a piano recital."

"Really?" she said. "What did you play?"

"*Blue Danube*."

There was a long silence.

"I would have gone. If I'd known."

I couldn't see why she'd want to hear *The Blue Danube*. "Sorry," I said.

"Listen, James. I was wondering if you wanted to go to the Barnes? Next weekend? We could take the train down to Merion, maybe walk around the galleries for a while?"

"That sounds fun," I said. The Barnes was this bizarre museum that some insane guy had started. It was famous for its crazy rules, like you couldn't get in on a Tuesday, or if you had red hair, or if you wore shoes that had a buckle instead of laces. For all that, they had one of the world's best collections of Impressionist art. The place was lousy with Degas and Chagalls and Monets, although it contained a lot of other stuff as well, such as toilet paper holders shaped like tiny outhouses and hex signs taken off of the barns of the Amish.

"And then maybe we could go to the Creperie for dinner. They make you all these crepes. You can put whatever you want inside them, like shrimp, or chicken. Cheese, if you want cheese."

"What's a crepe?"

"I don't know. It's sort of like a pancake, I guess."

"Uh-huh," I said. I liked pancakes all right. I wasn't so sure about pancakes with cheese, though.

"So do you want to do it?"

"I'm thinking," I said.

"Is it, like—a bad weekend or something?"

"Um. Kind of. I need to ask my parents, I think. Because we might have this thing we have to do."

"Oh," she said. I could hear the disappointment in her voice. "I'm not—You don't think I'm being—?"

"No," I said. "It's fine. I just have to talk to them, okay, because I might have to do this other thing. So how about if I call you? Can I do that?"

"Okay," said Sarah. She didn't sound like it was okay. "Let me know. I think it could be a ton of fun."

"It sounds great. I'll call you, okay?"

"Okay."

We hung up. I lay in bed for a while, the phone on my lap, staring up at the ceiling.

I got up and walked downstairs, through the second-floor hallway over to the big window on the landing. I'd imagined sitting here on this windowsill with Sarah, had thought about the afternoons she and I might gaze from here out on the whole wide world. Then I looked into my mother's study, the weird back room at the top of the stairs. Once again, something in there said, *Get out*.

I went into my sister's bathroom and splashed cold water on my face. There was a strangely shaped closet in one corner of the room that, according to the blueprints my father had found, had once been the site of a set of circular stairs that led up into the tower. After I flushed the toilet, I opened the closet door. I felt around, but there appeared to be no secret panels, no openings to any other dimension. It was a shame, really.

Hanging from a hook on the back of the closet was a green paisley skirt of my sister's, a blue peasant blouse with little mirrors sewn into it. *Okay, Jenny*, said the clothes. *Let's go*.

Oh for God's sake. Not tonight. I'm too sad.

Ah, come on. Hair of the dog that bit you.

I want to be in love. Is that so much to ask? To be in love with that beautiful girl? She likes me.

Is it really you she likes? Or the person you have to imitate in order to keep yourself disguised?

You know. Sometimes I get sick of this conversation.

I stood there, listening to the toilet flushing. It was still going. I was exhausted, my heart all cried out from camouflage.

Okay, Jenny, I said. Let's go.

I took the stairs two at a time. Did the presto-changeo. Then I sat down on my red chair, wounded and relieved. It was the same chair the ghost liked to spin around sometimes, just to show me she could.

You see, Sarah, I wanted to say. This is why I can't go to the Barnes with you.

I picked up Dottie's guitar and tried to play this Grateful Dead song I'd learned. I sucked, truly, on the guitar, and my singing voice continued to be an unpleasant amalgam of Emmylou Harris and Rochester. But that was all right. No one was listening.

And when you hear that song, come crying like the wind,
It seems like all this life was just a dream.
Stella blue.

I put the guitar down and had the sudden urge to smash it against the wall. I imagined the wood splintering into bits, the taut strings all loose and tangled. I went out into the hallway, saw myself in the full-length mirror on the back of the bathroom door. For all that, I looked like a relatively normal teenage girl. You wouldn't have guessed that there was anything so terrible about me if you didn't know better.

Then I saw the woman hanging in the air behind me. There was mist rising off of her, and her hair seemed wet, as if she had just emerged from a cold, raging river. She was wearing the long white nightgown. Her eyes were red and again I felt her sense of dread, as if something terrible were just about to happen. *Hey. Don't you know I can't swim?*

I inhaled sharply and turned around. A soft blue mist drifted across the hall and vanished into the Brown Study.

"I don't believe in you," I said, but that was all right. Apparently she didn't believe in me, either.

I woke to the sound of my mother screaming. I looked at the clock, but the power in the house was out. Judging from the gray light coming through the window, I could guess that it was an hour or so before dawn.

The house was roaring, as if we were in the midst of a great hurricane in the middle of the sea. I stepped out into the dark hallway.

The sound I heard was the sound of tons of rushing water.

I looked down the stairs. Water was circling through the staircase in a vast cascade. My mother screamed again. I heard my sister shouting. Sausage came out into the hallway and stood next to me and gave me a look. *What did you do?* she asked.

Me? I didn't do anything.

The dog rolled her eyes. *Fine. Have it your way.*

I pulled on a pair of jeans and walked down the stairs. My sister and my mother were standing in the hallway, calf-deep in floodwater.

"We're underwater!" my mother shouted. My sister looked over at her and shook her head.

"What's going on?" I asked.

Lydia nodded toward her bathroom, the one I'd used just the night before. The toilet was erupting. For the last seven hours, water had been pouring over the brim like a fountain.

How much water could one toilet produce, if allowed to gush uninhibited for seven hours?

A lot.

"No. Wait," said my sister, as she walked toward the second-floor landing. The river roared down the stairs. She looked down the steps toward the first-floor hallway. There was a foot of cold water down there, flowing swiftly to the kitchen and on toward the basement stairs. I couldn't even imagine how much water was in the cellar, if there was a foot of it on the first floor.

Enough to short out the electricity in the house, anyway.

"The water just kept running, and running," my mother said, in a trance. "And running, and running."

I sloshed into the haunted bathroom, and reached down into the water and closed the valve near the wall. The gushing ceased.

From downstairs came a sudden crash, as the kitchen ceiling collapsed and fell onto the floor in tiny pieces.

We walked down the main staircase into the living room—no easy feat, since there was a swift, cold current on the stairs. The water was up to the level of the electric sockets down there. Everything was drenched. Water poured down the walls, flowing over the face of my grandfather in his portrait, rushing down the slanted top of the piano like a flume. The ceiling over our heads buckled and bowed with the weight of water.

Sausage rushed down the stairs, like a cork carried along in a storm. There was a groaning sound from overhead, and then the living room ceiling burst. Plaster and pieces of wood rained down upon us.

"We're underwater," my mother began to chant in a strange, disembodied voice. Lydia looked angry, as if it were Mom's fault.

"Why didn't you protect us?" Lydia said to my mother. "Why didn't you stop it?"

"I didn't know how," my mother said helplessly. "I didn't think."

"This *always* happens," Lydia snapped, overcome with fury. "Now we have to live—in a *toilet bowl.*"

"Liddie," said my mother. "I'm sorry."

"You're *always* sorry," said Liddie.

Mom walked into the kitchen, where the ceiling lay upon the breakfast table. I went over to the basement steps and stared into the dark, watery depths. Bill Hunt wasn't going to be making any more potions in his secret laboratory, that much was for sure, especially the kind that turned him normal. For the foreseeable future, he'd have to stay just like he was.

I sloshed through the tide back to the front half of the house. The waters had freed some photographs from the rec room with the zebra-striped paneling, and pictures of my distant relatives were floating in a deep eddy near the bar. There was one of my uncle Sean taken during the war, an odd but dashing young man with half a mustache. Another showed my aunt Caeli standing next to my uncle Jack, the railroad detective. They lived above a train station in New Jersey.

In the dining room the water nearly covered the andirons in the fireplace. On the ocean floor were the swirling patterns of the Oriental rug, now destroyed. A saucer without its teacup floated toward the kitchen.

Out in the front hallway, the chandelier suddenly detached itself from the ceiling and fell with a great splash.

Slowly I waded through the waters, back into the living room.

I sat down at the piano, struck a chord. The piano sounded different, its soundboard soaked. My mother heard me playing and came into the black room, still wearing her robe. She sat down on a damp wing chair next to the fireplace. I played *The Blue Danube*. It wasn't so bad when you played it underwater.

My sister swung open the front door, and the river gushed out onto the porch and into the morning light.

In the days that followed, the house was invaded by a series of disaster specialists. A plumber came first, with a giant hose that sucked water out of the house and spewed it into the street. Then came a couple of stunned, amazed insurance agents. My mother led them, one after the other, to the second-floor toilet, and pointed to it, as if it were the mysterious Lake Itasca, source of the Mississippi. Plaster from the fallen ceilings was removed by a team of guys with brooms and shovels; the ruined rugs were hauled away by carpet resuscitaters to be dried and cleaned. As the waters receded the house seemed to look less like itself than ever before, and sheets of destroyed wallpaper peeled and fell off the walls, exposing the plaster.

More strange drawings and inscriptions were uncovered on the now-bare walls, including a poem on the wall of the second-floor hallway about a man who had been lost at sea. *To know him was to love him*, the poem suggested. All the electrical wiring in the house had to be replaced, and the floors removed, reinstalled, sanded, and stained; new ceilings would have to be plastered in the kitchen and the living room. This whole process would take at least a year, and in the meantime, we lived in the surreal ruin, which now took on an amazing smell of dampness and rot.

My father wasn't angry about the flood when he got home. For some reason, he thought the whole thing was funny. Maybe he saw the disaster as a clever way of getting State Farm to jump-start the renovations he'd been considering. At any rate, his primary concern upon his return was not the fact that his dream house now looked like the wreck of the steamship *Walter Scott*; the main thing he wanted to know was how *The Blue Danube* had gone.

I told him it was fine.

"Good, good," said my father contentedly, sitting in his wing chair in the destroyed living room. "I was in London when you were playing. Off Tottenham Court Road. I stopped and listened. Imagined I heard the music."

There were times when I wondered whether my father lived in a universe wholly different from ours. He looked at the members of his family, sometimes, as if he were viewing us through the inexplicable videoscreen of his intergalactic space destroyer.

He blew smoke toward the painting of Grampa. Old James Boylan, his features mottled now from the flood's flotsam and jetsam, looked down on me with disdain. *You*, he said to me. *You bastard. You drowned me.*

A few nights later I lay in bed wearing a halter top. There were grapefruit in it. I was reading *The Feminine Mystique,* by Betty Friedan. *Women in America*, she wrote, *found it harder to talk about the problem than about sex. Even the psychoanalysts had no name for it.*

Man, I thought. That is so true.

I picked up the phone.

"Hey, Sarah?" I said.

"Hey, Jaaames. I'm so glad you called!"

"Listen," I said. Now that I had her on the phone I wished I'd waited. It was wrong, what I was about to do to her. But lying to her was worse. There weren't a lot of good choices.

"I was thinking about that idea you had, about going to the Barnes this weekend?"

"Yeah?"

"It turns out I can't go. That thing I thought we had—I have to do. So I'm busy."

There was a long pause.

"I'm sorry," I said.

"Your voice sounds weird," said Sarah.

Shit, I thought. She could tell about the grapefruit.

"No it doesn't," I said.

"James," she said. "Can I ask you something? Honestly?"

Dear God, I thought. Please don't. "Sure."

"Are you seeing somebody else?"

I didn't answer right away. I wasn't quite sure what to tell her.

"You are, aren't you?"

"I really like you," I said to Sarah. "We've had a good time together. That night at the Wedgwoods', with the band playing 'Turn On Your Love Light.' That was so excellent."

"Do I know her?"

"Who?"

"The girl you're seeing."

It was a good question. She *did* know me, if it came to that, assuming that the girl I was actually seeing behind her back was my own bifurcated self. But it's fair to say there were things about me she didn't know, at least one of which, for instance, was the fact that even at this moment I had a pair of Florida grapefruit jammed down my halter top. Love was complicated, was my conclusion.

"I'll call you," I said. "Okay?"

There was a long pause. I could tell that Sarah was crying now. I didn't blame her. It's what I'd do, if a guy did what I was doing to me.

"Okay," she said, and hung up.

I lay there for a while, tried reading more Betty Friedan, but I wasn't in the mood. Somehow I got the sense that when Friedan was talking about the *nameless problem of modern women*, she didn't count me among its sufferers.

But you should, Betty, I wanted to say. *You should*.

I took off my girl clothes and stowed them in the secret panel in the wall. I walked downstairs and put the grapefruit back in the refrigerator.

Then I went back to my room, climbed softly into bed, and lay there staring up at the ceiling for a long time. I heard a freight train approaching the Somerset station.

Only a month earlier Sarah Towers had kissed me in a cornfield, had drawn small circles on my arm with a finger. Now I was lying here alone, listening to the sound of a distant freight. I thought of that despondent girl, the one who'd thrown herself beneath the Paoli Local.

Wait, wait, she thought, as she drifted through the air. *I've made a terrible mistake.*

PART II

At the Museum of Dummies, 1982

Don't worry, little brother, said Lydia.
Everybody feels like that.

Paranormal

· *Spring 2006* ·

I do not believe in ghosts, although I have seen them with my own eyes. This isn't so strange, really. A lot of people feel the same way about transsexuals.

Just because I'm skeptical, though, doesn't mean I'm not curious. The problem, of course, is that anyone earnestly desiring to learn more about zombies—or for that matter, transgendered people—has to first sift through a nearly endless pile of half-truths, religious bigotry, crazy postmodern theory, and just plain hooey. And scientists, who surely should be at the forefront of any exploration of the inexplicable, generally excuse themselves politely when these topics come up and head off to the men's room shaking their heads and muttering phrases like *Whoa, Scooby, this is, like, weirding me out!*—a sentiment with which I can only wholeheartedly sympathize.

Maybe someday researchers will tell us more about what makes people see things that are not there, or yearn to inhabit a body other than the one into which they were born.

In the meantime, when it comes to ghosts, or gender, we're all pretty much on our own.

In the absence of useful science, in the spring of 2006 I decided to take matters into my own hands and set about searching for a person whom I could only haplessly describe as a "paranormal investigator." I assumed that the odds of finding a trustworthy ghostbuster in the Philadelphia Yellow Pages were going to be slim at best, but in this, as in so much else, I was wrong. Thanks to the ever-dependable Internet and an organization called Meetup.com, I was able, with relative ease, to begin attending the occasional convocations of something called the Philadelphia Paranormal Investigators Group, and to befriend—in no time at all—a round, cheerful, extremely generous woman named Wendy, who had busted ghosts from all the way from Scranton to Atlantic City.

When I asked Wendy if she'd be willing to come out and do some tests on the Coffin House, she did not hesitate.

"Actually, Jenny," she said, "this is a good time for me."

"Really?" I asked.

"Sure," said Wendy without a hint of irony. "It's my dead season."

A few weeks later, Wendy stepped through the front door of the Coffin House and stood in the front hall for a moment, taking the house's pulse. The place had changed since the Flood of '73. But then, so had a lot of things.

"Whoa, Jenny," said Wendy. "There's a cold spot here." To her left was the old living room, the piano still in its alcove. The walls, now covered with tasteful cream-colored fabric, had ceased being black thirty years ago.

"What does that mean, a cold spot?" I said.

"A spirit, probably," said Wendy. She was wearing a T-shirt that bore the word BEWITCHED. "Or a portal."

"A portal?" I asked. I was wearing blue jeans and a knit sweater, my long hair held back in a scrunchie. "What would come through a portal?"

"You name it," said Wendy wearily.

My mother, who by almost any measure might be called a tolerant woman, came slowly down the stairs. She wasn't crazy about having ghostbusters in her foyer, but as always, she was determined to be generous.

"Hello, Mrs. Boylan," said Wendy. Her Philadelphia accent was shocking. I still remembered how surprised I'd been when I arrived at college in 1976 and found myself surrounded by people who had no marbles in their mouths. They'd been very hard to understand at first.

"Why, hello," said Mom, shaking Wendy's hand.

"Your house is so beautiful."

"It's our home," said Mom humbly.

Earlier, when I'd told her that I'd been meeting with a group of paranormal investigators, my mother had nodded thoughtfully. "Now, Jenny," she'd said. "When you say paranormal—do you mean, you know . . . *other transsexuals*?"

"You'll be back in an hour?" I said. She was going to the Acme to buy sweet corn.

Mom nodded. "You two have fun." She headed to the front door. "Oh, and Jenny—if you do find spooks, will you do me a favor?"

"Of course, Mom."

"Don't tell me about them."

"Okay."

"Also? I don't want anybody in my closets. You just promise me that."

"We'll stay out of your closets, Mom."

"Well, fine then. You have fun." Mom smiled, then went out the door. We listened as her car started up and rolled down the driveway.

"She's nice," said Wendy, opening up her bag of equipment.

"She is," I said. "When I was a teenager, and we came up with snotty nicknames for all of our friends' mothers, you know what we called her? Glinda the Good Witch."

Wendy smiled. "You could be called worse." She got out two long copper rods. As she held one in each hand, they swung freely, like antennae.

"These are divining rods," she explained. "They're pretty effective with places like this."

"How do they work?" I didn't know anything about divining. I had a vague image of hillbillies with Y-shaped sticks hunting for moonshine with hound dogs.

"They detect electromagnetic energy," she said. "If there's any disturbance in the field, they move. Spirits can move them, too. It's a good way to have a conversation with the spirits, if they feel like saying stuff. If the rods cross, that means yes. If they don't, it means no." Her stomach growled suddenly. "Excuse me."

"Are you hungry?"

"I'm good." She closed her eyes. "Is there anybody here?" she said, in a loud, commanding voice. For a moment the house was quiet. Then I felt that old sensation again, as if lightning was about to strike.

"Is there anybody here?" Wendy repeated.

There was a loud creak at the top of the stairs. We both looked up at the light pouring through the deep window on the landing. There was nothing there.

Then, one after the other, the stairs creaked with the heavy treads of descending footsteps.

The skin on my arms puckered into goose bumps, right on cue. Boy, I thought. This Wendy doesn't waste any time.

"Someone just came down the stairs," Wendy said.

"I know."

"Don't move."

We remained motionless for a moment. We could feel the presence of whatever this was, standing there on the bottom step.

"She's watching us," said Wendy.

"I know," I said, and thought, She?

"Are you lost?" said Wendy.

"Lost?" I said. The rods trembled, crossed before her, then uncrossed.

Yes.

"Can you point to where you're at?"

The copper rods trembled and swayed. Something cool passed through us, like a soft wind.

"Darn it," Wendy said. "She's gone."

"Where?"

Wendy's stomach growled again.

"Are you sure you're not hungry?" I thought about making her a sandwich. I'd baked some garlic bread that morning. It would be good with prosciutto and mozzarella, maybe some chopped basil.

After all these years, I was still good with cheese.

"I'm fine. Really."

We walked around the first floor for a while, but we didn't find anybody dead. It was hard at times to remember what the place used to look like, back in the days of its haunting. The zebra-striped paneling in the family room was gone, along with the wagon-wheel chandeliers and the bar. Now the walls were a cheerful, soft yellow. New skylights cast rectangles of sun onto the hardwood floors.

A passageway behind the place where the bar used to be led into an octagonal glass room my mother called the Conservatory. This was also new. It had a glass roof, a ceiling fan, and a round table in its center where my mother drank coffee and read the *Inquirer*. Beyond this was yet another new chamber, filled with couches and chairs and photographs of the grandchildren. My mother had built this room with the intention of using it as a first-floor bedroom in the event that she could no longer climb stairs. The years kept passing, though, and Mom kept going strong, still filled with the same buoyant energy, religious faith, and unquenchable optimism.

"Is that your dad?" said Wendy, pausing in front of a large framed photograph on the wall.

"That's him," I said.

In the photograph, he looked generous and kind, a little tired. There was a trace of melancholy in the eyes.

"He looks like a very gentle man," said Wendy.

"He was," I said.

We stood there looking at Dad for a while.

"And when did he die?"

"Nineteen eighty-six," I said."On Easter Sunday."

"You must miss him," said Wendy.

I nodded. I missed him, all right.

Since we'd come up empty-handed on the first floor—with the exception of those first, dramatic steps upon the staircase—we decided to try our luck upstairs. I led Wendy past my mother's room, past the new fancy bathroom with the Jacuzzi, past the second-floor room my mother now called the Library, lined wall to wall with leather-bound books. Once it had been my sister's bedroom, filled with her canopy bed and Jethro Tull albums, the trunk with her kittygirls over by the window.

My father had done the renovations himself, a few weeks after Lydia got married in 1978. According to the house's original blueprints, he said, there was a fireplace hidden behind a false wall. So he did what any reasonable man would do in the weeks after his daughter, age twenty, got married and moved to Oregon. He started destroying her room with a sledgehammer.

I'd stood at his side on that occasion. It had been odd to see him so worked up. He'd always been such a gentle character, shy and wistful. The afternoon he pounded apart my sister's room, though, I saw something in him I'd never seen before. I'd wondered what he was so mad about.

Dad took one final, furious swing, and all at once the head of his sledgehammer burst through a layer of bricks and into an open space. Cool air blew into the room from the hole he'd made.

Dick Boylan stood there in his plaid pants and Lacoste shirt for a moment, surveying the damage. Plaster dust was in his hair. Sweat trickled down his temples, which he mopped with a pocket handkerchief. He looked at me, a little embarrassed by the emotion he'd displayed.

I crept to the wall to check out the hole. With one hand I reached into the dark space. My fingers brushed against something unexpectedly soft.

"What is it, son?"

"I don't know," I said. My heart was beating quickly. There was something about the thing I was touching that frightened me. My hand closed around the soft form and lifted it out of the hidden fireplace.

My father's eyes grew wide. There in my hands was a mourning dove, dead. It must have flown down the chimney a day or two before, and gotten trapped behind the walls of the house.

"Whoa-*ho*," said my father, and his voice trembled. Dad put down his sledgehammer, then wiped his eyes with a handkerchief.

Then he came over to the place where I was kneeling, and touched the soft wings of the dead thing in my hands.

I led Wendy up the creaking stairs to the third floor. "My, my," she said cheerfully, as she arrived in the hallway. "There's a *lot* of activity up here." She put her hand on her heart, and, as if she was being drawn by magnets, slowly walked down the hall, beneath the trapdoor for the attic, and into the Brown Study. She went over to the haunted closet and opened its small wooden door. "It's in here," she said.

"What is?"

Wendy raised her rods.

"Who's in there?" she said. "Is somebody there?"

Yes.

"Were you a girl?"

Yes.

Wendy nodded. "I thought so. There's a *lot* of feminine energy up here."

Tell me about it.

"How old are you?" asked Wendy. "Are you under ten?"

Yes.

"Are you seven?"

Yes.

Wendy looked at me. I tried not to let my eyes betray the fact that I suspected this was all blarney. Her stomach growled again. I thought about the prosciutto.

"Okay," said Wendy. "Spirit. Does your first name begin with A?"

No response.

"B? C?"

No response.

"D?"

Yes.

"Your first name begins with D?"

Yes.

"Does your last name begin with A?"

No response.

"B?"

No response.

"C?"

Yes.

"Your initials were D.C.?"

My heart began to beat more rapidly as I remembered the name my father and I had seen written beneath the wallpaper in my room. *Dorothy Cummin.*

"Dorothy?" I said. "Dorothy Cummin?"

The divining rods began to swing wildly around the room, like wind socks in a hurricane. This went on for fifteen, twenty seconds. Then they were still again.

Wendy looked at me. "This is intense," she said.

I nodded.

"Did you die in this house?"

No.

"Ask her if she drowned."

"Did you drown?"

Yes.

The rods kept swinging crazily, like the compass of a ship being tossed by waves.

Wendy stood there with her eyes closed. "There's something weird here," she said.

This struck me as a rather modest assessment.

"Are you hiding from someone?" asked Wendy.

Yes.

"Are you hiding from your mother?"

No.

"Are you hiding from your father?"

The rods went wild again, crossing and uncrossing.

Wendy thought about this. Then she said, "Okay. Thank you for talking to us! Good-bye!"

She led us out of the Brown Study and back into the hallway. "What?" I said.

"There's something strange about that kid," she said.

"Strange how?"

"Like maybe she's not really a kid at all. I get the sense she might be lying to us."

"Lying to us?" I said. "They do that?" All this time, I'd been under the apparently mistaken impression that dead men told no tales.

"We call them trickster spirits," said Wendy. "When you run into one of these, it's impossible to get a straight answer."

I nodded. A trickster spirit sounded like the kind I'd wind up with. I thought about that line my father and I had found on the plaster beneath the wallpaper. *She was not of sound mind, and drowned.*

"Wendy," I said. "If a person is disturbed, say, in life. Are they disturbed when they're a ghost? Or does everything become clear to them?"

"Usually things become clear," said Wendy. "But then, getting lost can cloud them up again. This D.C. seems afraid of something. That's why she's hiding. And as long as she keeps hiding, she can never find rest."

"Uh-huh," I said. My heart went out to the child, hiding in the dark closet, even now.

Next on our tour was my old bedroom, which, like the others in the house, had changed a great deal over the years. The paneling with the built-in desk—and all its secret hidey-holes—had been taken down in the eighties. And the blue color my father and I had painted the room so long ago had now been replaced with a soft beige. There were blue curtains in the room now, and on one wall, a framed poster of a little girl holding a bouquet of flowers. My mother had put it up there for me. Little Jenny, she called it.

"Is there anybody here?"

There was no response.

"Is anybody here?" Wendy said again, more commandingly. She looked at me apologetically. "I'm not getting anything."

On a table near my bed were several framed photographs. One of them was of me, age fourteen. Next to it was a photograph of my sister taken at the same time. We both looked very young.

"Look at you," said Wendy, picking up the photo of Lydia. Speaking of ghosts.

"That's my sister," I said. I'd told her about the Ol' Switcheroo a few weeks earlier. "This is me."

Wendy looked at the photograph of the cheerful, wild-eyed Young James.

"Whoa," she said.

I nodded. *Whoa* pretty much summed it up. I looked at my sister for a while. She'd been gone a long time, too.

"Hm," said Wendy.

"What?"

"I'm getting a weird energy from this photograph," she said.

I didn't know what to tell her.

"I'm sorry," said Wendy. "Is she—?"

"Tell you what," I said, unwilling to go into the gory details. "Let's go back downstairs."

Wendy put the photograph back down, next to the one of Young James.

We walked down the creaking stairs again. "You know who we haven't found," I said. "This old woman who appeared in the mirror. When I was a kid, I saw her a couple times, always in that bathroom mirror, looking over my shoulder."

"Maybe that's who this D.C. was," said Wendy.

"I thought she was a child."

"Yeah, well," said Wendy. "Like I said, she might be lying."

"I don't know," I said. "That woman in the mirror. She always felt like someone else."

"Maybe she only *thinks* she's a child," said Wendy. "She was an adult, but she doesn't remember growing up. That happens."

I understood this, too. Something along these lines had happened to a lot of the people I knew.

We were standing in the middle of the second-floor hall. Wendy clutched her heart suddenly. "Whoo," she said. "Did you feel that? Another cold spot."

I hadn't felt it, actually. I wondered how many signs of the supernatural I had come to ignore in the house, and whether I'd grown, over the years, nearly as oblivious to the paranormal as my mother, for whom the house was a place of warmth and light, a museum of bright memories.

"Do you want to check out my mother's room?" I said.

"Is it okay?" said Wendy.

"As long as we don't go in her closet," I said.

"Whoa," said Wendy again, as we stood in the center of my parents' bedroom. "Do you feel that? I think we hit the jackpot."

I didn't feel anything, other than a vague sense that we shouldn't be in here. It seemed wrong. After all, my father had died in this very bed, my mother at his side. My sister and I had been downstairs that Easter Sunday, drinking coffee. He'd been sick a long time.

But here he was again, a soft, curious presence, coming closer.

"Is there anybody here?"

Yes.

The Monadology

On the last night of my sophomore year at Wesleyan, I was up in the college belfry. I had everything I needed: my electric Smith-Corona typewriter, a stack of erasable onionskin typewriter paper, a six-pack of Billy beer, and the *Monadology,* a hilarious work by the German philosopher Gottfried Leibniz. Through the open window I could hear the sounds of the campus: the Stones blasting out of the Eclectic house, the boys over at DEKE draining a keg to the music of Lynyrd Skynyrd, the Grateful Dead Live at the Fillmore over in West College. On the steps of South College, the building that housed the carillon, my friend Lucy Potemkin was playing "Morning Morgantown" on the guitar. Earlier, she'd shouted up to the tower: "James, come down out of there."

But I wouldn't come down.

The belfry was reached through a spiral staircase at the top of the building in which Wesleyan's president had his office. Now and again I'd pass President Campbell on the stairs, on my way to or from the belltower, and he was unfailingly nice to me, which speaks well of him, especially considering the fact that on another occasion a group of my friends had seized the place by force. The way they figured, if they took over Colin Campbell's office, there wouldn't be apartheid in South Africa anymore.

He wasn't surprised his office got taken over. After a few years as Wesleyan's president, he'd learned it made sense to keep a suitcase packed. He wished the students well and headed out, locking the door behind him. It didn't take my fellow Marxists too long to realize there wasn't a bathroom.

But some of the smarter radicals had anticipated this gambit and had brought along a bunch of Hefty trash bags. So they used those instead. They had a good time in the president's office, too, even used his phone to have pizzas delivered, along with Sicilian spinach pies.

Eventually they declared victory and handed the president's office back to Colin Campbell, who, a few years later, gave up being a college president and signed on as the CEO of Colonial Williamsburg. My friends the radicals cleaned up his office before they left, making sure that he didn't think any worse of them just because they'd thrown him out of his office and declared him a capitalist stooge. They took the big bag of poop, too.

Wesleyan was like that in the late 1970s, Marxists walking around with bags of poop, women turning their dorm rooms into giant uteruses. (The door was the vagina, *and men weren't allowed in.*) Then there was Phyllis Rose, and Robert Hayden, and Annie Dillard, and William Manchester, writing out their books on legal paper in the library. One of the fraternities, Eclectic, had an electric chair you could sit in. If you were very, very good, they'd give you a shock, although usually this was not enough to kill anybody.

A couple of the guys who eventually became the Blue Man Group were walking around the campus too, although, of course, back then they were not blue. No more than anybody else, anyhow. Another guy I knew, a magician, got a Fulbright to travel in Iran with the Whirling Dervishes. He was bound for med school and a career as a psychiatrist. His theory was that, when it came right down to it, Dervishes, Freud, and the Amazing Kreskin were all pretty much in the same line of work.

It was like going to college in a giant space station.

"James?" Lucy Potemkin shouted from the front steps of South College. "Are you done yet?"

I went over to the window and stuck my head out. "Maybe I could catch up with you later?" I yelled down to her. "I'm right in the middle of things."

"Okay," said Lucy. " 'Cause I want to make sure we get to talk later. Okay? I think we need to talk."

"All right," I said. "We'll talk. That'll be good."

I was having a hard time coming up with a conclusion for the Leibniz paper, in part because of the bat problem in the belfry and in part because I knew Lucy was sitting out on the steps waiting for me. I had a pretty good sense of what this talk we needed to have was, too. Over the years I'd have plenty of talks just like it.

The music department hadn't exactly given me permission to start living up in the bell tower, but then they hadn't specifically said I couldn't, either. There was a bed in the attic of the Old South College building where the bell tower was, and I slept up there sometimes when I didn't feel like going back to my room. I wasn't crazy about sleeping in the tower, though, given the bat issue. I didn't like listening to the sound of their leathery wings while I lay there dreaming about bosoms.

Still, the set of nearly two dozen giant bells hanging over my head provided some consolation. The Flintstones song sounded good on the carillon, as did the *F Troop* theme, "Smoke on the Water," "Teddy Bears' Picnic," "George of the Jungle," and "(I Can't Get No) Satisfaction."

I'd arrived at Wesleyan a dissolving personality, determined to find a way to change genders before I graduated. But I hadn't been there very long before I decided that—who knows?—maybe I'd be able to keep the whole boy thing going a little longer. My theory was, if I was creative and funny and fast enough, it might all still work out. Maybe I wouldn't be the person I was supposed to be, I thought, but what the heck. A lot of people don't get to be themselves, and you had to admit that if you couldn't be a woman, living up in a bell tower and playing "The Hokey Pokey" on a carillon was the next best thing.

The bell tower was divided into two rooms, one on top of the other. The top chamber contained the bells, mounted on a giant steel superstructure inside a white cupola. Wires connected to the clappers ran through the floor and emerged in the ceiling of the clavier chamber below. The wires terminated in the rosewood clavier, a set of long wooden bars arranged like the keys of a piano. In order to play the bells, the carilloneur punched those sticks like a prizefighter. There were times when I'd come down from the bell tower with my fists black and blue.

I'd spent the term studying the empiricists with Professor Bendall. I'd made a breakthrough earlier that spring when discussing the work of Leibniz with my friend Thurman, who was a philosophy major.

"So this guy Leibniz?" I said. "His theory is that the world consists of these tiny little nuggets, called monads?"

"That's right," said Thurman, whose go-to guy was Immanuel Kant. Thurman was doing an honors project on the *Prolegomena to Any Future Metaphysics*. "Each of the monads is nonextended and indestructible."

"So they're, like, little goobers," I said.

Thurman nodded gravely. "Yes, James. In a sense they are goobers. Each monad perceives all other monads and reflects it. Beings are clusters of mirroring monads. Which means, of course, that in Leibniz's view, the world is not really spatiotemporal."

I thought this was rather nice of him to say, considering that Thurman had once stuck his entire ass out the window as I walked by his dormitory with my parents.

"Okay," I said. "But the thing is—when Leibniz talks about monads and everything? He's really just, like, making it all up. Right?"

Thurman, a very tall, lean man with sunken eyes, looked at me sorrowfully. "What do you mean? You're saying that the construction of his philosophy is itself an act of the imagination?"

"No, man," I said. "What I mean is, monads don't really exist. Right?"

"James," said Thurman. "That's hardly the point."

"But it *is* the point," I said. "Basically, when it comes to monads—he just invented them. Okay? I mean—the idea that the world is made up of these little sparkling goobers—he's wrong. Isn't he? Because the world's not made up of sparkling goobers."

Thurman sighed and touched his forehead with his fingers. "James," he said. "James."

"What am I missing?" I said.

"It's not about whether he was *right*," said Thurman, once more picking up the *Prolegomena to Any Future Metaphysics*. "It's about the felicity of his invention."

Pretty soon I'd be working on a prolegomena of my own, and if anybody thought they'd start up with any future metaphysics before considering it, they'd be sorry. It was, in fact, this very prolegomena that I was supposed to be finishing up in the university bell tower. In the morning, after the paper was handed in, I'd get in the car and head back to the Coffin House, and my parents, and my summer job as a teller at Continental Bank in Philadelphia.

And so, I typed, on the Smith-Corona.

As we behold the unfolding of the monads like the movement of a sunflower to the sun we can understand that human nature is beholden to a focus beyond its control even though they might be very small. Or not exist at all. This is important for you and important for me as well. By learning about monads and the way they reflect things on a truly deep level we learn about ourselves. Who also reflect things back to ourselves and move in ways that we ourselves think are mysterious beyond fathomability, which makes you think, alot.

I could almost imagine the remarks Professor Bendall would add to this.

I pulled the sheet of onionskin out of the typewriter, turned the dial to off, and listened as the power drained out of the Smith-Corona. My sophomore year was done.

It was time to celebrate. I climbed on board the bench of the rosewood clavier and began to ring changes on the ear-shattering carillon. True: it was eleven o'clock at night, but that didn't matter. My music always cheered everybody up.

When I came down out of the bell tower, I found Grace Finney sitting on the steps of South College, smoking a cigarette. I didn't know her very well, but I'd seen her around. She was an actress whom I'd first seen onstage in David Mamet's *Sexual Perversity in Chicago*, at the '92 Theater. Grace was a beautiful woman who wore leather jackets, a leather cap. She had a reputation for being very tough. All my friends were in love with her.

"Hey Grace," I said.

"James," she said. "I thought you'd be along."

"You did? How come?"

She blew smoke out into the spring night. "Nobody else plays heavy metal on the college carillon, James."

"What are you doing?"

She had a book in her lap. "Reading. I got a philosophy exam."

"I just finished a philosophy paper. About these monads."

"Monads?" she said. "What are monads?"

I shrugged. "I don't know," I said.

She held up a volume of Hegel. "I'm writing about dialectics."

"Dialectics," I said. "You mean, like, Scientology?"

She smiled. "No, James," she said. "That's *Dianetics*. Dialectics is the philosophy of opposites."

I thought about this. "How do you make a philosophy out of opposites?"

"Well, you know how people are. They like to see things in black and white? Up or down, male or female?"

She had my attention now. "Uh-huh."

"Well, dialectics says that's all bullshit. That life is not about opposites, but about finding balance between all those extremes."

I tried to sound less interested than I actually was. "How do you do that?" I said. "Find balance, I mean."

"By paying attention," she said. "By trying to see how everything also contains its opposite." She took a drag on her cigarette. "Because if you live your life at the extremes, you go nuts. If you want to make any sense out of the world, you have to live in the gray."

"That sounds hard," I said.

"The hell yes it's hard," she said. "People don't like the gray. It makes people uncomfortable." It occurred to me that there was something delightfully gray about Grace Finney herself, in fact, this gorgeous woman in tough-guy leather.

Grace reached into her jacket and pulled out a flask, then took a slug. "You want some?"

"What is it?"

"Jim Beam."

I took a nip from her flask. "Thanks," I said. "I should go." I stuck my paper under one arm. "I'll see you around, okay?"

"Okay, James," she said. It sounded like it was just fine with her, whether I stayed or left. I wondered, as I walked off down Brownstone Row, whether she'd been waiting for me. "Hey James," she shouted.

"Hey what?"

"I like the way you play the bells," she said.

"Yeah?"

"Yeah. You make me laugh."

"Thanks," I said as I headed back to my dorm. It was a nice thing for her to say. It was one of my hidden talents, as it turned out: the ability to make people laugh.

Grace didn't know it yet, but I could make her cry, too.

It was a beautiful night in Middletown, Connecticut, the stars twinkling overhead, the long brownstone buildings all in a row. To my right, as I walked back to my dorm, was the Memorial Chapel and the '92 Theater and Judd Hall, the psychology building. Beyond these was the great green expanse of Foss Hill, at the top of which was a huge observatory, covered in ivy. As I watched, the dome of the observatory spun around. Somebody was in there, looking at the heavens. I wondered if she was working on a *Monadology*, too.

I walked toward the observatory, going the long way around Brownstone Row, then took a right at the Public Affairs Center. I headed past Olin Library, and Clark Hall, which was where the studios of WESU-FM were located. I saw a friend of mine framed in the window, naked, talking into the big microphone. This was David Zucker, doing his weekly *Nude Radio* program.

I entered Foss One, and headed down the stairs into the tunnels, in order to make my way over to Three. The tunnels were poorly lit, covered with wild murals and graffiti. On this particular evening, someone had broken into the storeroom that contained all the stuffed animals from the now-closed zoology department and left them posed at unexpected locations. I passed a bunch of people sucking nitrous oxide out of a big cold tank next to a stuffed walrus. A little farther down the hallway Ned Stockman was playing "Delia Was a Gambling Girl" on acoustic guitar next to a giant kangaroo. I was crazy about Ned Stockman. Later he joined the CIA.

"Hey James," he said. "Good episode tonight."

"Thanks," I said.

He was referring to a radio drama that I'd written and Dave Zucker had produced called *Squid Family*. It was a fifteen-episode underwater soap opera that took place among a group of squids: Widley, Didley, and their parents. In episode one, the squids had moved out to Great Salt Lake in hopes of better things.

But in this they were disappointed.

Squid Family was a hit, at least by the insular standards of the campus. It was the first thing I'd ever written that anybody said was any good. Everywhere I went people now thought of me as that *Squid Family* guy.

I'd arrived at the school half-translucent. Now, after two years of bell-ringing and *Squid Family* and monadology, it seemed as if I was turning out to be a solid person after all. It felt wonderful and strange. I wondered if this was what everybody else felt like all the time.

I approached a stairwell that led out of the subterranean realm. Just as I reached it, I found the point of a sword at my throat. John Moynihan was standing there wearing a long black cape, an eye patch, a hat with the skull and crossbones.

"Moynihan," I said. I loved Moynihan. He had a girlfriend who thought she was Nancy Sinatra.

"Avast, matey," he said. "Time to walk the plank!"

"Now?" I said.

The point of his sword jabbed into the soft part of my neck. I raised my hands above my head. "All forms," he observed, "are an imperfection of the Void."

I said the only thing I could in the situation. "Aye-aye, Captain."

He lowered his sword, put a map in my hand. "Guard this," he said.

He flapped his cloak theatrically, and in an instant was gone. I heard his footsteps disappearing down the dark tunnel. I looked at the map he'd given me. There was a large X in the middle. All around this were various dangers: *The Swamp of Nerds, the Amnesia Forest*. At the edges were dark waters of an uncharted ocean. There were serpents in it wearing top hats. *Here be dragons*.

I headed up the stairs.

My roommate, Bert Spivak, was sitting at his desk when I arrived. We had something called a "divided double," which was two conjoined singles. Bert had the outer chamber. He'd come to college with exactly one Samsonite suitcase full of clothes, and it had lain on the floor, open, for the full year. Bert was an economics major, and smelled bad. I couldn't figure out what it was that generated the stench in his room, seeing as how he had so few possessions. Sometimes I wondered if an animal had died in his suitcase, and he just hadn't worked his way down to it yet. It would have to be a pretty big animal, though, to create an aroma like this. Maybe, I thought, the thing that had died was Bert himself.

He looked up as I came in, and pointed with his thumb to my room. "Lucy's waitin' for ya," he said.

I had forgotten about my impending chat with Lucy, and I dreaded the conversation I knew was coming. Women loved the fact that I was so sensitive, that I wanted, mostly, to talk to them, to drink cups of coffee and eat Nilla Wafers, but my lack of interest in actual sex eventually wore them down. In my experience, straight women like it when a guy has a feminine sensibility, an enthusiasm that goes right up to—but unfortunately does not quite include—his being an actual woman.

The same thing, I found out years later, is true in reverse for men: guys who don't know any better, these days, are generally charmed by the fact that I am a woman with an affection for baseball and whiskey. Men like it when a woman can be one of the guys. Except, of course, when she actually used to be one. When boys figure out that part of it, their enthusiasm wanes somewhat. And their faces take on a look similar to that of a nine-year-old who's just found out that what he's purchased under the name of "sea monkeys" have really turned out to be brine shrimp.

All in all, I had not come very far from my salad days with Sarah Towers, whose heart I had broken the night before I cleverly filled my parents' house with toilet water.

"Hey James," said Lucy. She was sitting on my bed.

"Lucy," I said. We kissed. "Hey."

"I'm leaving tomorrow," she said. "Back to New Jersey. And so I wanted to say good-bye."

"Well de well de well," I said. This was one of my endearing catchphrases, the *well de well de well*. So far as I knew, I had invented it myself. "Isn't that nice. The ol' happy trails thing. What does it all mean? Indeed."

"I made this for you." She handed me a piece of heavy paper covered with a wash of pastel watercolors, with clouds drawn against this in black ink. It was a beautiful thing. At the bottom she'd signed it, *For James with Love Always. Lucy.*

"Wow," I said. "This is really nice. You didn't have to do this."

"I wanted to," she said. She reached out and touched the side of my face. "You're special."

I was special, all right. I leaned forward and kissed her. I loved the way it felt. We held each other. Lucy raised her lips to my ear. "I brought my diaphragm."

"Did you," I said. "Well de well de well."

"Let's make love," said Lucy. "Please?"

"Well," I said. My heart was pounding. "I don't know."

"What do you mean, you don't know?" She looked at me, hurt. "Don't you want to?"

"Well, sure I want to, I mean, you're great. But it's like—I don't know, I feel like I want to save that, for when things are more aligned."

"Aligned? With what?"

"Well, you know. With the time when that happens."

"When what happens?"

"The very thing we're talking about."

Lucy opened her mouth, then closed it. She didn't say anything for a while. Then her eyes filled with tears. "Oh my God," she said. "I'm such an idiot."

"No you're not. You're great."

"I can't believe—"

"Please," I said to her. I held her. "Don't be sad. You know I love you."

"I love you, too," she said. "Really. I've never met anybody like you."

"Let's write letters this summer," I said.

"Really? You're serious?"

Of course I was serious. I loved writing letters. As it turned out, I was a lot better on paper than I was in person.

We exchanged addresses, then we made out on the bed. Things got all hot and heavy. I got her shirt off, messed around with her breasts for a while. They were globey!

"Okay, well," I said, when she started moaning. "I really oughta hit the hay."

"The hay?" she said.

"Yeah. You know, I don't want to open a door without knowing what's inside."

"A door," she said, sitting up, little moons and stars floating around her head.

"You know how special you are to me," I said, and kissed her on the cheek. "A lot."

Lucy blew some air through her cheeks. "What's wrong with you?" she said. "Come on. Let's just fuck!"

"Ah, well, now. We talked about that."

"Did we? What did we say?"

"I thought we decided to keep that for a time when, you know, things don't hum so much."

"What does that mean?" said Lucy. "Hum? I don't hear any hum!"

"Listen," I said, and I put my arm back around her. She had her shirt in her lap. We were very still for a minute. "Do you hear it?"

"What?"

"The sound of the universe!"

We sat still for a little longer. Lucy looked at me, tears in her eyes. "I think I hear it?" she said.

"And that," I said. "Is why you're so special."

"Oh James," she said. "James, James."

I kissed her again. "I'll write you," I said.

"Okay." Lucy stood up and pulled her shirt on over her head. She leaned down and kissed me. Then she went to the door.

"Listen," she said. "James. I'm sorry. Really."

"It's okay," I said. "There's nothing to be sorry for."

But I was wrong about this. There was plenty to be sorry for. *Hey you,* I wanted to say. *Don't get me started.*

Lucy nodded and then headed out. I'd dodged another bullet.

I took off my pants and got into bed, turned out the light and lay there for a while. All around me I heard the sounds of Wesleyan University. Guys typing papers on electric typewriters; people shouting and laughing out by the quad. Someone down the hallway was listening to Frank Zappa. *Oh no, I don't believe it. You say that you think you know the meaning of love. Do you think it really can be told?* It was a sentimental number, but Zappa had other tunes as well, including one about the relationship between a donkey and an enchilada.

The phone rang. I looked at the clock. It was after midnight.

"Hello?"

"Hey," said a woman's voice. "Jimmy. It's your sister."

"Hey." I turned the light on. Lucy's watercolor was still sitting on top of my steamer trunk, next to my big box of records.

"What are you doing?"

"Nothing. Sleeping." I could hear the sound of the static on the phone line. She was calling me long distance from Minneapolis, having transferred from Carleton to the U of M after her freshman year. She'd been dating a guy named Eamon O'Flynn, who went to school there. In my sister's case, *dating* someone meant, you know. Actual dating.

"I have some news for you," she said. I sat up in bed now, worried.

"What?"

"I'm getting married."

I regret that the first words I said in response to this were, "You think so?" But I said them.

"I *know* so."

"Well," I said. "Well de well de well."

"Aren't you going to congratulate me?"

"Of course," I said. "That's great. Good for you." I hoped my disappointment wasn't audible. It was the worst news I could imagine. I hadn't even met this Eamon. All I knew was that he wanted to go to law school, and that he liked Jimmy Buffett. It says a lot about me, probably, that I would have liked Eamon better if he wanted to be unemployed and had a predisposition for that Frank Zappa song about the donkey having sex with Mexican food.

"When's this going to be?"

"This summer."

"Where?"

"The Bryn Mawr Presbyterian church. The reception is going to be at the house."

"Just don't get some accordion band, okay?" I said. "People at weddings always get these accordion bands, and you wind up wanting to shoot yourself in the head."

"Jimmy," she said, hurt. "We haven't *talked* about the band yet."

"Are you going on a honeymoon, anything like that?"

"Yeah. I think we're going camping."

"Well de well," I said. "Camping sounds like fun."

"And then we're moving to Oregon."

"Oregon? What's in Oregon?"

"Lewis and Clark College. I'm transferring there."

"Why?" I said. It would be her third college in four years.

"Well, Eamon's going to law school in Portland."

"You don't want to finish up at the U of M?"

"I don't think so," she said, like this was a stupid idea.

"What do Mom and Dad say?"

"Oh, you know," she said. "We had some big fight about it. Then they said they were happy."

"Are you wearing Mom's wedding dress?"

"No way! Hers?"

"Yeah," I said. "I bet you'd look good in that." I wasn't thinking of how she'd look.

"There's another thing," she said.

"What?" I was getting tired of this conversation. It was already clear to me that she was making a terrible mistake, and there was no point in trying to talk her out of it. She wouldn't put up with any crap about the sound of the universe humming, either. Lydia was going to marry this Eamon O'Flynn whether I told her she could or not.

"I want to know if you'll be an usher. At the wedding."

"An usher?" I said. It didn't sound like much fun.

"Please?"

"Okay," I said, although I wasn't happy about it. I didn't have the sense that this was any kind of honor. I thought it was like being asked to be the doorman.

"Oh, thank you, thank you," she said. "Eamon loves you."

"He's never met me!" I said.

"Yeah, but I've showed him all your cartoons."

"Well, okay," I said. The way I figured, cartoons were probably a good way to get to know me. "Listen, Lydia," I said. "I'm only going to ask you this one time, all right? Why are you doing this? I mean, you know marriage is just a legal way to keep women enslaved? The iron fist of the patriarchy?" I was very serious about this.

"Hey little brother," said my sister. "Don't worry about it. We won't stop the revolution, okay?"

"I'm serious," I said. "Don't do it. You don't need some piece of paper!"

"But Jimmy," she said. "I'm in love."

I started to say something, but then stopped. It wasn't the last time I'd find myself in this situation, asking for an explanation for something and getting that answer: *Because I'm in love*. Even now, thirty years later, I understand that when someone tells you that they're taking a trip to Neptune, or starting tap-dancing classes, or changing their name to Tiffany-Chiffon Murfreesboro on account of their being in love, the only thing you can do is wish them well, and get out of the way.

"Well," I said to my sister. "I'm glad."

But I was the opposite of glad, and after I hung up with her, I lay in the dark thinking for a long time. I thought about Lucy Potemkin and her diaphragm, about being an usher at my sister's wedding, about all the hippies I knew lying around unconscious next to a big happy tank of nitrous oxide and a stuffed walrus. It seemed as if everyone I knew was going to wind up a man or woman.

It was hard not to feel, sometimes, like I was standing on a dock as all my friends slowly sailed out to sea.

I got out of bed again and put my pants on.

Bert Spivak didn't wake up as I snuck through his fragrant chamber.

The campus was still in full-on party mode, even though it was going on two A.M.; classes were over and lights were on all over Wesleyan as students drank tequila and listened to Elvis Costello and howled at the moon, up in the big cemetery. I walked down Foss Hill, past the observatory where the telescope was still pointed up at the stars, back to the bell tower.

And there I sat down on the front steps and cried, until my eyes were tired.

Goddammit, I thought. *Goddammit to hell.*

As I sat there, John Moynihan walked by, with his eye patch and his cape. I wanted to say *Well de well de well* to him, but I couldn't.

I loved my buccaneer friend, but Moynihan felt that obvious displays of emotion were a violation of the pirate code. He caught a glimpse of the tears on my cheeks and kept moving. I heard his voice, though, singing a rock and roll tune as he walked away from me. *'Cause celluloid heroes never really feel any pain*, he sang. Moynihan was a big Kinks fan. *And celluloid heroes never really die*.

I watched him disappear into the undergraduate night. The clock in the steeple of Memorial Chapel tolled the hour.

But Jimmy, she said. *I'm in love.*

Squeezebox

My grandmother screamed with joy as Lydia opened up the box that contained the antique panties.

"What are these?" Lydia asked, horrified. We were all sitting in the family room in the Coffin House—my parents, Lydia, me, Gammie, and Hilda. Eamon O'Flynn sat on a chair at my sister's left. There was a big pile of presents on the floor.

"My lucky pantaloons," said Gammie.

"You're giving me your underpants?" said Lydia.

"They're great for makin' babies!" said Gammie.

A new dog had joined the family since the flood, Matt the Mutt, and at this moment he came into the living room and stared at us with hostility. He was covered with white bushy hair and had two large black spots that overlapped his ear and eye on each side. He'd been raised in my sister's freshman dorm at Carleton, and she'd brought him home after her first year and handed him over to my parents.

He looked at Gammie's underpants and barked.

"Quiet," said my father. The dog had no interest in him.

"Whoop? Whoop?"

"Hilda!" shouted Gammie. "I gave Liddie my lucky pantaloons!"

"Whoop," said Hilda.

"I said they're great for making babies!"

Matt the Mutt barked again.

"Whoop?"

Gammie sighed happily. "Did I ever tell you about the night your father was conceived?"

Everyone in the room shouted, "YES!" Even Hilda shouted it. Gammie finished her vodka and sat back happily. "We were in Atlantic City," she said.

"No!" said Lydia. "Please!"

"September 1927. Your grandfather had just gotten kicked upstairs at Johns Manville."

"We know the story," said my mother kindly. "You really don't have to tell it again."

"Well," said Gammie. "Over dinner Jim turned to me and sang."

"Dear God," said Lydia.

" 'When our love was new! Each kiss an inspiration!' " My sister covered her face with her hands. "That's 'Stardust'! Hoagy Carmichael. A popular song. A *very* popular song."

"You sing it very nicely, Mrs. Redding," said Eamon O'Flynn. He was a short, square-jawed man with a mop of brown hair. His eyes twinkled.

"And then he kissed me! Right at the table! And I kissed him back."

"Who needs a drink?" asked my mother. "Can I get anybody anything?"

"And I kissed him back," said Gammie. "That is what I did. And he took me in his arms and we went up to the room, and you know what happened then?"

"We know what happened then," I said.

"Don't say it," said Lydia, her face still covered by her hands. "Please don't say it!"

"Best screwin' of my life!"

"Whoop? Whoop?"

"I said, best screwin' of my life, Hilda! With Dick's father! In the Claridge Hotel, in Atlantic City. *Best screwin' of my life!* Nine months later, out pops Junior!" Gammie looked at her enraptured audience. "Did I ever tell you about the day Dick was born?"

The six of us who were not Gammie shouted once again, with one voice, "YES!"

"HE SLID RIGHT OUT!"

"Whoop? Whoop?"

"HE SLID RIGHT OUT, Hilda!"

"Please make it stop," said my sister. "Please."

Matt stood up, went over to the wall, and lifted his leg.

"No," said my mother. "Bad dog!"

Matt gave us a look like *Some people*.

"I'd always heard these stories of childbirth," Gammie said. "Girls yelling and screaming. And so on and so forth. Not your father. He was as gentle as a lamb!" She leaned back in her chair. "Such a good boy," she said. "A spoiled brat! Who's a spoiled brat?"

My father twinkled softly. "I am," he said.

"And those," Gammie said, pointing to the underpants that still lay in my sister's lap. "Those were the pantaloons I was wearing. That night. That special night in the Claridge. In Atlantic City. That is what I was wearing."

"We know," said my sister.

"My lucky pantaloons!" Gammie sighed. "After that, Jim always called me Stardust. That was his name for me. After the song."

"Don't sing it again," said my sister.

" 'Ah, but that was long ago!' " sang Gammie. " 'And now my consolation, is in the stardust of a song!' "

Hilda looked around. "Whoop?" she said.

Gammie raised her glass in the air and shook the ice cubes around. "Vodka," she said.

My father got to his feet. "No," said Gammie, pointing at Eamon O'Flynn. "The *boy* will get it."

Eamon stood up, took the glass from my grandmother, and walked through the house back to the kitchen. My grandmother stared at his receding form.

"He's awfully short," she said.

"How about this one?" said my mother, handing my sister another elegantly wrapped present. "This is from Mrs. Waxwire, down at the Radnor Hunt."

My sister looked up. Her face was red. She cast a withering glance at my grandmother. As was usually the case the withering glance bounced off of Gammie like a tiny pebble bouncing off the windshield of a speeding truck on the interstate. "I don't know any Mrs. Waxwire," said my sister. She sounded tired.

"Ted Waxwire works at Ballard Spahr," said my father. He was wearing plaid pants and a shirt with a little alligator on it. "He's a top man."

It wasn't a surprise that Lydia and Eamon were getting presents from people they'd never heard of, now that my father was a vice president at the bank. More gifts arrived for them each day, and a lot of them were from strangers.

Lydia opened up the box. "It's a Mr. Coffee," she said.

"Oh, they're supposed to be very good," said my mother. "You know Joe DiMaggio recommends them."

"The Yankee Clipper," said Gammie wistfully.

"Whoop?"

"The Yankee Clipper!" Gammie shouted, at Hilda. "We're talking about Joe DiMaggio. The baseball player."

"Oh," said Hilda, disappointed. "I've never understood American baseball. It just seems like someone's made a dog's dinner from rounders."

Gammie shook her head. "Queen Elizabeth over here."

"Who's this one from?" said Lydia, as my mother put another present in her lap.

"Mrs. Dalrimple."

"I don't *know* any Mrs. Dalrimple," said Lydia.

"Mrs. Dalrimple?" said my mother. "The violinist?"

"Her husband works down at Fidelity," said my father.

Lydia unwrapped the box. "Towels," she said.

"*Monogrammed* towels," my mother observed.

"Whose initials are these?" asked Lydia. The towels were stitched with the letters LBO'F.

"Why, they're *your* initials," my mother said. "Or will be."

"My initials?" said Lydia, still working it through.

"Lydia Boylan O'Flynn!"

"I haven't decided whether I'm taking O'Flynn yet," said Lydia. "I thought I might keep Boylan."

"What?" said Gammie, incredulous.

"I said I thought I might keep Boylan."

Gammie looked astounded. "He's going to be your *husband*," she pointed out.

"A lot of women keep their own names now," I said. "Just because you get married doesn't make you someone's property! You know what a woman without a man is like? A fish without a bicycle!"

The members of my family considered this insight.

Gammie snickered. "You wait."

My mother looked at my sister, alarmed. "Well, you can write a letter to Mrs. Dalrimple telling her you don't want her nice monogrammed towels," she said. "You can be the one to explain the way you're repudiating other people's kindness!"

"I'm not repudiating anything, mother," said Lydia. "I'm just saying, I get to choose my own name. Don't I?"

Eamon came back into the room with Gammie's vodka. He handed it to her politely and gave her a small cocktail napkin as well.

"Can I get you anything else?" he said.

Gammie thought it over for a long, long time. Then she said, "No."

Eamon looked at my sister, who was on the verge of tears. "What's wrong, Lids?"

She held up the monogrammed towels. "These," said Lydia. "They've got the wrong initials."

"They're from Mrs. Dalrimple!" said my mother. "They're very expensive!"

"Bob Dalrimple is a top man at Fidelity," said my father, peacefully smoking a cigarette.

"She says she's keeping her own name," Gammie explained. "After the marriage. She's rejecting O'Flynn. *Rejecting* it!"

Eamon shrugged. "That's her choice," he said. "Isn't it?"

Everyone looked stunned at this. He held his hand out to Lydia, and she took it. Eamon pulled her to her feet and gave her a big hug. Lydia rested her head against his shoulder. We all sat there watching this, not speaking.

"I think we'll take a walk now," said Eamon, easing my sister out of the room. "We'll open more presents tomorrow."

"But we have a very big stack," said my mother, and it was true. There was a pile of boxes towering up to heaven.

"There's plenty of time," said Eamon with a smile. "Excuse us now."

He walked with Lydia out of the room, led her through the dining room. We heard the front door open, then close.

Gammie sipped her vodka. "I give 'em a year," she said. "Tops."

The house to which I had returned after taking my leave of Wesleyan University in the late spring of 1978 bore little resemblance to the place that had been flooded five years earlier. In part, this was because the insurance company had been surprisingly generous with the post-flood reconstruction funds, allowing my parents to bring the house well into the twentieth century.

But there was more to the house's transformation than this. In the years that had just passed, my father's star had risen. Now, in my father's powerful middle age, the Coffin House—though no one called it that anymore—had changed again.

My parents had hired a gardener named Ziggy, a huge Italian guy who not only cut the grass but also cleaned the pool and weeded the perennial garden. When he was working, I'd come through the door and sing, in my best David Bowie voice, " 'Ziggy played guitar, jamming good with Weird and Gilly, and the spiders from Mars.' "

My mother would look at me confused. "Ziggy doesn't play guitar," she'd say, thoughtfully. "Does he?"

No one, in the old days, could have mistaken the Boylans for a family of means. Now, as I stood at the edge of adulthood, it seemed we had become something else entirely, a family with its own gardener.

All of this created the other big difference in the place. As the walls were repainted, the drywall sealed, the new floors stained and buffed, the windows and doors replaced, the house felt less and less haunted. By the time I got out of high school in 1976, I could feel the difference: its spirits were gone.

By the time of my sister's wedding two years later, all that haunting seemed like a crazy memory, something I'd imagined or invented out of boredom or confusion, a dementia born out of sheer loneliness. Had any of it been real, when you came right down to it? I wondered, sometimes, whether my memories of my own life could be trusted.

" 'He took it all too far,' " I'd sing to my mother. " 'But boy could he play guitar.' "

"Who's this we're talking about?" she'd ask.

So it was with some surprise a night or two later that I heard Sausage lift her head off the floor and growl at something that could not be seen. I turned on the light.

"What is it?" I said. "What do you see?"

The dog was staring at the door of my room. I swung my feet onto the floor, walked across the room, and opened it. The hallway was still. The mirror on the back of the bathroom door reflected nothing unseemly. From downstairs came the sound of my father snoring.

Sausage growled again. I went back to my room, pulled on my pants, and headed down the creaking stairs.

I passed through the second-floor hallway, with its new wallpaper and new floorboards, past the rooms that contained my sleeping family. I passed the deep window on the landing. It was dark outside. Stars shone down.

The front door of the house was open, and as Sausage stood on the landing, looking down the stairs into the ornate front hall, I thought of Detective Arbogast falling backward down the stairs in *Psycho*, after being slashed by a knife. Crickets and cicadas sang in the night.

I walked down the stairs, one hand trailing along the banister like a tendril. Since the flood, my mother had needlepointed a custom design for each of the risers, which were intended, in their own cheerful way, to tell the story of our family. At the top of the stairs was a family crest, with an eagle on it. On the next step down was a needlepoint Sausage, one paw extended in friendship. As I descended the stairs I passed over the following images: a man reading in a library; the masks of comedy and tragedy; a woman surrounded by tulips in a garden; a bear and a bull surrounded by ticker tape; the Wesleyan cardinal; a piano keyboard encircled by crazy notes; a sower sowing seeds into the wind; two members of the Philadelphia Flyers; my sister going over a jump on Checkmate; and ba-BOING! asleep on a pillow.

The last riser, at the bottom of the stairs, was an ornate needlepointed image of the house itself.

Gazing on these risers a few years later, a girlfriend of Zero's would shake her head and say, "This is the WASPiest thing I have ever seen in my life." She didn't mean it as a compliment exactly, but I loved those risers. I *still* love them, primarily because my corklike mother made them, stitch by stitch.

I walked out onto the porch. A set of stone stairs led down into the yard. There was a man sitting on the steps by himself, his back to me. Sausage went up to him and licked his face, which was odd since of course she detested human beings on principle.

Eamon turned back to me and said, "Hey, Jim." His words were garbled slightly because he had something in his mouth. I went down the steps and sat next to him.

"Hey."

We sat there together listening to the sounds of the night.

"You want a chaw?" He held a small tin toward me.

"No thanks," I said. He smiled, put the tin back in his pocket.

For a while we did not speak. Now and again Eamon would hock a big saliva-ball of chewing tobacco into the hedges. Not too often though.

"Your family always have Dalmatians?"

"Yeah," I said. "Since I was little."

"Fire dogs," he said.

"Matt's the first dog we had that's not a Dalmatian."

Eamon smiled. "Poor little buttfucker."

"Excuse me?"

"That's the name they called that dog in the dorm at Carleton. Buttfucker. Or B.F. Back when he was little he liked humpin' things."

"Charming," I said.

He hocked another big cheekful of sauce into the hedges. "I guess you don't like me much," he said.

"Like you?" I said. This was uncalled for, so far as I could see. Of course I didn't like him. Part of the reason I didn't like him was that he didn't seem to understand that if you didn't like someone, the last thing you'd do on the Main Line was talk about it. On the Main Line, you generally treated the people you hated and the people you liked about the same. "Sure I like you. Why wouldn't I like you?"

"I don't know," said Eamon. "Midwesterner. Catholic. Stealin' your sister. You'd have lots of reasons, if you wanted any."

"I don't judge people that way," I said.

He reached out and patted Sausage on the head. "She thinks the world of you, you know."

"Well," I said. "She's pretty great."

"Got a fuse on her, though, don't she."

"She does," I agreed.

"My sister's got a fuse on her," he said. "Anybody wanted to marry her, I'd try to kill him, too."

"I'm not trying to kill you."

"Maybe not." He spat some more tobacco. "I'll try to take care of her, okay. The best I can. That's all I can tell you, Jim. I hope that's good enough for you."

"For me?" I said. "You don't need my blessing, Eamon. You can do what you want. It's a free country."

"You think?"

We sat on the big stone steps for a long time after that without exchanging any more words. Sausage lay down on the porch and went back to sleep.

I looked up at the summer stars. "There's the Northern Crown," I said. "That little curve. My favorite constellation. It looks like a tiara."

Eamon looked up. I waited for him to ask me to point it out for him, but he didn't. Instead he nodded.

"Arcturus looks pretty bright tonight, too," he said. "In the Herdsman."

"I know where Arcturus is," I said, annoyed. "There. Right above that planet. I think that's Saturn."

Eamon O'Flynn, from Minneapolis, Minnesota, considered the heavens. "That's Mars," he said.

"You know the stars?" I said suspiciously.

Eamon nodded humbly. "Eagle Scout," he said.

The front door opened softly behind us. A woman stood there in a white nightgown, her long blond hair hanging down. For a moment I thought it was that ghost I used to see in the mirror. But that would be unlikely. *This house is clean.*

"Hey," said Lydia. "What are you boys doing?"

"Nothin'," said Eamon. "Stargazin'."

I could see from Lydia's face that she was pleased we were getting along so well. "Hey Eamo. You got any chaw?"

He got the tin out of his pocket and handed it to her. "Okay so," he said. I thought, Eamo?

I watched as my sister stuck a wad of seaweed in her mouth, like Popeye the Sailor Man. It was possible, although not certain, that my sister was now strong to the finich.

"Can you make me a milk shake?"

I was just about to respond when I realized she wasn't talking to me.

Eamon nodded. "All righty," he said, and stood up. He turned back to me. "You want one, Jim?"

They stood there on the porch, the big house behind them. Their cheeks were great with chaw.

"No," I said. "I'm good."

On June 22, we sat in front of the fireplace opening more engagement gifts. There were cutting boards from Dansk, crystal wine decanters, good china and cutlery. Ted Sullivan from Pittsburgh National gave them another Mr. Coffee.

"You can exchange that," said my mother.

"Might be a good thing, having a couple a Mr. Coffees," said Eamon. "One for regular, one for decaf."

Matt the Mutt went over to the hearth and peed on the fireplace tools.

"No," said my mother. "Bad dog."

It was my twentieth birthday, and I wasn't entirely sure if this had been forgotten, or what. I didn't want to say anything, in case it had slipped everyone's mind. There was a lot going on.

Lydia opened up her last present, which turned out to be a salad spinner. Then she sat back, exhausted.

Finally, my mother brought out a square box and put it in my lap. It was fairly heavy, so that ruled out panty hose.

Slowly, I opened the box and held up, for all to see, the thing that lay inside.

Everyone sat there for a moment in stunned amazement.

"It's—a squeezebox," said Eamon, impressed.

"A concertina," corrected my mother.

"Jeez," said Lydia. "Now all you need is a monkey."

I pushed on the buttons and opened the bellows. The room filled with a wild, rasping honk, like the sound of someone playing harmonica through an iron lung.

My mother looked concerned. "Do you like it?"

I grinned from ear to ear. "It's a miracle," I said, honking the concertina some more. "It's too cool!" I got up and hugged my mother.

"What is it again?" said my father.

"It's an Irish concertina," I said. "For playing all the old songs." I honked it again.

"All right, then," said my father, grinning. " 'It's a Long Way to Tipperary.' In seven-eight."

"Don't," said Lydia. "Please."

" 'Good-bye, Piccadilly,' " I sang. " 'Farewell, Leicester Square!' "

"Dear God," said my sister. "Make it stop!" The concertina was surprisingly loud. The dogs started barking.

" 'It's a long way to Tipperary! But my heart's right there!' "

My sister shook her head sadly. The dogs were still howling. My mother sat in her chair with a happy smile on her face.

"Well," I said to her, overcome with joy. "Well de well de well."

"Mama's got a squeezebox," noted Eamon. "Daddy never sleeps at night."

My father looked perplexed. "What's that, Eamon?"

"The Who," said my sister.

"I don't know," said my father. "That's what I'm asking."

The day after my birthday, I headed out to Chocolate World with Doober and Zero and Otto. We drove through Hershey, Pennsylvania, beneath the streetlights shaped like Hershey's Kisses, past the union hall for Chocolate Workers Local 464, past the roller coasters and Ferris wheels of Hersheypark. On the stereo was Dean Martin singing "The Peanut Vendor."

If you haven't got bananas don't be blue; peanuts in a little bag are calling you.

"Totally *excellent* version of the peanut vendor song, man," said Doober. He passed the joint to Otto.

"Stan Kenton did the original," said Otto, who was an authority on most things, especially jazz. He'd fractured his skull in a Mazda during our senior year, but he was all right now. You wouldn't even notice the scar unless you knew where to look.

"I heard Desi Arnaz do this one time," I said.

"Oh man," said Zero. "Desi Arnaz is excellent."

"Stan Kenton's band stretches it out more, though," said Otto. "There's more experimentation."

"I think Desi Arnaz was pretty experimental," I said. "You ever watch the *Lucy* show? Definitely fringe material."

Zero shrugged. "Lucy never did anything for me."

"Get out," I said. "That Meata-Vegamin bit? It's a classic." He turned up the peanut vendor song.

In those days, my friends and I listened to everything—classical, traditional Irish, Javanese gamelan, cool jazz, Indian raga, Frank Zappa, Gregorian chants, Rahsaan Roland Kirk. The only thing completely off our radar was disco, which we assumed appealed exclusively to the stupid. Inevitably, it's disco that people now associate with the era of my adolescence. Whenever I go to any kind of reunion of the people I knew then, the room always fills with the very sounds we once detested. And as for the music we loved? Even we don't listen to it anymore.

"I had some of that," said Doober. He'd quit Cornell just that spring. "In Berkeley."

"Some of what?" asked Otto as we pulled up in front of Chocolate World.

"Meta-vitamin. It's awesome."

We got out of the car. "What are you talking about, man?" said Otto. "It's a joke. There's no such thing."

"Well, that's where you're wrong," said Doober. " 'Cause I had some, dude."

The air was redolent with the fragrance of chocolate.

"It's not meta-vitamin, man," I said. "It's Meata-Vegamin."

"It's *Vita*-Meata-Vegamin," said Zero. "Okay? And it's a joke. Which is why you couldn't have had any." We walked up to the Chocolate World admission booth. They waved us in. Chocolate World was free.

Doober looked disappointed. "Dude *said* it was meta-vitamin. *Denied!*"

"Did you smoke it? Or was it—needles, or what?"

Doober was shocked. "Needles? For meata-vedge-a-vitamins? I don't think so."

"It's *Vita*-Meata-Vegamin," said Zero.

"Not what I had," said Doober. "It comes in a bag. You sniff it."

We let this sink in. Then Zero said, "You mean—it's glue. You're talking about sniffing glue, in a bag."

"It's not glue," said Doober, hurt.

"Can we stop talking about this?" I said. "What's the difference?"

Doober now spoke in the voice of the Cowardly Lion. "Put 'em up!" he said. "Put 'em up!"

"The difference," said Otto, "is he's saying he got high off of something that was a joke on *I Love Lucy*. Something that doesn't exist."

Doober, wounded, said, "My family didn't have a TV."

"Dude," I said. "I've *watched* TV at your house. I think I've watched fuckin' Lucille *Ball* at your house."

"Maybe you did," said Doober. "In your *mind*."

Before us was the glowing, throbbing turntable, from which the Chocolate World workers eased us onto our moving cars. It was like the Haunted Mansion at Disney World, or at least that's what people said. I'd never been to Disney World, but I'd been to Hershey.

We settled down in our car and sailed into the dark of Chocolate World. We heard macaws squawking in the jungle. *This*, said a narrator over the amplifiers, *is the story of cocoa. And the story of one man. Milton Snavely Hershey. A man with a dream.*

"Snavely, man," said Doober.

Sometimes it was great, being one of the guys.

We watched as the story of chocolate unfolded in front of us. Cocoa beans were harvested, then packed onto cargo ships by audio-animatronic Ugandans. This always reminded me of the time Gammie had somehow managed to take me and my friend Liam Kennedy to the Philadelphia Naval Shipyard, when I was eight years old. A somber, regal Colombian officer in epaulets showed us around his ship, which was unloading bags of cocoa beans, just like the ones in Chocolate World. That outing had ended badly, though, when Liam and I got separated from Gammie and wound up wandering through the ship, lost. Finally we found Gammie up in the captain's quarters, having a formal luncheon, with silverware and a tablecloth. The captain looked deeply satisfied. Later he took Liam and me up to the bridge, where we got to blow the ship's horn.

"Heard your sister's getting married," said Doober.

We were passing through the conching room, where scores of paddles were stirring an ocean of chocolate. It smelled especially chocolaty in here.

"Yeah."

"What's he like?" asked Otto. "The lucky fellow."

"He's a good guy," I said. "Comes from Minnesota. Wants to be a lawyer."

"Huh," said Otto. There was silence as we passed out of the conching room and left that brown ocean behind. All the guys, except for maybe Doober, had entertained crushes on Lydia at various times. "Well. I hope they're happy," Otto said wistfully.

"Me too," I said.

"I hope they're *snavely*," said Doober. "Ha ha ha."

"Sssh," said Zero. "Here it comes."

A happy song began to play from the loudspeakers. It was kind of like "It's a Small World," only larger. *It's a Hershey's Chocolate, a Hershey's Chocolate, a Hershey's Chocolate World! Wherever you go, whatever you do*. We all sang the chorus together: *Hershey's, the great American chocolate bar!*

The song rose to a climax, and then we passed through the dark veil that separates Chocolate World from our own. We wound up in a large area that sold T-shirts and candy bars. Doober bought a Krackel bar the size of his head.

"You know what's really weird about Krackel, man," said Doober as he started up his car, and we left Chocolate World behind. "You never see a full-size Krackel. They're incredibly rare. You see mini-Krackels all the time, though."

"They call that the Fun Size," I noted.

"Fun Size, sure, but where's the regular-size Krackel? It's like the government's got them all stockpiled or something."

"I don't think the government gives a fuck about Krackel," said Otto, looking out the window. "Do we have to talk about this?"

Zero was firing up the car bong. On the stereo was a bootleg of the Grateful Dead performing a composition entitled "Cryptical Envelopment."

"That's where you're wrong, man," said Doober. "Government's got the Krackels locked up tight."

"Can we listen to something else?" said Otto, with a sigh. Zero handed him the bong. "I am so fucking tired of the Grateful Dead."

Doober couldn't believe his ears. "Tired?" he said. "What does that mean, *tired*?"

We were back on the Pennsylvania Turnpike by now, heading east. Otto declined the car bong.

Zero reached into the bag of cassette tapes and put the Dean Martin back on. The car filled with the sounds of timbals and horns.

"Peanut vendor song, man," he said.

"We just *heard* this," said Otto.

"Different each time though, isn't it."

We drove through the farmland, toward Pennsylvania Dutch country. *If you're looking for a moral to this song. Fifty million little monkeys can't be wrong.*

"Hey Zero," I said. He was a philosophy major. "Did you ever read Gottfried Leibniz? *The Monadology*?"

"Sure," said Zero. "He's one of the German empiricists."

"What did you make of the monads? Do you think they're real?"

"What do you mean, make of them?"

"The way they're supposed to reflect everything? I wrote a paper on it."

"It's nutty," said Zero. "A world of mirrors." He reached down and stopped "The Peanut Vendor," then hit rewind.

"What are you doing?" said Otto. Zero hit play. The song began again from the beginning.

"Sometimes I can't wait until it's over," said Zero. "Before I start it again."

Doober stared at the road that lay ahead. "Snavely," he said.

That Sunday, three days after my birthday, my father turned fifty. My mother gave him a cocktail shaker. I gave him an inflatable rubber boat.

Then we set up the stereo by the pool and played all his favorite records. He'd never been a big fan of amplified music, but then he'd never heard the Toccata and Fugue in D Minor that loud before either.

My father floated in the pool in a rubber boat, a martini in one hand, as Bach blasted over the rhododendrons and the azaleas. His wife and his children and his future son-in-law sat on lawn chairs watching him drift around happily. Gammie and Hilda came over, along with Aunt Nora, and everybody had a drink, even Aunt Nora, who miraculously did not feel chilly sitting in the blazing sun. She'd made my father a kittyboy with a tiny felt cigarette in one paw. We had the hibachi grill going: burgers and dogs. Jimmy Carter was president. Smoke from the cookout drifted across the manicured lawn.

We raised our glasses and toasted the birthday boy. "Actually," my mother noted, "we ought to toast *you*, Gammie. You're the one who actually did all the work."

"Well, if you look at it that way," said Gammie. "We really ought to toast his father." She sipped her drink. "Did I ever tell you about the night Dick was conceived?"

"Yes!" we all shouted.

My sister sighed. "Dear God in heaven," she said.

"Atlantic City, New Jersey," said Gammie. "September 1927. The Claridge Hotel."

"Actually, Mrs. Redding," said Eamon pointedly. "You told us that story just the other day. I'm sure you don't want to repeat yourself."

Gammie thought this over for what seemed like a long time. "No," she said, at last, begrudgingly. "I suppose not."

And just like that, he had shut her down. I looked at Eamon O'Flynn, the miracle worker. My sister smiled triumphantly, as if to say, *You see? He's got superpowers you don't even know about.*

As far as I was concerned, if Eamon O'Flynn had the ability to keep Gammie from repeating the story of my father's conception over and over again, he had all the superpowers he needed. For a while, I sat there stunned, amazed at the man's hidden talents. Then I realized something else, something that perhaps accounted for his super-strength.

Eamon O'Flynn had an Irish grandmother of his own.

When the Toccata and Fugue in D Minor was over, I got out the Beethoven Symphonies. We started out with Number Five. Dad had a cheeseburger in one hand, an L&M King in the other. When he'd finished the burger, my sister made him another martini. "Thus," announced my father, listening to the first four notes of the Fifth, "fate knocks on the door."

After Five we gave him Seven; after Seven we gave him Nine. My father floated on his raft. The sun moved across the summer sky.

That night, I was awakened again by the sound of Sausage growling. I checked the clock: 1:30 A.M. I got out of bed, went to the bathroom, and looked out the window. My sister and Eamon were sitting on the stone steps of the porch, three stories below. I heard their soft voices as they talked, but I could not make out the words. I saw their faces draw together for a kiss.

I went back to my room and lay down on the bed for a while. Beneath the blue paint on the walls of this room were Dorothy Cummin's drawings. I looked at the wall, imagined that I could see the griffin and the dragon and that empty staring face.

In the corner, lying in two pieces by the radiator, were the splintered fragments of the Stella guitar, broken into pieces like the shards of Narsil. One night, in a fit of anger, I'd thrown the Stella out the window. The neck had snapped off as it hit the ground.

I looked at the dog. You think I should do it?

The dog looked discouraged. *You're going to do what you're going to do,* she said. *I don't think anybody else's opinion makes much difference to you.*

You make it sound like I'm a complete egotist. Like I think the whole world revolves around me.

The dog laughed bitterly.

What?

I think you're jealous, said the dog.

Jealous? Of who? Of her? Of him?

Of the both of them.

The dog was way out of line, as far as I was concerned.

You resent her, the dog went on. *You resent her getting to have a life.*

Shut up, I said, and went to the closet. Just shut up.

I got out a candle. Who knows? It might well have been the same one that Lydia and Tammy and Lexi had used during the séance. Then I walked across the hallway to the Brown Study. I opened the door to the haunted closet.

"Olly olly oxen free," I whispered.

Then I went to the window and threw up the sash.

It was another tropical Pennsylvania summer night: humidity hanging in the air, crickets cheeping in the primordial thicket. I swung my leg out the window and climbed out onto the roof above my mother's haunted office, and then began to ascend the treacherous slope up to the very top of the house.

I climbed onto the flat roof and sat there beneath the stars, my heart pounding. I could hear my sister and Eamon talking quietly far below me.

Then I lit the candle and sat there watching the flame. I wasn't sure how to proceed. I'd never done anything like this before.

Come, I whispered.

This is stupid, I thought. Why am I doing this?

Come, I whispered again.

I looked at the lightning rods on top of the house, two sharp spikes covered with verdigris. I imagined the lightning hitting them, the whole house shaking with the violent blue current.

Come back, from where you have been. I need you.

There was no wind whatsoever, but the candle flame flickered.

Stop them, I said.

I swallowed. *Curse them. Stretch out your hands and strike them.*

Strike them? I thought. Have you totally lost your mind? We're talking about someone you love.

Curse them. Strike them. Crush their hearts.

The candle flame grew large. Then it went out. A line of gray smoke curled toward the heavens, then vanished.

I stayed up there for a while looking at the heavens, at the delicate necklace of the Northern Crown, at the bright red planet near the Herdsman.

As I looked at it I realized the bastard was right. It *was* Mars.

Later I climbed back down the steep roof, slid down the gully of the dormer window, and stepped off the rain gutter onto the lower roof outside the Brown Study. Then I crawled back inside. The door to the haunted closet was still open.

I climbed back into bed and looked over at my old dog. The Dalmatian gave me that look: *I'm not angry. I'm just terribly, terribly disappointed.*

I thought about picking up the concertina. *Leave the Strand and Piccadilly, or you'll be the one to blame. Love has fairly drove me silly, but I'm hoping you're the same.*

Instead I turned out the light and laid my head on the pillow. I had only lain there in the dark for a few moments when I felt that old sensation. It had been a long time.

The footsteps began again in the attic. They sounded tentative at first, as if the walker had been asleep for a long time and was only now regaining her footing.

Sausage lifted her head and growled. The door to my room slowly creaked open, a little at first, then all the way.

The Onion Patch

A little old lady with peculiar glasses came up to my teller's window. "I'd like to cash this, please," she said, in a rich Texas drawl. She handed me a piece of torn notebook paper upon which she'd written the words *twenty-seven dollars*.

"Okay," I said. "But first you have to sign the back."

She turned the paper over and signed her name. *Ladybird Johnson*.

I was a teller at Continental Bank for the summer. It was right in the heart of the city, across the street from City Hall and down the stairs from a sculpture of a giant clothespin. Unfortunately the clothespin was kind of a nut magnet, a veritable lighthouse for lunatics.

"Okay, Mrs. Johnson," I said. "How would you like this?"

"Fives and sevens," she said.

I thought it over. Mrs. Muhammad, my supervisor, looked over anxiously at me. I drew a ten, two fives, and a seven on a piece of stationery, and handed it to the former First Lady. I'd drawn a picture of LBJ on the seven, which I think raised her spirits somewhat. She'd been down in the dumps since Tet.

"Thank you so much," said Ladybird Johnson.

"How is the highway beautification project coming along?" I said. "All the wildflowers?"

Ladybird Johnson looked discouraged. "Everything gets choked by weeds in the end," she said, and headed out.

"Jim," said Mrs. Muhammad. "Next time she comes to your window, I want you to get the guard."

"But she's harmless," I said. "Really."

"Get the guard," Mrs. Muhammad hissed.

My father had gotten me the job at Continental. The idea was that I was supposed to float around from branch to branch, replacing various tellers as they took their two weeks off. But they never moved me out of the clothespin branch, perhaps because there were some doubts about my tellering skills. In addition to cashing pieces of notebook paper, I spent some of my time in the teller's cage writing a long poem entitled "The Kiwi," which used as its central image the New Zealand bird that has no wings and cannot fly.

It's also a brand of shoe polish.

A sour-looking woman came to my window and signed a personal check. I checked her balance—holy cow, she was loaded!—then I counted out the money and placed it on the counter. My customer looked at the stack of bills and raised one eyebrow. "Um," she said. "I think this is four thousand dollars."

"That's right, ma'am," I said. I was afraid I'd hurt her feelings. "Is that okay?"

"No, it's just that—" She looked around the bank at the other tellers. "My check was for four hundred."

I looked at her check again. Sure enough: four hundred.

"Whoops," I said. "Darn those pesky decimal points."

The woman looked at the stack of bills. "So—do you want to count this out again?"

"Oh yes," I said. "Well de well. Absolutely." I put all the money back in my drawer, started over. "I'm an English major," I said. "Ha ha!"

She didn't laugh, just gave me a sucking-on-lemons face and said, "I used to be an English major, too." What she didn't say, but what was clearly implied, was *But then it went into remission.*

As a poet and a bank teller I sucked in similar degrees. No matter how many times I counted up the money, no matter how many quatrains I invented, I always had an imbalance. "Kiwi," for instance, was unique in that it had a whole section of couplets that ended with words that rhymed with *orange,* including *door hinge* and *porridge.* Another word I used to rhyme with *orange,* was, of course, orange itself, although when I used it to rhyme with itself it was always a *different kind of orange* I was talking about.

As a teller one of my signatures was forking over cash in unexpected denominations. My favorite forms of legal tender were the two-dollar bill and the Eisenhower silver dollar. A nice thing about working in a bank was going into the cool, silent vault, where there were towers of twos and hundreds, big rolls of Eisenhower dollars, Kennedy half dollars all in a stack. Some of the other tellers claimed they'd seen five-hundreds once in a while, a strange, grainy note with William McKinley on the front. Mrs. Heffernan, the head teller, said she'd seen a thousand-dollar bill one time, which had either Grover Cleveland or Salmon P. Chase on it, she couldn't remember which. Mrs. Heffernan was a wild-haired, oddly cheerful woman who spent a lot of time humming "What the World Needs Now Is Love" to herself. Over time, Mrs. Heffernan's good cheer was slowly worn down by my incompetence, but at the beginning of the summer, she still believed, impossibly, that my skills would improve.

On the other side of Mrs. Heffernan was Miss D'Alanzo, who was about my age. She was a firecracker from South Philly. Miss D'Alanzo, who chewed a lot of gum, was a big Firesign Theatre fan. *Her* favorite song was "How Can You Be in Two Places at Once When You're Not Anywhere at All," which she liked to sing while she was using the passbook savings machine. She also liked to randomly quote the dialogue from the Firesign's playlet, "I Think We're All Bozos on This Bus."

"Say," said Miss D'Alanzo, casting an eye my way. "You're a bozo, aren't you? I could tell by the big red nose!"

"Honk, honk," I'd reply.

"Enough with the bozo talk," said Mrs. Heffernan, counting up twenties.

"It's Firesign Theatre," said Miss D'Alanzo.

"I don't care what it is," said Mrs. Heffernan. "We are not clowns." Mrs. Muhammad shook her head sadly, as if she knew something about our situation that Mrs. Heffernan did not.

At the end of the day I balanced out my drawer. Sometimes I had a couple hundred dollars no one could explain, not even me. Mrs. Heffernan didn't really mind it so much if you were over. When your drawer was under, though, that was a problem, especially if you were under by a couple thousand dollars, as I so often was. When there was that much missing, Mrs. Heffernan made us all go through our drawers again, on the assumption that I'd handed the cash over to another teller by mistake. Most of the time the trouble was the result of bad addition or subtraction, but once in a while I'd find a missing fifty on the floor, or a band of twenties that actually contained fives. Other times, though, the cash had just vaporized, like breath on a mirror. "James, James," said Mrs. Heffernan crossly. "You're costing us *money*."

The highlight of my week was Thursday afternoon, when a man with a gnarly face and a red bow tie would come up to my window and cash a check. He wore a straw hat and a seersucker suit, like some dapper gent out of the 1930s. He treated me with a strange adoration, as if he knew full well that teller was not my true calling. Mr. Bow Tie would wait in my line, even if Miss D'Alanzo or Mrs. Muhammad was free. "That's all right," he said cheerfully. "I'll wait for my favorite teller."

I could not for the life of me figure out why I was his favorite teller. One time, Mr. Bow Tie asked that I cash a check for $48.75 for him in "fives and twenties, and the rest in silver." By silver, of course, he meant quarters, but that's not the way I heard it. I decided he wanted twenty-five dollars in silver reserve notes, six Kennedy half dollars, and three quarters. When I placed this stack before him, he looked astonished. "Why, whatever's this?" he said.

I explained what it was.

"Oh, I didn't make myself clear," he said. "I'm so sorry."

"No, it's my fault. Sometimes I don't know where my head is."

"Don't worry," he said. "You're just a little petunia in an onion patch."

Then he winked. As he walked away, he whistled happily, as if I had just given him a great gift. Mrs. Muhammad glared after him, as might anyone who had been called an onion.

By the time I balanced my drawer, prepared the float for the next day, and locked the excess in the vault, it was going on four o'clock. Then I passed through the revolving door of the bank and entered the underground train concourse, which was twenty or thirty degrees hotter and filled with the smell of hot pretzels and fire. The route to the Somerset train was through a long series of tunnels and escalators, none of which gave any access to fresh air. The moment that I stepped off the train at Somerset was usually the first moment I'd been outside since stepping onto the same train on my way in to work, nine hours earlier.

Then I'd walk back to the house, where there'd be a few hours of quiet before everyone else arrived home from their summer jobs and my sister and Eamon started opening up their presents again. During this time, I would sit in my room, put on Miles Davis or John Coltrane, and turn on the air conditioner.

Then I'd open up a secret panel, and see what lay inside.

A few days after I cursed him with my humble voodoo, Eamon O'Flynn came down with a profound set of mysterious allergies. His nose turned scarlet. His head filled with mucus. He sneezed ceaselessly and explosively. His throat ran freely with a grotesque postnasal drip. My mother took him to our GP, the hilariously named Dr. Payne, but he couldn't figure out what was wrong with him. Dr. Payne had never seen anything like it.

To his credit, Eamon O'Flynn kept right on going in to his summer job at the law firm throughout his illness, even though no one would have blamed him if he'd opted to spend the rest of July 1978 lying in bed. Some days, as Eamon and I rode into Philadelphia together on the train, it seemed that all he did was blow his nose.

"Shame about your sinuses," I said happily.

"I feel like my head's gonna explode," he said.

"Poor you," I said.

At the bank, I continued to misplace money by the hundreds. Usually this was offset by the amount of money that I mysteriously earned. Sometimes I mistakenly bound up pieces of my epic poem with the twenties.

"What's this?" said one of my customers, looking at a scrap of paper that contained the line *I carried the bear on my back toward the heavens.*

"Well de well de well," I said. "During my freshman year there was this one time a whole bunch of us rented the Outing Club cabin, up in New Hampshire? And there was this stuffed bear in the place. This one night? I carried it outside and did this whole dance with it. We were *laughin'*."

The customer took this in, then exited onto the streets of Philadelphia.

"Jim," said Mrs. Muhammad. "They don't need to hear about the poem."

"Well, she *asked*," I said.

At the end of that day, as I balanced out my drawer, I could tell I was going to be short. I was used to misplacing a couple hundred either way, but on this day it looked especially bad. As I did my calculations, Miss D'Alanzo quietly performed the Firesign Theatre to herself.

"Back in the saddle again," she sang. "Out where an Indian's your friend."

I pushed the button for TOTAL on my adding machine. How much was I short? $10,000.00.

"Something wrong, Jim?" said Mrs. Muhammad, seeing the look on my face.

"I'm short," I said, and thought, But not as short as Eamon O'Flynn!

Mrs. Muhammad looked at my total, and her eyes grew wide.

"You find that money," she said. "You find it now."

Mrs. Heffernan, the head teller, was also singing. "What the world, needs now, is love, sweet love! That's the only thing—" She stopped singing when she saw the expression on Mrs. Muhammad's face. "How much?" she said.

"Ten thousand dollars," I said.

She went pale. The branch director, Mr. Hutch, was sitting across the platform talking on the phone. We all lived in fear of Mr. Hutch.

"Well, James," she said. "You have your work cut out for you."

"I know."

"Where's the money?" she asked.

"I don't know."

"I think you had better find it," said Mrs. Heffernan. "Or maybe you're going to jail."

"No," said Miss D'Alanzo. "You wouldn't send him to jail!"

"Not if he finds the money," she said cheerfully.

"Okay," said Mrs. Muhammad. "Now retrace your steps."

It was like something out of *It's a Wonderful Life*, with me in the role of forgetful, drunken Uncle Billy, except that there was no villainous Mr. Potter. I had lost that cash, somehow, all by myself.

"I'll check your tape," said Mrs. Muhammad. "You retrace your steps." She turned to Miss D'Alanzo. "You help."

"Everything all right?" said Mr. Hutch, coming over to our teller windows.

"We're working on it," said Mrs. Heffernan. Mr. Hutch decided not to ask any more questions for the moment.

Miss D'Alanzo went into the vault with me. "Ten thousand bucks," she said, laughing. "That's a lotta clams, James."

"They wouldn't really send me to jail, would they?"

"No," said Miss D'Alanzo. "She's just trying to scare you."

"Well, it worked," I said, counting out the money in my drawer in the vault. "I'm scared."

"Even if you *do* go to jail," she said, "it wouldn't be for long."

"I'm not going to jail, okay?"

"Jeez, relax," she said. "Hey, can I ask you a question? What's this poem you're always working on?"

The money was not in the vault. "It's about a bird," I said. "That can't fly."

"Whoa," said Miss D'Alanzo. It was cool in the vault. I could have reached out and touched the side of her face. "That sounds sad."

"It starts out sad," I said. "But things work out in the end."

"Really?" said Miss D'Alanzo. She licked her lips. "So it learns how to fly?"

"I don't know," I said. "I haven't written the end yet."

We stood like that for a second, Miss D'Alanzo and I. I could almost feel her breath on my throat. It was funny how we had grown closer after I'd apparently lost—or stolen—ten thousand dollars. I wondered how far I could get with her if I lost, say, a couple million.

Mrs. Muhammad came into the vault holding a big stack of money. "Does this look familiar?" she said. It was ten thousand dollars, in hundreds, all banded up.

"Hey," I said. "There it is! Where'd you find that!"

"By the coffeemaker," she said.

"Whoa," I said. "No way!"

Miss D'Alanzo started laughing.

"By the *coffeemaker*," Mrs. Muhammad said again.

"Now I remember," I said. "I was going to put it in the vault. But I got sidetracked."

"Sidetracked?" said Mrs. Muhammad. It seemed like a lot of money to lose just because you got sidetracked.

"Is it ten thousand exactly?" I said.

"It is." She was now looking at Miss D'Alanzo as if she were somehow part of the caper.

"So I balanced my drawer," I said. I hadn't hit it exactly on the nose for a few days.

"You—" Mrs. Muhammad didn't know what to add to this, so she didn't add anything. She walked toward me and slapped the pile of money into my arms.

Miss D'Alanzo laughed. "Honk, honk," she said. "Say. You're a bozo, aren't you?"

"Yeah," I said. "I guess."

Thick, dark clouds were boiling up in the sky that night as I walked from the train station to the house. When I got home, there was a strange gloom in the place. I felt it the moment I walked through the back door. Matt the Mutt, who could usually be counted on to knock me to the floor, only lifted his head and rolled his eyes. Sausage was nowhere to be seen.

As I walked into the living room, I saw my sister rush by, tears streaming down her face. Eamon followed close behind her. "Lydia," he said. "It's all right. Really." Then he paused to blow his scarlet nose.

I heard my sister run up the stairs. "We're *doomed*," she said, and her footsteps receded. There was a slam as her bedroom door closed.

I walked into the room with the zebra-striped walls and the empty fish tank above the fireplace. My parents were sitting on the couch.

"What's up?" I said. I was still wearing a gray suit. On my lapel was a button with the Continental Bank's friendly slogan: YOU'RE ALWAYS NUMBER ONE!

My mother sighed. She started to speak, but then found she could not.

"Your sister and Eamon's wedding rings have disappeared," said my father.

"Disappeared? How?"

"They don't know."

"They put the rings in the boxes," said my mother sadly. "Then they put the boxes on the bar. That's the last they saw of them."

"But they couldn't just vanish," I said. "They have to be somewhere."

"They've looked everywhere," said my mother. "We're thinking that maybe they got thrown out with the trash."

This seemed unlikely, but not totally out of the question. A big pile of boxes and wrapping paper had to be hauled out of the family room each day to make room for the next batch of Mr. Coffees and monogrammed ice buckets.

Then they asked me something unexpected.

"You don't know anything about the rings," said my father. "Do you, Jim?"

I couldn't imagine what they thought I'd be doing with not one but two rings that did not belong to me. What did they suspect—that when I was out of their sight I was busy trying to marry myself?

Actually, the more I thought about it, the more it sounded *exactly* like something I'd do. But no one was supposed to know that.

"I don't know anything about their rings," I said, although this was not technically true. It seemed clear to me that there was a direct connection between the curse I'd laid on them and this disappearance.

My father sighed. "Your sister's pretty upset," he said. "Maybe you could help cheer her up?"

"She has Eamon for that," I said bitterly.

My father seemed surprised by the tone in my voice. He reached out and put his hand on my shoulder. "Just because she has him," he said, "doesn't mean she needs you any less. Do you understand that?"

I was going to say, *Of course I understand that, what do you think, I'm an idiot*, but my throat closed up so I couldn't talk. I nodded.

"Okay, old man," he said.

I went out to the kitchen and looked up the back stairs. I could just barely see, from where I was standing, my mother's paneled office. The dark clouds outside seemed even darker. There was the far-off rumble of thunder.

It was fortunate, I thought, as I opened up the freezer, that we had vanilla ice cream. I put a couple scoops in the blender, some Hershey's chocolate syrup. Then I hit the button that said liquefy.

Lydia's door was closed, and she didn't respond when I knocked at first. "Hey, open up," I said. "It's me."

After a moment, the door swung open. She looked as if she'd half cried out her brains. The last time I remembered seeing her look like this was when her horse was hit by the car and she'd stayed in bed for days, lost.

I held up the milk shake. "I made you this," I said.

She looked at me for a long time, then she reached out and took the shake from me. Eamon wasn't in her room. Lydia sat down on her bed. I went over to the chest of drawers and sat down on the pile of kitty-girls.

She sucked on the shake. "Thanks, Jimmy," she said. "This is good."

Doober called me on the phone a few hours later. He wanted to know if I wanted to buy some glue.

"I don't *think* so," I said.

"You seem pretty sure," he said. "For somebody who's never even tried any."

"Doober," I said. "It's *glue*. Is that what it's come to? Sniffing glue in a bag? What's next? Drinking cough syrup?"

"It's not glue," he said, irritated. "They make it special."

"Whatever," I said. "You can count me out."

There was silence on the other end of the line. "I'm outta here," he said. "Day after tomorrow. Out to San Francisco."

"Really?" I said.

"I'm sending your sister a present. Okay? I know she thinks I'm bogus and everything. But I'm leaving her something to remember me by."

"Well de well," I said. "I hope you have fun out there."

"Oh don't you worry about that."

"Doober, you ever think about going back to school?"

"Not likely."

"No?"

He thought things over. "You think everybody is so stupid."

"Stupid? What are you talking about?"

"You got it all figured out, don't you? Well, you don't. You're nothing. You're like a single baked bean on top of a marshmallow. If that."

"What are you so mad about?" I said. "Is this about the glue?"

"It's not glue," he said. "And when you call it that? You prove my point."

There was a sudden crash of lightning outside, and I jumped. Sausage, lying on the couch, jumped, too.

"Listen, I have to get off the phone," I said. "There's a storm coming."

"Don't you tell *me* about the storm that's coming," Doober said.

There was another crash of lightning. I wished Doober well and hung up on him. I wouldn't talk to him again for twenty-eight years.

Sausage looked at me fearfully. The lights in the house flickered out, and for a moment the dog and I were plunged into darkness. Then they came back on again.

I think I made a mistake, I told the dog.

I told you it was a bad idea, she replied. *I told you all along. Would you listen? Oh no.*

I didn't think it would actually work, I said.

Well, what are you going to do now? Climb up on the roof in the middle of a thunderstorm? Tell them you were only kidding?

Rain began to hammer against the window. I could see the dark outlines of the trees swaying wildly in the storm.

Maybe.

I went across the hallway into the Brown Study. The door to the haunted closet stood open. From downstairs I heard the sound of Eamon sneezing his brains out in the guest room.

There was another crack of lightning, and then all the lights in the house went out again.

Shit. The door to the Brown Study slammed shut behind me, all by itself, as if it had been thrown closed in anger.

I went to the window. Lightning flickered in the sky.

Stop it, I thought. Let's call this off.

The rain fell in sheets. There was no response.

Seriously. I don't really want them crushed.

The door behind me slowly creaked open. A moment later, the dog came into the room. *What are you doing?* Sausage inquired. *Backpedaling as fast as you can?*

I shrugged. It's just that I can't stand how easy it is for them.

You're all convinced no one will ever love you, said the dog. *Is that the long and the short of it?*

Pretty much.

What makes you so sure of what the future holds, Jenny? You've got the gift of prophecy now?

Let's say it's a good guess.

You're breaking my heart, you and your miniature violin.

You tell me, Sausage. How can you be loved, if you can never be known?

The lights came back on. The dog was standing in the doorway, brown jelly running out of her eyes. She heaved a weary sigh, then walked back to my room.

You're pathetic, said the dog.

Just let them be, I thought. They didn't do anything. If anybody ought to be cursed, it should be me.

There was an ear-shattering crack, and the house shook. My sister screamed from downstairs, and again all the lights went out. Eamon O'Flynn sneezed. As the lightning hit the house I found that I could imagine exactly what it looked like, up there on the flat part of the high roof. The two lightning rods, covered in verdigris, were consumed by blue electricity, just as I had been on my first day in this house, when I'd stood by the door and imagined, in the far-off future, the day of my wedding.

The next day at the bank, Mrs. Heffernan sat me down and we had a little talk before I opened my window. I was on probation. No more stacks of money by the coffee machine, she said. No more lyric poems bound up in the twenties.

"You just have to focus," she said. "Focus on the job at hand."

I decided to try it Mrs. Heffernan's way, and suspended my work on *Kiwi* for the duration. It wasn't that hard to do. My poem wasn't really going all that well, mostly because I'd reached the part of the ballad where the bird with its pathetic nubby wing-stumps has to figure out a way to take off.

I took a break toward the end of the day to reduce my float. This was one of Mrs. Heffernan's suggestions: if I kept the actual amount of money in my drawer low, I wouldn't hand over an extra thousand dollars to someone by accident.

While I was in the vault, I heard the voice of Mr. Bow Tie, talking to Mrs. Muhammad.

"Where's my favorite teller today? Is she sick?"

"What?" said Mrs. Muhammad. "Who?"

"My girlfriend," said Mr. Bow Tie. "That sweetie pie who sits next to you."

"If you're talking about Jim," said Mrs. Heffernan, "he's in the vault."

"He?" said Mr. Bow Tie, as I came back into view. He looked me up and down and understood something he had not understood before. His face turned crimson, and then he fled.

Later in the day, Ladybird Johnson climbed down the circular staircase that orbited around the giant clothespin, came in to the bank, and appeared at my window. On a piece of notebook paper she'd written *fifty-eight dollars*. "Ah need to get this cashed," she drawled. "Sevens and threes."

I looked at the sad old woman in her long soiled raincoat, her hair covered with a scarf tied beneath her chin. I felt bad for her, felt bad for everybody.

"Guard," I said.

The Attic

Dearly beloved. *We are gathered here in the sight of God and in the face of this company, to join together this man and this woman in holy matrimony; which is an honorable estate, instituted of God, signifying unto us the mystical union that is betwixt Christ and His church.*

My sister and Eamon O'Flynn stood before the altar. Lydia held a bouquet of flowers. To Eamon's right stood his best man, a student of animal husbandry. On Lydia's left was her maid of honor, her freshman roommate from Carleton, a Palestinian woman named Dena who, if you pressed her, wouldn't have ruled out the idea of total world revolution.

Which holy estate Christ adorned and beautified with His presence and first miracle that He wrought in Cana of Galilee, and is commended of Saint Paul to be honorable among all men.

My parents and I sat in the front row, holding hands. Tears twinkled in my father's eyes. My mother's smile was so enormous she looked like the happy sun in a child's drawing. Beyond all expectation, I had survived my responsibilities as usher. When the last guest had been seated, I'd even been disappointed, briefly, that no one else needed my guidance.

Lydia looked beautiful, and happy, and slightly scared. The Bryn

Mawr Presbyterian church was packed. Sunlight streamed through the old stained-glass windows.

And therefore is not by any to be entered into unadvisedly or lightly; but reverently, discreetly, advisedly, soberly, and in the fear of God.

Behind us sat Gammie and Hilda and Aunt Nora. Gammie was uncharacteristically reserved, her face pale and remorseful.

The evening before, she'd called Lydia on the phone and drunkenly informed her that her marriage was doomed. "He's too short," she said. "Too. Short. Go ahead, show him those pantaloons I gave you. What difference will it make? When you're little like he is, underpants are all the same."

Lydia hung up on her, hung up on her for good. Not long after that, she was in her room, with the door closed, weeping into her pillow.

This time, though, milk shakes could provide no solace.

Into this holy estate these two persons present come now to be joined.

Across the aisle were the O'Flynns, a huge and generous crowd of Minnesotans. The father, a wry, kind, brilliant attorney, liked to chomp on cigars. He'd told me some off-color jokes at the rehearsal dinner. The more I got to know them, the more I liked the O'Flynns. I especially liked their oldest daughter, Molly, who had hiked the Appalachian Trail from end to end. She'd told me about traveling the country, about swimming in the Pacific Ocean with dolphins.

Mr. O'Flynn was short, too.

If any man can show just cause why they may not lawfully be joined together, let him now speak, or else hereafter forever hold his peace.

For a moment the church was silent. There were plenty of reasons why they shouldn't get married, but we assumed no one would raise them. After all, there are always reasons why people shouldn't get married, and if we gave heed to every misgiving, no one would even bother. When, ten years later, it was my turn to get married—in the Bethlehem Chapel at the National Cathedral—this same question was posed again, and once more there was a dramatic silence in response. I stood there with Grace Finney, the woman who had changed my life, the woman whose love made me feel, at age thirty, as if I were cured, as if I could finally be a man at last, and felt the silence in that room.

What do you think? Would my spouse's life have been better, truly, if someone had raised his hand at that moment, and said, *I don't think they should go through with it! After all, the groom's a woman! What kind of a marriage is that?*

Okay, so. Maybe I'm a bad example.

I could hear people shifting in their seats, a lawn mower in the distance, children somewhere calling to one another. For a moment it appeared that this second would pass without objection, and the minister looked upon the bride and groom again with a smile. He was just about to carry on when we heard a voice.

"Whoop? Whoop?" said Hilda. For just a moment she'd forgotten where she was, and sat there whooping, as if it were 1919 again, and Hilda herself was the innocent, beautiful girl in the white dress, her entire life before her.

At the reception there was an accordion trio. The bride and groom's first dance was to "The Tennessee Waltz." When the band took a break, I played some of my sister's favorite songs on a stereo I'd set up in the front yard beneath the tent. There were the Beatles and the Stones and Jethro Tull and the Grateful Dead. I even put some Jimmy Buffett on there, to which the Minnesotans reacted with a raucous cheer.

The reception passed in a blur. My grandmother sat silently at her table, picking at her poached salmon with a fork. For once in her life she had no stories to tell. When, late in the day, the accordion trio played "Stardust," she looked up wistfully, her eyes full of tears.

There was a crazy moment when the Dead's "Cumberland Blues" came up on the mix tape, and Lydia danced, wildly, with my friend Gordo. Eamon sat to one side, quietly chewing tobacco, observing his bride's last, desperate watusi.

And then husband and wife were rushing out the front door of the house and climbing into my parents' Oldsmobile Omega, as we all threw Raisin Bran at them.

The Raisin Bran was my idea.

There was a cheer and a shout, and then the Oldsmobile was disappearing in the distance. For a moment I stood at the end of the driveway by myself, staring in the direction in which their car had gone.

Well, I thought. I've finally lost her. I'd cursed them, then uncursed them, then thrown Raisin Bran. It all led to the same place.

At the time I felt bad about this, felt like I'd never make her a milk shake again in my life. But I was young, and the world was wide, and there were many things I could not yet imagine.

I'd have the chance to lose her all over again, in the years that lay ahead.

I went back inside. On a table near the piano was a pile of presents. One of them was from me. Another Mr. Coffee.

There was also a large rectangular present from Doober, who'd left for California days before. I could tell what it was from the shape.

He'd given her his Krackel.

I climbed the long staircase and then paused at the top, turning around by the deep window on the second-floor landing. As I looked back down at the first floor, I remembered the night I'd descended these stairs and found Eamon O'Flynn alone, looking at the stars.

There was no one on the second floor. The house seemed exhausted and drained. Already people were passing out on various couches, making out with strangers.

My sister's wedding gown hung from a hook in the hallway at the bottom of the third-floor stairs.

It was a good dress. My aunt Nora had stitched the whole thing together herself, using the same basic skills she employed in the creation of kittygirls, although to a somewhat different end. My sister, apparently, was now a kittywoman.

I grabbed the dress on my way up the stairs, reached the third floor, closed the door to my room, and stepped in. It was a good fit. I spun around. The lace swirled against my ankles.

Sausage, asleep on my bed, raised her mournful head. *Oh for God's sake*, said the dog. *You're absolutely pathetic. You know that, right?*

I headed out into the bathroom where the Hunts' monkey used to live. The dress made a rustling sound as I walked. In the mirror on the back of the door I saw the reflection of a young woman with long blond hair.

It was dispiriting, being the kind of person who had to behave in such a manner. But then again, Lydia was done with the dress. Was it so wrong that it get a second wearing, from a girl who would surely never have a wedding of her own? I looked good, as I stared at myself in the mirror; stranger than that, I looked *normal*. It was hard to believe it was me.

After a few moments, though, the feeling of sadness trumped the sensation of wonder. After all, it wasn't my sister's dress, or for that matter, her life that I wanted. It was my own.

I rustled back into my bedroom and took a slug off of a bottle of Jack Daniel's that stood upon the dresser. I remembered the look of wild abandon in my sister's eyes as she had danced, one last time, to the Grateful Dead. I thought about Gammie, sitting there by herself as the band played "Stardust."

Then I sat down in my red swivel chair and picked up the concertina. It had all come to this in the end.

Good-bye Piccadilly, farewell Leicester Square!

At that moment, from over my head, I heard the sound of footsteps.

I looked up at the ceiling, took another slug of Jack Daniel's. I walked back out into the hallway, still wearing the wedding gown, and stood beneath the trapdoor in the middle of the hallway that led up to the attic. A string attached to the trapdoor dangled down.

All right, you bastards, I thought. Let's talk.

I pulled on the string, and the trapdoor yawned open. I pulled down a wooden ladder attached to the door. Its legs straddled the hooked rug on the floor. Above me now was a vast black space. The sound of footsteps stopped.

I got a flashlight from my room, then slowly climbed the ladder that led up into the darkness.

The old rafters in the attic slanted in every direction, and sharp nail points from the roof jutted out at me from every angle. I shone my flashlight around. The floor was covered with an ancient granular insulation, like Styrofoam peanuts. There were a few old pieces of furniture up there as well—an old-fashioned wardrobe of the Hunts', as well as my grandfather's pipe rack, with the pipes still in it.

In another corner was a trunk that had belonged to my mysterious uncle Sean, the shaman of the family. He'd spent his whole life traveling around on freight trains, moving between the twin poles of Stone Harbor, New Jersey, and Treasure Island, California, a tiny speck of land beneath the Oakland Bay Bridge. We'd wound up with his trunk after he died on board a train just outside of Salt Lake City. It contained his books—the poetry of Emily Dickinson; the philosophy of Carl Jung and Carlos Castaneda—as well as the unfinished manuscript of his life's work, a poem called *Goldenrod*.

I'd read the first page of Uncle Sean's book, before Ziggy put the trunk up in the attic. It started like this:

> *This is the beginning! The all-soul time is coming! Now shall be the all New, all Soul, all One. The darkness has dwelled in our hearts and blocked the sun. Now comes the bright star, the light of knowledge and love. No more shall all be two. Now comes all one, all soul, all heart!*

Once, when Uncle Sean visited us, he'd promised me that he was going to tell me the secret of the universe when I turned eighteen.

"But why can't you tell me now?" I'd asked. I was only ten at the time.

"Because," Uncle Sean had said, "it's too horrible."

The wall of the attic behind Uncle Sean's trunk was made of a slightly different kind of wood than the rest of the house. My flashlight played off the timbers. I could now see that this was where the tower once had been, the spire from which, according to neighborhood legend, a child had fallen to her death. I inhaled sharply, seeing it all at once in my mind's eye, the girl standing here, a bird landing on the edge of the balcony.

The child took one step, and then another.

From below me, I heard the sudden sound of footsteps on the third-floor stairs. I moved quickly toward the trapdoor, but I realized that I wasn't going to be able to get down the ladder in time. As I looked through the hole in the floor, I saw that the person now arriving on the third-floor landing was my father, still wearing his morning coat and cravat from the wedding.

I was in a tight spot. I tried to reach around my back, so I could undo the buttons of the wedding dress, but there were a lot of them. Anyway, even if I did get the dress off, I'd be naked, up in the attic, and that wasn't a good option either. My father would be perplexed. *What happened to your clothes, son?* he'd ask.

Oh, I'd reply. *Nothing*.

I clicked off the flashlight.

"Hello?" said my father's voice. He was standing at the bottom of the ladder now. "Jim? Are you up there?"

I remained frozen in place, and silent. My father stood motionlessly, looking up toward the attic. Surely he must have thought that it was odd that the trapdoor would be open. What possible reason would anyone have for going up there, and on the day of his daughter's wedding, no less?

"Hello?"

We stood still, in stalemate, my father and I.

A moment later, I heard him knock on my bedroom door. "Jim?" he said. It creaked open. I pictured him looking around my room, with its Allman Brothers posters and Indian tapestries on the wall. On the floor were my cuff links, my coat with its boutonniere, my fancy pants.

"Jim?"

He walked out into the hallway again. I backed toward the corner of the attic and hid behind the trunk that contained my uncle Sean's life story. My father walked across the hallway and into the Brown Study. His footsteps creaked over to the corner of the room, and he paused for a moment as he looked into the dark recesses of the haunted closet. Then he came out and walked across the hall to the Gammie Room.

I wasn't in there, either.

The door of the Monkey Bathroom swung open. There were towels on the floor, water dripping slowly from the bathtub faucet.

He looked into the Haunted Room, with its single lightbulb suspended from the ceiling, the boxes of horse-show ribbons and Christmas decorations on the floor.

I moved slightly, and the floor beneath me creaked. I heard my father walk back into the hall, toward the bottom of the attic ladder. I knew what he was doing, because it was what I'd so often done myself—looking up at the ceiling, wondering what those footsteps were, up in the attic. Except that this time the haunted, hidden thing was me.

Slowly my father began to ascend the wooden rungs that led to the place where I lay.

I huddled behind Uncle Sean's trunk, hoping that it would be enough to keep me hidden. I gathered the hem of my dress into a tight ball so that I would not be unveiled by the train.

Dick Boylan's head peeked through the floor. He didn't have a flashlight, so it was hard for him to see. All around him were the shadows of the junk in the attic, the Hunts' wardrobe and the old pipe rack and the trunk that contained the sheaf of papers upon which were written the words *Now is the time of joy, of all men in each man, entering heaven on earth time space. We are all heart because we all are one! No time shall be the time of no love! All shall be all heart, all time, all one soul!*

"Is anybody there?"

He paused. Was it possible that he sensed some spirit up here, some phantom that lurked where he could not see? Did he know, as he stood there atop his ladder, that his son was gathered in a baroque clump behind an army trunk in the corner? Did he see, edging from behind it, the telltale train of the dress my aunt Nora had sewn by hand?

He crept up the ladder a little farther. I made myself as small as I could. I could hear him breathing as he drew nearer, and nearer. Light from downstairs filtered through the open trapdoor.

My father took one step toward the place where I was hiding. Then another.

He stopped a few feet away from Uncle Sean's trunk. Then he made a soft moaning sound.

There was a long, agonizing silence. Then, with one hand, he reached toward his father's pipe rack and picked up one of the pipes.

I heard him sniffing the pipe, and then he moaned again softly, as if the ghost of that smell had transported him back to the days of his own youth, to the time when he was a child playing piano for *his* father. The old bastard sat there in his white linen suits and smoked his Norwegian Wood, while my father sat at the Cable-Nelson and plowed his way through the *Pathétique*, murdering—as my father put it—a thing of beauty.

He put his father's pipe in his mouth and sucked on it. Then he took the pipe out of his mouth and looked at it for a long time.

Minutes passed. Dick Boylan stood there in the attic, holding his father's pipe, not speaking. It was the night of the day on which his daughter had been married, the day she had left him at last. My father stood there for a long time, lost in thought.

Then, finally, he put the pipe back in the rack. I heard him sigh. A moment later, Dick Boylan backed down the rickety ladder. The last thing he did was to fold up the ladder and close the trapdoor.

I was now plunged into darkness, trapped for good up in the attic of the Coffin House. There was no way to lower the ladder from up here, not unless I called out for help, either wearing a wedding dress, or nude.

I sat there in the corner, next to the place where the tower once was, and listened to the sound of my father's footsteps receding. It was very quiet in the place where I was now presumably entombed forever. I wondered if King Tut had felt like this, three thousand years earlier, when they plastered him in his sarcophagus.

Something drifted over my face, like gauze, or the webs of spiders, and I shuddered.

But it was only the veil.

From the far end of the attic a board creaked, and then another. "Hello?" I said, softly. "Hello?"

I peered into the darkness. I saw nothing. That attic was as dark as the ink of squids in the Great Salt Lake.

Slowly I crept toward the place where the trapdoor was. I reached forward with my blind hands and felt my fingers close around something.

It was one of my grandfather's pipes. I raised it to my face and smelled the faint scent of tobacco. For the first time, I imagined this other James Boylan as a living man—not as the frowning bastard in the painting downstairs, but as a person of flesh and blood.

I took another step forward, and then another.

All at once the floor gave way beneath me. That trapdoor was on a spring, and I'd managed, in the dark, to step blindly onto it. The door swung down. I bumped over the chute of the unopened ladder on its underside. Briefly, I flew through the air, a streak of white, an inverted angel in a downward flight, like a character out of *Paradise Lost*. Then I landed in the middle of the third-floor hallway with a tremendous crash. A moment later, Grampa's pipe fell from the ceiling as well and knocked me on the head. The trapdoor, recoiling on its springs, snapped shut.

I heard a voice from downstairs. "Jim?" said my mother. "Is that you?"

I sat there for a moment stunned and amazed by my flight through space. In no time at all I had traveled from a dark, sealed tomb and back to this world of light. The dress was covered with insulation and dust. There were cobwebs on the veil.

I called downstairs. "I'm okay, Ma!" I said. "I'm okay!"

PART III

Baltimore, 2005

Now, now, he said. That's enough of that.

All at One Point

· *Spring 2006* ·

"Is there anybody there?"

Yes.

"Can you point to where you're at?"

Wendy and I stood in my mother's bedroom, watching the tips of the divining rods tremble. A neighbor's dog howled. Water dripped from the faucet in the bathroom.

The divining rods swung toward the bay window, where filtered sunlight streamed through the curtains.

"He's very intense," said Wendy. "Do you feel him?"

I felt him.

"Were you a boy?"

Yes.

"It's my dad," I said.

"Are you Jenny's dad?"

Yes.

I felt my throat close up and tears rush to my eyes. And as I felt these things I thought, Jenny. Remember. This is all total bullshit.

"He's very warm," said Wendy.

"Hi, Dad," I said.

"Do you want to hold the rods?" said Wendy.

"I don't know how to use them."

"Here," she said, placing the copper rods in my hands. "Just hold them steady."

I can't believe I'm doing this, I thought. This is such crap.

This was not idle conjecture. A few weeks earlier I had interviewed a well-known paranormal debunker, Mr. James Randi of the Randi Educational Foundation, a.k.a. the Amazing Randi. "Of course dowsing rods move," he'd said wearily. "They move because of the way they're built. It's called the ideomotor reaction. It's physically impossible to keep them steady."

Randi's theory was that people who believe in ghosts are more often than not the victims of charlatans taking advantage of the vulnerable and the deranged.

Why is it, I wondered, that people need to believe in a world other than the one in which they live? Some of the people in Wendy's paranormal investigation group seemed to need to believe in ghosts in the same way that New Englanders needed to believe in the Red Sox.

"What do I do now?" I said to Wendy. The sticks pointed into the room.

"Talk to him."

I felt strangely self-conscious. I didn't know what to say to my father, assuming that it was his spirit that now was hovering before me, which it wasn't. There were so many things I wanted to tell him.

But I didn't know where to begin.

There's a certain phase in a young person's life in which it seems like all you do is leave home, for the last time, over and over again. You write your suicide note, you drink your last glass of Guinness, you kiss those you love and hope they'll forgive you for the inexplicable journey that you've chosen. Then you head out into the dark world.

A few months later, surprise: you're back, ready to have your heart broken all over again. As my friend Cedric—an English teacher at Colby—would observe many years later: *All good-bye, ain't gone.*

On Veterans' Day 1980, a big U-Haul was parked in front of the Coffin House. Reagan had been elected the week before, just a few days after the Phils improbably won the World Series. I was off to New York, to begin the adventure of my adult life. Such as it was.

Somewhere in the depths of the overloaded U-Haul was a copy of *The Last Battle*.

I went back inside to find my mother in tears. "Mom," I said. "Don't be sad. I'm going to come back and visit. All the time."

"I know," she said.

I climbed into the cab of the truck and drove off, down Somerset Road, toward the Pennsylvania Turnpike. I heard the sound of all my possessions rattling around in the back of the truck. Sitting alone behind the wheel, I hollered at the top of my lungs, as if I were surfing on a big wave of molten lava.

I was moving into a marginal apartment on 108th Street and Amsterdam, one floor above an S&M dungeon and right next door to a health food store that sold no health food. If you walked into the store, you found yourself in a dark space with walls painted black, and a wire fence with a hole in it at one end of the room. You slid five dollars into the hole, and a moment later, a tattooed hand grabbed the money. After the hand with the money disappeared—like the action on some sort of antique bank—a small manila envelope containing marijuana slid out. The envelopes were stamped with the single word: HEARTBEAT.

I lived with a young filmmaker named Charlie Kaufman, who was working at the time as a production assistant on a Woody Allen film that turned out to be *Zelig*. Charlie wasn't allowed to talk about the movie, though. Woody made everyone take a vow of silence, like Ezra Pound after he got out of the nuthouse. For my own part I was working at *American Bystander* magazine, the "American *Punch*" spearheaded by the first cast of *Saturday Night Live,* and edited by former *Lampoon* editor Brian McConnachie. The fact that the magazine seemed destined never to come out did not discourage me. "We are in a dark tunnel," I said to the comedian Harry Shearer one day, when he stopped by to check us out. "But we're going over the top."

When I wasn't Bystanding, I worked on my first novel, *Ammonia Quintet*. The plot concerned a wizard held hostage by a pack of wild waffle irons. The only possible antidote for this, the wizard learns, is to fill their mouths with batter, which he has to leave in the griddles for a precise amount of time in order for the counterspell to succeed. How much time?

Until the steaming stops.

In time I was joined in New York by my sister, after her divorce from Eamon. She entered the graduate program at NYU, studying medieval poetry, and lived in an apartment on Jane Street in the West Village. I'd meet her once a week or so, under the big street clock on the corner of Forty-third Street and Fifth Avenue. We'd walk around the city looking in shop windows, head up to Rumplemeyer's for hot cocoa.

Sometimes we ordered the Coupe aux Marrons—candied chestnuts in syrup over vanilla ice cream, covered up with whipped cream—and two spoons.

She was fragile in the months following her divorce, laid low by shame. Lydia was convinced she'd let everyone down by leaving Eamon, that she'd broken a promise she had sworn to keep. It was a strange time for us, the only time in our long history when I seemed like the older sibling. She was so thin and sad in those first few months that I was afraid anything might carry her off, that she could blow out like the flame of a candle. I tried to take her under my wing, even though, by almost any measure, my wings weren't much bigger than hers.

One night in 1982, I went down to the West Village to join Lydia for dinner. As I walked down the hallway to her apartment, I encountered one of her neighbors, an elderly woman with a nose like a mynah bird. "Too late," she said, nodding. "Too late, too late, too late."

My sister's door was ajar, and I entered her apartment to find her sitting in a chair, looking through her open window, with tears streaming down her face. She'd just put in window boxes the week before, and filled them with violets. But my sister wasn't looking at her flowers.

In her hands she held a small glass horse. "Liddie," I said. "It's me. It's your brother."

She gazed sorrowfully at me. "Oh Jimmy," she said, and more tears leaked out of her. "Oh Jimmy."

"Are you okay?" I said, even though it was clear she wasn't.

From the other side of her wall, I heard Lydia's neighbor talking to herself. *Too late,* she said.

"I wrecked everything," said Lydia.

"Who says? You didn't wreck anything."

"I did," she said. "I disappointed everybody."

I sat down next to her. "You could never disappoint me," I said. "You know why?"

She shrugged. Her eyes fell again to the small glass horse in her hands.

"Because you have *pizzazz,*" I said, in my Gammie voice.

One corner of her mouth rose in a half smile.

"You know where pizzazz comes from?" I asked her.

She whispered something so soft I could barely hear it. "*Yr bsm,*" she said.

"What was that?" I said. "I couldn't quite hear that."

"Your bosom," she said. The other half of her mouth rose.

"You know what might make you feel better?" I said.

"What?"

"If you ate some dirt. You know that's the problem with kids today. They don't eat enough dirt."

My sister looked at me, the tears still rolling out of her eyes. She took a deep breath. "Whoop," she said faintly. "Whoop? Whoop?"

I brushed the tears off her cheeks. She made some more.

"I hurt, little brother," she said. "I hurt."

I put my arms around her and hugged her. "It's okay, Liddie," I said. "You won't always hurt."

"I hurt now," she said.

I held her in my arms. "I know it," I said.

I didn't get back to Pennsylvania much during those years, mostly because I didn't have the money for the train or, for that matter, anything else. When I did come back, I was surprised that life in the Coffin House had continued on without me. My parents built a greenhouse on the south side of their house, filled it up with orchids. My father spent hours in there, quietly tending his cattleyas and dendrobiums.

One Thanksgiving Liddie and I stayed up all night with my friend Curly, watching the guys inflate the balloons for the Macy's parade. On the street outside the American Museum of Natural History, we saw a half-inflated Superman restrained by giant nets, like Gulliver. We waited until the parade began, then found a coffee shop and ate a couple stacks of pancakes.

Curly took us down to Penn Station later that morning, and my sister and I rode the Amtrak train back to Philly, changed over to the Paoli local, and stepped off at Somerset station just before noon. Then we walked the streets toward home.

Liddie and I came in the front door to find my parents and Gammie and Hilda and Aunt Nora sitting around the fireplace beneath the watchful gaze of Grampa in his oil painting. Sausage, now a hundred and eleven years old, looked up feebly at me. *You resemble someone who used to live here, I think. I can't remember.*

My mother rushed toward us each in turn. My father twinkled from his wing chair, a cigarette in one hand. The house smelled like turkey and stuffing.

Aunt Nora, draped beneath a blanket, shuddered sweetly at us. "I'm so cold," she noted happily.

Gammie raised her empty glass at us and rattled her ice cubes.

"Vodka," she said.

One evening I was in my seedy apartment with Charlie Kaufman, who'd had a bad day. Earlier, he'd called up Jerry Stiller and Anne Meara, to whom he'd been told he might be able to sell some jokes. To Charlie's surprise, it was Anne Meara herself who answered the phone when he called. She immediately demanded that Charlie start reeling out his wares if he was supposed to be so damned funny, telling one gag after the other. Anne Meara wasn't impressed with Charlie, and it's fair to say that he wasn't impressed with her, either. The two of us sat around drinking beer after that, and watching *The Prisoner of Zenda* on my aunt Nora's black-and-white 1966 Zenith television set.

During a commercial Charlie and I got in a heated discussion about which popular song we wished we'd written. Charlie chose "Dancing Cheek to Cheek." I was trying to make the case for "Chim Chim Cheree."

Years later, when Charlie made *Being John Malkovich*, a minor part of the plot involves the Cameron Diaz character realizing she wants to be a man. It's all very funny, the whole transsexual business. Even I think it's funny, sometimes. Kind of depends on the situation though.

Malkovich, Malkovich, Malkovich, Malkovich.

I went to bed that night on my mattress on the floor. The windows, which had bars on them but no screens, were wide open to the New York summer night, and flies buzzed around my head. In the alley behind our building, German shepherds barked. People yelled at the dogs and threw glass bottles at them out of upper-story windows. The bottles smashed into a thousand pieces as they hit the cement. There was salsa music and car alarms.

From the S&M dungeon downstairs, a young man sobbed, *Stop, please stop. I'm dying, please stop.*

A year or two later, I woke up in the Coffin House. It was the middle of the night, and I heard, inexplicably, the strains of Beethoven's Ninth. I was lying on a fold-out couch in the Brown Study, in the room with the haunted closet. The door to the closet was wide open. It had been closed when I went to sleep.

The room flickered with a red strobe, pulsing like a heartbeat. From somewhere in the house came a strange crackling sound, an alien voice that seemed to be coming to us from a great distance. *Are you there?* it asked. *Are you there?*

I sat up in bed. The room pulsed red again. I heard voices from downstairs. I swung my feet onto the floor and pulled on a pair of jeans, then went out into the hallway. Paramedics were standing in the second-floor hallway. The red strobe I'd seen was the beacon of the ambulance. A guy with a white lab coat spoke into a walkie-talkie.

I had thought, when my sister left for her honeymoon in a car filled with Raisin Bran, that we had come to the end of my family's first life, and that the four of us would never again live beneath the Coffin House's crazy slanting ceilings together.

But I'd been wrong about this. It wasn't so surprising. I'd been wrong about a lot of things. Here we all were, the four of us, living in the Coffin House together one last time, as my father fought his final round with melanoma.

The voice crackled over the walkie-talkie again. "Are you there? Are you there?"

The paramedic raised the transmitter to his face. "I'm right here," he said. "Over."

I went down the stairs and into my parents' room. Guys in doctor's coats were running all over the place, plugging in machines with ornate oscilloscope displays. My sister and my mother stood at the foot of my father's bed, tears streaming down their faces. My father lay flat in the bed, bald and frail and supernatural. For all the world he looked like the astronaut at the end of *2001: A Space Odyssey*, lying on his back, pointing up at the universe of stars in the heart of the unknowable monolith.

It was three o'clock in the morning. I had not hallucinated Beethoven's Ninth, either. It was playing on WFLN, the classical music station, on my father's radio. We were in the heart of the third movement, the uncanny *"Adagio molto e cantabile."*

"How old is he?" asked a man with a clipboard.

"Fifty-seven," said my mother.

"Eighty-seven," said the man with the clipboard, writing it down.

"*Fifty*-seven," said my sister, annoyed, as if the paramedic had never seen a cancer patient before.

"Fifty-seven?" said the clipboard guy, and gave us a look like, You're sure?

"What's going on?" I said. I couldn't believe that all of this had been happening while I was asleep. Didn't they know how helpful I could be in situations like this one?

Actually, the more I thought about it, the more I understood why they'd let me sleep. I wasn't known for my social skills. At twenty-seven years old, I was a strange, feminine, praying mantis–like creature. About the only thing I was good at was comedy, and comedy was just about the only thing that the current situation did not require.

A large woman named Jolette, the home-care nurse, turned to me and said, "Your daddy's had himself an event."

My father lay motionless beneath the white sheets. His heartbeat, broadcast into the room by the monitor, fluctuated wildly.

"What happened?"

"About an hour ago," said Jolette, "he started thrashing around, yelling out for help. We called nine-one-one, got these guys in here." It was clear she didn't think much of the EMTs. "He's been quiet for a while now."

"I think he's stable," said one of the EMTs. "You should have a discussion with his primary care physician in the morning; see what sort of options you have."

"But what's happening to him?" I asked, as if it were some mystery.

"If he has tumors in the brain, he's going to have episodes like this," said the man. "As those tumors grow, more and more of his functions will shut down. These seizures are like the body fighting back, trying to keep from shutting down."

"He should keep fighting," said my mother. "He said he wanted to fight as long as he could!"

"We done here?" said the guy with the clipboard. It was clear he was, anyhow. He started unplugging some of the machines.

"We're done," said the other guy. "Keep him on oxygen." He looked at my mother and sister. "You all hang in there."

We nodded. We'd hang in there, together, for whatever time remained.

A little after four in the morning, I climbed the creaking steps back up to the third floor. I was sleeping, for the first time in my life, in the Brown Study, because the bed in my own room had mysteriously collapsed on my first night home, and I'd woken up in the middle of the night to find myself lying at a strange angle on a mattress surrounded by splintered wood.

I lay down on my fold-out couch in the Brown Study and stared up at the ceiling. There was no red strobe in the room this time, and the radio static was gone. I could still hear, through the floor, the erratic beep of my father's heart, as he continued to make his way between the worlds of the living and the dead.

I opened my eyes sometime before dawn with the distinct sense that something was in the room with me. Dim gray light shone through the window to my left, the one that led out onto the roof. My father's heartbeat continued to be audible through the floor. It was slower now.

The entity emerged from the closet in the corner, a blacker shadow within the darkness of the room. There was something shiny and dense about it, like oil. I had the sense that if I touched it, my hand would emerge from its mass shiny and wet. It was vaguely human-shaped, and fine white streaks, like kite string, moved through it.

In all the years that I had lived in this house I had never been in the presence of whatever this was. It had two armlike appendages and a head, although the face was not visible, being enclosed in a kind of hooded shadow. It had no legs.

It moved in what I later thought of as *clicks*, which is to say that rather than floating, or walking, it disappeared and then reappeared a foot or two closer to the bed. It did this again and again, clicking toward me until it stood at the foot of the fold-out couch. It raised one of its arms toward me. There was something like a baton or a wand in its hand. The white lines in its heart pulsed.

For a long while it stood at the foot of the bed. I sat there in a kind of trance, unwilling to scream. I did not understand what this thing was or what it wanted, and as it looked at me, I got the sense that it had formed something of the same opinion about me. Its hoodlike head tilted to one side, as if it was thinking, *Who the hell are you?*

I don't know how long we lingered in that stalemate, the thing and I. It may have been twenty seconds. But after a while it clicked to a different place in the room—a position a few feet closer to the window. Then I watched as it clicked to the far side of the room, where the sun was now coming up through the curtains. It stood there for a while and did not look back at me. Then it vanished completely.

I lay in the fold-out couch for a long time as the room grew lighter. From outside came the sound of birds. A car came down the street and paused before our house. A man threw a copy of the morning newspaper onto the drive, and it landed there with a soft flap, as if this were a day like any other.

In the afternoon I went into my father's room. He was lying in his bed, propped up on pillows, smoking a cigarette. WFLN was still playing on the radio.

"Hey," I said.

"Good morning," he replied. His eyes twinkled. "Is it morning?"

"It's just after lunchtime," I said.

"Ah, well," he said. "I'm doing a lot of traveling, so I don't know."

"Traveling?" I said.

He didn't elaborate. They'd turned off the heart monitor, but the room still had a lot of equipment in it. A urine bag connected to his catheter hung off the end of the bed. The oxygen hoses wrapped around his face.

"Last night was pretty dramatic," I said.

"Oh, did you like that?" he said. "I thought it might be fun to give everyone a turn."

"You gave us a turn, all right."

He didn't say anything for a while, just looked at me with his bright, sad eyes. "Sometimes," he said at last, "I feel like I need to go. But I don't know how. They tell me—I'm not supposed to think about that."

"I don't think you should worry about anything right now," I said. "I don't think you're going anywhere." It was amazing to me that I could say such a thing to him. Clearly the events of the night before suggested that he was going somewhere, and he was going there sooner rather than later. And yet, here I was, putting on what I imagined to be my game face, talking as if he were going to get over metastasizing brain tumors by looking on the bright side.

"I don't mean—that," he said, exhausted by my incomprehension. "I mean go—to the bathroom."

"Ah," I said. Now I understood. He meant the catheter. He'd forgotten he had one. "Yeah, that's supposed to take care of itself." I pulled back the sheet and showed him the hose. "See how this connects to you? All that pee just runs out of you and into this bag."

"Oh," he said, fascinated by *how it connected to him*. "I've become an experiment, in science."

He was more tranquil now that he had figured out the business of going. He looked at me. "After I'm gone—" he said, and paused.

"You're going to be here for a long time," I said, again, like an imbecile. "You're going to get better."

"Well, that might be. I don't really know—what is happening to me."

"You had a seizure last night. There were paramedics here. Do you remember?"

He thought it over. "They were playing Beethoven," he said slowly. "Maybe I dreamed that."

"No, that's right," I said. "When I came down the third movement was on."

He took a long drag from his cigarette. "The *adagio*." He sighed. "I wasn't here for that. I had to travel. Then—I came back."

"I'm glad you came back."

"When I'm gone—" he said again.

"Dad—"

"What will you do—" he said. "To the house?"

This was not the question I was expecting. "To the house?"

"When your mother and I are gone. What—will you build?"

He looked at me with his piercing eyes. It was a good question.

"I don't know," I said. "Maybe—I was thinking, maybe I could put the tower back on."

My father's eyes widened. "Yes!" he said. "The tower! Rebuild the tower!" He squeezed my hand, hard. Then he let it go, exhausted. "The tower," he said again.

"And sometimes I think about repainting the living room. Black, like it used to be."

He smiled. "That black. Well, you can paint it then. If your mother is gone." He took one last drag off his cigarette, then tapped it out in the ashtray. "But then. Your mother will live forever."

Jolette knocked on the door with a tray of lunch things: some soup, a carton of Ensure, some wiggly lime Jell-O.

"I want some spiced wafers," he said, looking at her.

"Some what?"

"They're his favorite cookies," I said. "Spiced wafers."

"Yes, well, Mr. Boylan," said Jolette, putting the tray down. "The world is full of things people want. Most of 'em, they can't have."

I took a long walk with my sister that afternoon. A church bell was ringing from the steeple of the Somerset church down the street, pealing somberly over and over again.

In the haze of the strange days we were living in now, we had completely forgotten it was Good Friday. We saw people in dark clothes walking from their cars toward the tiny church.

"Are you okay?" she said.

"Not really. You?"

Lydia shrugged. She was back at NYU now, beginning her dissertation. My sister was studying a medieval poet who'd written a mysterious work called *The Pearl*, about a man who unexpectedly loses his jewel and finds himself transformed by sorrow.

We walked past the church, down the long, quiet streets of our hometown. Behind iron gates were the manicured lawns of the rich. A woman with dark glasses walked a cocker spaniel with a leather leash.

"You guys should have woken me up last night," I said. "When he first had his seizure. I should have been there."

"I know," said Lydia. We paused at a small bridge that ran over a stream. The brook below us ran toward a house occupied by the family of my friend Beansie. They had ghosts, too. Beansie and his mother used to complain about them all the time. There was a particular problem with Beansie's grandfather, who used to pass through the living room while everyone was trying to watch television.

A few years later, Beansie's family moved out of the place and baseball player Lenny Dykstra moved in. Lenny chewed a lot of tobacco, just like Eamon O'Flynn.

"I think we were afraid he was going to die that second," said Lydia. "And that kind of paralyzed us."

"And yet today, he's sitting up and talking," I said. "Every time I think he's on his deathbed, he rallies."

"He's a fighter, isn't he?" she said.

"So are you."

She stared out at the stream, full of the rushing waters of spring. She didn't say anything, but she put one arm behind my back and I put my arm on hers. We watched the stream. There was a gnarled tree standing on the banks, its roots stretching toward the creek.

I thought about the thing I had seen in my room the night before, too, the dark hooded face, the arms that reached out toward me, asking the question for which I had no answer. *Who are you? What are you doing here?*

Then we turned from the stream and started walking, for the last time, back to the house where our family lived.

"Jimmy," said Jolette, coming into the study. "Can you come in? It's your daddy."

It was late at night, and my sister and mother were asleep. I was reading *Cosmicomics*, by Italo Calvino, a story called "All at One Point," a nostalgic narrative written from the point of view of the beings who had all been together at the beginning of the universe, back when everything was connected, and all men and women were part of a single entity.

"What's wrong? Is he failing?"

"No, but you come in here and look. He's talking funny."

I walked across the hallway to see my father sitting up in bed, pale as milk. "Jim," he said to me, his eyes fearful. "Jim."

"What is it?" I said. "What's wrong?"

WFLN was playing Mozart. "Did you see him?"

"Who?"

"The conductor."

"What conductor?"

"I'm wakin' your mama," said Jolette.

"I was lying here, you see," my father said. "And then he came in. He was all in black. With the white bow tie. He had his baton." He looked at me beseechingly. "Did you see him?"

"I think I know who you're talking about," I said. I thought about the entity that had stared me down that morning. It had come into the wrong room.

"He scared me," said my father, and I couldn't think of his ever having been scared by anything before, except maybe that time I got shot full of the blue electricity, on the first day we'd stepped into this house, and I'd fallen to the floor, and he'd held me in his arms.

"He said he wanted me to go away with him."

"And do what?"

"And conduct his orchestra."

I sat by my father's side, as Mozart played on the clock radio. It was eleven-thirty at night.

"But I didn't want to go with him," my father whispered. "Because *I did not know the music.*"

Dad didn't say anything more for a while. He just lay there, listening.

"What *is* all this music?" he said finally. His voice was barely audible. "What is it?"

"It's Mozart, isn't it?" I said. "*The Magic Flute*?"

He looked over at me with the same look he used to give me when I screwed up something on the piano.

"Not *that* music," he said.

Two days later, when he died, Beethoven's Ninth was on the radio again. The last movement.

Joy, beautiful spark of the gods,
Daughter of Elysium. Inspired by fire, we enter thy sanctuary.

I wasn't there when it happened. My mother was sitting next to him, holding his hand. Afterward she came down into the kitchen, where Lydia and I were drinking coffee. We had the radio on downstairs, too. "Your father just died," she said.

We all embraced, a threesome now. Then we went back up into his room and opened all the windows. He was lying on his back, his mouth slightly open, as if in surprise. Bells were ringing from all the steeples in the town. It was Easter Sunday.

"Were you close to your father?" Wendy asked me, twenty years later, as I stood in what had once been his room, holding her ridiculous copper divining rods.

I didn't know what to tell her. I thought about the way he used to get me to play songs backward on the piano, the way he'd stop us in the middle of dinner and order us all to argue the reverse of whatever we had been advocating thus far.

"Yeah," I said. "We were close."

"Well, just talk to him like you used to talk to him," said Wendy.

"Dad?" I said. "It's me." *Guess you heard about the sex change?*

Yes. The rods moved all by themselves, as I held my hands perfectly steady.

The ideomotor reaction, probably.

"Are you okay?"

Yes.

It struck me that there had to be a better question to ask someone who had returned from beyond the grave than this. But I couldn't think of anything. It was hard to turn an inquiry into the nature of the immortal soul into a yes or no question.

"Do you remember when you saw that conductor?" I said.

Yes.

"Did you ever meet him? And conduct his orchestra?"

Yes.

I looked at my hands. I was trying, desperately, to keep them steady.

"So now—you know the music?"

Yes.

Tears spilled over my eyes and down my face. Each of the rods in my hands swung outward, one to the right, one to the left. They swiveled all the way around until they were flat against my sides. They stayed like that for a while. Then they swung back straight ahead.

"I thought he might do that," said Wendy. "We call that the invisible embrace. When they move the rods around you. I see that all the time."

"Okay," I said, and thought, This is the corniest thing I have ever done in my life. And remember, this is coming from a woman who once attended the National Ventriloquists' Convention in Kentucky, mistakenly hoping that she might write the story for *The New Yorker*.

"Well, okay, Dad. Take care of yourself."

The rods quivered back and forth.

"You were a good father," I said. "Are a good father."

No.

"You are. I wish you could see the boys, Dad. Luke and Paddy. I see you in them, sometimes."

Yes.

"Dad," I said. My tears rolled down. "I just wanted to say—I'm sorry. If I wound up—a disappointment—"

And then, incredibly, I felt his hand on the side of my face.

Now, now, he said. *That's enough of that.*

Don We Now Our Gay Apparel

In December 1997, I climbed the stairs up to the Haunted Room to get out the Christmas decorations: the tree stand and the glass reindeer, the angel merry-go-round and the giant pinecone, the tinsel-rope and the nutcracker and the plastic mistletoe fairy. I was still a boyo then, would be one for just a little bit longer.

I swung open the door, and there was all the family's old junk, just as it had been twenty-five years before. Snow ticked softly against the small square window in the corner.

Formal dresses hung in garment bags, bathed in the fragrance of mothballs. There was the blue crinoline gown my sister had worn when she was a bridesmaid at my wedding. My wife, Grace, had a gown hanging here, too, a strapless thing she'd bought for the garden party my mother threw us when we got engaged. And there was a black dress Mom wore to funerals. That one had gotten a lot of use lately.

In a box in the corner were a few remaindered copies of my first collection of short stories, *Remind Me to Murder You Later*, as well as a few of my first novel, *The Planets*. On the cover of the novel was a quote from a reviewer at *The New Yorker*. According to a critic at that publication, I was *wacky*.

Dude, I wanted to say. *You don't know the half of it.*

I picked up the box of decorations and carried them downstairs. The house was silent, except for the soft sound of snow against the windows and the deep murmuring of the boiler in the cellar. I was the only one home.

I reached the first floor and looked at my watch. My mother would be back in an hour, and I'd hoped to have the tree decorated for her by then. Grace and the boys were coming down from our home in Maine the next day.

I put the box of decorations down in the front hallway of the Coffin House, in the living room that was black now only in memory.

On the side of the big box, written in my own six-year-old script, were the words CHRISMAS DECERASHUNS.

I reached in and got out the first container. On the top of this box were the words THE NAMED ONES.

There, in protective partitions, were two dozen balls, each one marked with black felt-tip pen. Gammie had started this tradition back in 1957. She wrote the name of a member of the family on a ball and then hung it from the tree. As our family grew, so did the inventory of the Named Ones—there was one for Lydia and for me, marked with the years of our birth, as well as balls for Aunt Nora and Hilda Watson. There was one for Gammie's third (or was it fourth?) husband, Hal. There was one for the mouse, DIAMOND, and another for the cat that died in 1971, SNEAKERS. Another bulb bore the plaintive word BA-BOING!

The first balls on the tree were always my parents', ELEANOR and DICK. We hung them side by side, with a bell-shaped ornament ringing just above them. Back in the days when my sister and I would decorate the tree together, LYDIA would go over on "her" side, the right, and JIMMY went over on the slightly messier (but in my opinion more artistic) left.

I picked up NORA and held it in my hand. It was a plain ball, nearly fifty years old. It made me a little sad to look at it now and remember her. As I looked at the ornament with my aunt's name, one of the steps on the long first-floor staircase creaked. Then another. I looked up.

"Hello?" I said.

The footsteps worked their way all the way down to the first floor, and then they stopped. I could see the bottom of the staircase from where I was standing. There was no one there.

"Hello?" I said again.

My mother and I hadn't been sure who'd make it to the service for Aunt Nora, back in 1995. When we got to the funeral home, we were a little surprised to find my cousin Declan standing there in a blue suit and a long ponytail. Declan is about ten years older than I am, the son of my aunt Maeve. At one point, he'd been a respected scientist, taught organic chemistry at an Ivy League school. Now, though, he only ate plums. In the summers he lived in the desert down in Mexico, doing peyote.

We walked across the room to say hello. The only thing in the room besides the three of us was my aunt Nora, stretched out in a casket and wearing makeup. The night before, the funeral home had called us and asked for a photograph of Aunt Nora, so they'd know what she was supposed to look like. It took us a while to find one in which she looked like herself.

Cousin Declan hugged my mother. "She's okay," he said. "She's part of the universe now, all right?"

Declan and I shook hands. We hadn't seen each other since his first wedding, back in 1968. "How've you been?" I asked him.

"Good," he said. "I'm good, all right?"

We stood for a while, the three of us, then we turned to look at Aunt Nora, all stretched out. We didn't say anything. After a bit my mother started to cry. She ran her fingers through Aunt Nora's hair.

"Poor thing," she said.

Later we all drove out to the cemetery. We'd been there a lot recently: first for Gammie, then Hilda Watson. Those two had decided that when they died, they wanted to donate their bodies to science. They wound up cadavers at Jefferson Medical School. We couldn't talk them out of it. "Cadavers," my mother said, fed up with the both of them. "What next?"

I told her I didn't think there *was* anything next. Once you reach *Be a cadaver* on your to-do list, your work is probably pretty close to being finished.

But I can't say for sure. It's not like I'm some big expert.

After Aunt Nora's funeral we went back to the Coffin House with Declan and drank a pint or two. It was nice, sitting around the kitchen with my mother and my cousin, lifting a few jars, telling stories of Aunt Nora, Uncle Sean. My uncle Jack, the railroad detective. Uncle Rufus, the night watchman. Aunt Caeli, who played one of those organs that made its own percussion. She lived above a liquor store in Jersey and rode a red bicycle. When last seen, she'd grown her fingernails out so that they were nearly a foot long. It was quite a crew.

We wound up all misty-eyed and singing "The Salley Gardens," the song Yeats got all wrong in his collection of ballads:

And I wish I was in Belfast town, and my true love along with me;
Money in my pocket, to keep a single company.
Liquor to be plenty, a flowing glass on every side.
Hard fortune would ne'er daunt me, for I am young and the world is wide.

I liked my cousin Declan. For a guy who only ate plums, he sure could put away the beers.

Before Declan left, I climbed up into the attic, got out Uncle Sean's manuscript, and gave it to my cousin. I figured it might make more sense to him than me.

"Just so you know," my mother said kindly, as I handed him the old, yellowed pages. "It's gobbledygook."

Declan nodded, and stared down upon the opening words of *Goldenrod. All time shall be all soul, and we will all be all one all soul, One Love.*

"Oh yes," said Declan, his eyes growing wide, as if at long last he'd found the answer to a question that had been haunting him for years. "Yes," he said again, reading onward. "Yes, yes, *yes*. All right?"

I put the ornament marked NORA in the center of the tree, not far from the ones for GAMMIE and HILDA. We didn't have a ball for cousin Declan. That time I'd seen him at Aunt Nora's funeral was the first time I'd laid eyes on him in twenty years. And the last.

I reached into the box and found a decoration marked EAMON. For a moment I wondered if I should throw it away; after all, Lydia had divorced him fifteen years before. It was one of the very few pieces of evidence in our house that Eamon had been alive. Still, the idea of throwing his ornament away struck me as bordering on voodoo. Surely, if these decorations had any intrinsic power, there'd be some effect on Eamon, wherever he was now, when the glass ball with his name on it was destroyed.

I briefly considered putting Eamon's ball on the back of the tree, in the area we now called the Pet Cemetery. This was the place where our now-dead pets resided—Sausage, Matt the Mutt, and of course, ba-BOING! But that didn't seem especially dignified either. I placed Eamon's ball back in the box where it had rested these last fifteen years. It wouldn't do any harm there.

I recalled Eamon, and the wild days that had led up to his marriage to Lydia. I remembered my sister finding us outside on the porch, late one summer night.

What are you boys doing?

Nothin', said Eamon. *Stargazin'*.

The next four balls in the box all belonged to Lydia's children: ASTOR 1989, JULIA 1991, CHARLES 1994, and the brand-new MARGARET 1997. Next to these was one for her husband, Aidan. They lived in a huge, five-hundred-year-old mansion in Scotland, a stone's throw from Loch Ness.

I'd been to Lydia's house in the Highlands once, and it was remarkable to me to see how she'd re-created many of the elements of her own childhood in this entirely new culture. And so, while she developed a shocking Scottish accent and actually served things like blood pudding and haggis for dinner, she also rode horses and raised chickens in a henhouse.

She was a great mother to her children as well, stricter than I was with my own, but still clearly loving. I was crazy about my nieces and nephews, too, who, in spite of the crazy Scots argle-bargle that emerged from their mouths, were also largely Boylans at heart. My older nephew, Astor, was the most like me of the bunch, and I gladly gave him gifts I knew he'd enjoy, including a product called Fart in a Can, a gift that made him laugh so hard that for a long time he couldn't even talk; he just sat there with his Fart in a Can, shaking and trembling with joy, made mute by his own astonishment.

Until recently, Lydia and her brood had always come across the Atlantic to spend Christmas with Eleanor at the Coffin House, but after the third child was born, it had become too difficult to uproot the whole family every December. In addition to this, my mother had reached an age at which she could no longer endure the long transatlantic flight. So we all came together only once a year now, in summer. Those were still great days: the six grandchildren running around the yard, Lydia and I sitting on the back porch, watching them and drinking iced tea.

The last time Lydia had come back to Pennsylvania for Christmas, Eleanor sat on a worn, comfortable couch by the fire in the living room with her grandsons and granddaughters gathered around her in a child-pile on Christmas Eve, and read *The Polar Express* out loud.

> *At one time most of my friends could hear the bell, but as the years passed, it fell silent for all of them. Even Sarah found one Christmas that she couldn't hear its sweet sound.*

We all wept when she got to the end; then we laughed at ourselves for weeping.

Then we wept some more. We sat there for a long time, all of us, weeping and laughing, as the logs on the fireplaces burned into the night.

I put up the balls for LYDIA and AIDAN and the cousins, and then I reached into the box and picked up a red ornament with a multifaceted surface, like a mirror ball. In my sister's handwriting, in black Flair, was written CHECKMATE.

For a moment I looked at this one, and thought about Lydia's horse, and the way that loss had shadowed us, in some vague way, all these years. I put CHECKMATE in the back of the tree in the Pet Cemetery, along with DIAMOND the mouse and BA-BOING!

The footsteps creaked again in the front hallway, and I looked through the big arch toward the stairs.

"Who's there?" I said. "Hello?"

The old house seemed very quiet. I looked at my watch and wondered when my mother would be coming home. Outside, the snow was beginning to stick. I didn't like the idea of her being out in this weather, behind the wheel of a car. She was already late, and the light outside was beginning to fade.

The next bulb read GRACE. I'd started dating Grace Finney, the tough girl in leather from Wesleyan University, in the mid-1980s, and on Christmas Eve 1987 I picked her up from work in Washington, D.C., and drove her to the Coffin House for her first Christmas with my family. She had been orphaned in her early twenties, and the idea of spending the holidays in a big house with lots of people was very appealing to her, reminding her, in some way, of the house that she had grown up in and the holidays she'd spent with her two sisters and her brother, before the loss of her parents.

Grace had noticed I seemed withdrawn and somber that night, and after Gammie and Hilda and Aunt Nora had finally retired, she and I sat before a roaring fire in the family room, the place that had once been the swingin' bachelor pad with the zebra-striped walls. My friend Zero was there, too. He'd been spending the holidays with us since my father died, adding his own weird humor and fundamental kindness to our gatherings. For the most part, his presence changed our ritual just enough for us to feel the ache of my father's absence a little less. He flirted ruthlessly with Gammie, who flirted right back. Sometimes he could go too far, though. Once he'd mooned my aunt Nora, right at the dinner table, when she started into one of her harangues about her great inventory of chills. Aunt Nora never quite got over that, and years later would occasionally ask me, "How is your friend? You know, the one who showed me his bottom."

"Why don't we sit down?" Grace said to me, as Zero went outside in the snow to walk his dog, Alex.

"Okay," I said.

We sat down by the fireplace, and Grace put her arm around me.

"I love your family," Grace said. "Your mother is the nicest person in the world."

"I'm glad you don't think they're all insane," I said.

"I didn't say they weren't insane," said Grace. "I said I loved them."

She pulled out a small present and handed it to me. "I wanted you to have this tonight," she said.

In the box was a watch with a yellow face and a moon that revolved and displayed its phases. It was the most beautiful thing I had ever seen.

"I have something for you, too," I said, and got the small box out of my pocket.

She knew what it was. Her face turned pale, and her mouth dropped open.

"You know how your grandmother said for you to call her sometime?" I said. "And she said that if you had big news, you should call her collect?"

"Uh-huh," she said.

"Well, maybe you'll want to call her collect."

She opened the box. There was the ring. The diamond sparkled in the firelight.

"Oh Jimmy," she said. "What have you done?"

"What I wanted to know," I said. "Was if you wanted to get married."

At that moment, Zero returned from outside and walked straight into the family room with the dog. Grace popped the ring box closed and stuffed it in her pocket.

"Hey guys," said Zero. "What's going on?"

I looked at Zero, and then I got up. "Let's get some drinks," I said. Zero and I walked into the kitchen and poured out a couple of Irish whiskeys.

"I'm thinking I need to talk to Grace in private for a little while," I said.

"What's going on?" he said. "Are you proposing?"

"I'll talk to you about it *later*," I said, picking up the whiskeys.

Zero clapped me on the shoulder. "Good luck," he said. Then he climbed the back stairs with his dog. I watched him ascend.

When I got back to the family room, Grace was sitting on the couch, looking at the ring. It was still in its box.

"So," I said. "You never answered my question."

She looked at me.

"Do you want to get married?"

Grace nodded. "Uh-huh," she said.

"Really?"

She nodded again. "Yes. I do."

I put my arms around her. "Me too," I said.

We kissed.

A little later, as we walked up the stairs to my old bedroom, I passed my sister's old bedroom, now the library. There, for a brief moment, I saw Gammie and Hilda and Aunt Nora gathered around the television, watching *It's a Wonderful Life*. For a split second I made eye contact with Zero. I gave him the thumbs-up sign, and he smiled.

The next morning, I woke up in my bedroom, the one that, a long time ago, had borne on its walls the lyrics *O dig my grave both wide and deep*. There was a sharp, piercing pain in the middle of my chest. For a moment I did not know what this was.

Then I saw the diamond in Grace's ring. Her hand was resting on my chest, and the ring had turned on her finger so that it was digging, urgently, into my heart.

"Listen," I said to Grace. "You can take the ring off this morning. If you don't want to have a whole big scene with my grandmother and the aunts. We can tell everybody later if you'd prefer."

"Jim," she said. "I'm never taking this ring off. Ever."

She kept her word about that, too. Even now, twenty years later, long after her husband became a woman, she's wearing it still.

I hadn't told Grace my secret when we got engaged.

I think the expression people use is *My bad.*

I can tell you I should have. I don't think there's much question about that.

But let me ask *you* something for a change.

Would *you* have told her, if it had been you instead of me? After all those years of *petitioning the Lord with prayer,* praying desperately that love would cure you? Would you have looked Grace in the eyes and told her that until the day you met her you suspected you did not exist, that you had spent your whole life up to that point like some kind of sentient mist?

Would you have had the courage to turn to the one person you loved, and to speak the words you knew might well make her turn her back on you forever?

Maybe you would have. Maybe you'd have found those words, somewhere within you. In which case, you are a person of integrity and courage, and I can only say I wish I were more like you.

But then, I've wished that I were more like you from the beginning.

That same night, Zero woke up from a restless sleep in the Haunted Room. He felt the presence before he saw it. Then, slowly, it flickered into view. Later, Zero said the figure appeared "like a set of horizontal lines all folding into view, like a set of venetian blinds."

Then my father stared at my friend, and my friend stared back.

He looked at Zero for a long, cold moment, then smiled. Zero heard him think, *And who else were you expecting? John Gielgud?*

My father was wearing his own clothes—plaid slacks, a button-down shirt. In his hand he had a cigarette, which if you ask me is an odd thing for a ghost to have. But my father always had a cigarette, and perhaps old habits are hard to break.

Zero said that he didn't feel scared of my father. He felt protected, as if my father was making a set of appointed rounds, checking up on everyone to make sure they were okay.

My father floated at the foot of the bed for a while, and then at last he turned and passed through the door out into the hallway. *I have other things I have to do. Other people I have to watch.*

Zero looked at the door for a moment, then put his head back on the pillow. It was a long time, he said, before he fell back asleep.

He didn't tell me about the ghost until years later. By then I was a woman, and he was an MIT professor.

"Why didn't you tell me about it when it happened?" I asked. "Were you afraid it would have freaked me out or something?"

He nodded. "It *would* have freaked you out, Jenny. Wouldn't it?"

I thought about it: my father appearing in my friend's room on the night I got engaged. Zero was probably right.

"What was he like, when you saw him?" I asked. "Was he scary? Did it seem like he wanted something, or like he had unfinished business?"

"He was *still*," said Zero.

I put the ball marked ZERO on the tree not far from the one for GAMMIE. We had one for Zero's dog, ALEX, too, and so I hung that one close to his master.

Next out of the box were the ornaments for my own boys, LUKE 1994 and PATRICK 1996. I put these next to GRACE. I couldn't wait until my wife and children arrived the next day, bringing with them the lobsters and the presents and all the Christmas energy. It would be nice, I thought, to have the house filled once more with the sounds of raucous children.

Something creaked in the front hallway, and once more I felt the old familiar feeling of electricity upon my skin.

"Hello?" I said once again, looking into the dark hallway. "Is anybody there?"

The house was silent.

Jenny, something inside me said. *You know you're still a woman in your heart.*

Oh for God's sake, I thought. I just want to live a normal life. Is that so fucking much to ask?

Jenny.

You know, sometimes I get tired of this conversation.

I turned angrily back toward the box of ornaments and took out the last one. It was a decoration I had made in third grade, in Miss Voron's class at Culbertson Elementary. My name was spelled out on it in glitter glue.

JIMMY.

I picked up the ball and hung it on the tree, between Grace and my mother and my sister.

The electricity prickled on my skin, and I turned once more to the hallway, and looked at the bottom of the stairs, waiting for the blue mist to appear. Something was going to happen any moment. The entire house was waiting for it.

Jenny.

One of the limbs of the Christmas tree began to bow, as if it were being drawn downward by an unseen hand. Then the ball that read JIMMY slipped off of the branch, and shattered on the floor.

"Oh," I said, and bent down. The glass was everywhere. The lights in the house flickered off for a moment. I was in the dark. My heart pounded in my breast.

Then the lights came back on. I drifted through the house, through the big front hallway with the long staircase, through the dining room, where my father used to sit at the head of the table and encourage us all to *Argue the opposite,* through the kitchen where I used to eat a Hostess cupcake and drink a glass of milk after school, all the way to the back pantry, the very room where, on my first day in this house, I had first been blasted with Sith lightning.

Jenny.

I got out the broom and dustpan from the closet, then went back to the living room.

I got down on my hands and knees, surveying the damage.

Then, shard by shard, I began to pick up the pieces.

The Pearl

The last time I saw my sister's face was in the spring of 1999. We were in a pub in a hotel in Dublin, drinking Guinness, doing shots of whiskey. Somebody was singing in the corner.

As she stepped away from me and she moved through the fair
And fondly I watched her move here and move there
And then she turned homeward with one star awake
Like the swan in the evening moves over the lake.

I'd come to Ireland to spend a year as visiting faculty at University College Cork, and to shepherd my own students from Colby College in Maine through the UCC system. Grace took a yearlong sabbatical from being a social worker and spent the year happily working out at the Brookfield Health Center, shopping at the English market for fresh salmon and brown bread, and occasionally visiting the Jameson's Irish Whiskey distillery in Middleton with me to take the Jameson's Irish Whiskey Tasting Challenge. Luke and Patrick, now five and three, went to a Montessori school that year, where they played pennywhistles, drew pictures of airplanes with chalk, and stuffed sponges into cans.

Every couple of months, Lydia crossed the Irish Sea and stayed with us in Cork. Or, there'd be occasions like this one, when we'd all converge in Dublin for a long weekend. Among my other responsibilities as director of Colby College's program in Cork, I'd chaperone my students in Dublin as they attended the National Theatre at the Abbey and careened down Grafton Street. Lydia had accompanied Grace and me on some of these adventures—on a trip to Trinity College to see the Book of Kells, then on to the Joyce Museum, where I sat down at Joyce's piano to play one of his favorite songs, "I'm the Man Who Broke the Bank at Monte Carlo," only to find the cover mercifully sealed with a small padlock.

"We'll have another round," I said to the bartender, who nodded and began to pour another couple of pints for my sister and me.

"I'm not finished this one," Lydia said.

I shrugged.

It felt strange, the two of us together after forty years, sitting on barstools in the Old Country. Sometimes, when I saw my sister, I felt as if we'd been army buddies. *You and me, Liddie*, I wanted to say. *We were in the Big One.*

What she did not know was that I had already begun the process that would take me from the world of men and eventually leave me washed up on the shores of womanhood, blinking and half-drowned, but hopeful that I would find some signs of life in the new green world before me.

I'd come out to Grace, slowly, timidly, and that year in Ireland I was trying to negotiate some kind of middle ground. I wanted to stop living a lie, but I also wanted to avoid plunging into turmoil the lives of the people I loved. So I cross-dressed occasionally, after the children were asleep. Grace and I sat by the peat fire in our flat in Cork, with me in a Coldwater Creek skirt, and her doing the crossword puzzle in the *International Herald Tribune.*

Grace wasn't crazy about my cross-dressing, but she seemed to understand that it was important to me, so she tolerated it. Quite frankly, I wasn't crazy about cross-dressing either, since, as always, whatever I felt was not primarily about clothing. But it was a start.

As that barman slow-poured another Guinness for me, my sister looked into my face, and saw, perhaps, that her brother was beginning to look a little willowy.

I don't know. I can't tell you what she saw.

At the time I had pierced ears, and my hair, which had always been thick and blond, had grown down to my shoulders.

I was still nine months away from the moment of no return, a morning in January 2000 when I would find myself frozen, back in Maine, at a railroad crossing, unable to move forward in the world, even as the train passed by and the crossing bell ceased and the barrier rose into the cold New England air.

The barman put our pints in front of us. The balladeer sang from the corner of the pub.

Last night she came to me, my dead love came in
So softly she came that her feet made no din.
As she laid her hand on me and this she did say,
"It will not be long, love, till our wedding day."

Lydia finished her pint, then picked up the next. "Cheers," she said, and we clinked glasses.

"So," I said. "You ever think about finishing your degree?"

She licked the foam from her lip. "Someday," she said wistfully. "But you know, with four children, I've got a lot going on. Writing a dissertation about medieval poetry doesn't feel like it's at the top of my to-do list anymore."

She'd finished all the requirements except for the dissertation at NYU, before my father's death brought everything to a screeching halt. She took a job with a company in Edinburgh the fall after he died; that was when she met Aidan. The next thing she knew, she had four children and a couple of horses and a whole chorus of chickens out in a henhouse near a haunted mansion by Loch Ness. I could easily understand why she'd never finished the dissertation, even though it was all that stood at this point between her and the Ph.D.

"I know," I said. "You know I'm incredibly proud of everything you've done," I said. "Your family, and Aidan. You're such a good mother. Who knew?"

She shrugged. "One thing you learn when you raise children. You begin to be a little more forgiving of your own parents." Lydia drank from her pint. "Maybe you start to be more forgiving of everybody."

She never spoke of her marriage to Eamon anymore, and I knew better than to embarrass her by mentioning our time together in New York, when she'd been so fragile. I remembered standing next to her, in the final days of her marriage, by the sink in the Coffin House, as we did the dishes together and the tears rolled down her face. "How long are you going to wait before you decide to make yourself happy?" I asked her. "Until you're forty? Until you're ninety?"

"I know," she'd said. "I just hate to disappoint everyone."

Perhaps it was not so strange that my sister's area of scholarly study had been the Middle Ages, that like my father she had found a certain mystery and charm in the literature of the twelfth century. Among other poets she'd studied was the author of *The Pearl*. I'd studied *The Pearl* myself during my capricious time as a graduate student at Johns Hopkins, and was both moved and infuriated by it. The poem tells the story of a man who has lost a "precious Pearl," variously interpreted as his daughter or a lover, who has fallen into the "herb garden" of a graveyard. It's written in that nearly incomprehensible Middle English, which always sounded to me like two-thirds Elvish and one-third pig Latin.

Allas! I leste hyr in on erbere;
Þur gresse to grounde hit fro me yot.
I dewyne, fordolked of luf-daungere
Of þat pryuy perle wythouten spot.

[Alas I lost her in an herb garden—
Through grass to ground it from me got.
I dwindled, done in by love-distress
For that prize pearl without a spot.]

"Are you all right?" Lydia asked me. "You seem kind of—I don't know."

She looked at me hard. My eyes fell to my pint. I wondered whether this was the moment I'd been waiting for, all these years. *Listen, there's something I need to tell you.*

I'd thought about this conversation a thousand times since childhood, but I'd never gotten further than that sentence. *What is it*, she'd reply, and I'd just shudder. *You can tell me. No matter what it is, you know I'll always love you.*

The boys in the corner of the bar began to play something sad and slow, a tale of emigration.

"Listen," I said.

"What?"

I drank my pint. In my heart I wondered if she already knew. Surely, at least once over the last forty years I'd let escape some telltale sign of what I was? Had she never looked in my eyes and seen a girl looking back at her?

"What?" she said. "What is it, Jim?"

I took a deep breath.

I have a problem. I don't even have a language for talking about it. I'm afraid if I say what's in my heart you'll turn your back on me. I don't want to hurt you.

"This song," I said.

She raised an eyebrow. "What about it?"

Farewell to the groves of shillelaghs and shamrocks
Farewell to the girls of old Ireland all round
May their hearts be as merry as ever I would wish them
When far away on the ocean I'm bound.

"It's sad," I said.

She sipped her pint. "You're worse than Gammie," she said. "You've turned into such a sentimentalist."

"You know what you need," I said, in my Gammie voice. "*Pizzazz.*"

She smiled. "You're not kidding."

"*Now where—*" I said, continuing on. "*Where do we find pizzazz? Is it in a store?*"

"Stop."

"You can't buy pizzazz in a store!" I shouted. I picked up my pint.

"That wasn't what you were going to say, before," said Lydia.

"What?"

"When you said *listen*, like that. I know you, little brother. And when you say *listen* like that it's because you want to say something."

"I was just thinking of Gammie," I said. "If she were here she'd be standing on the bar, singing."

Lydia sighed. "I like men," she said, in her own Gammie voice. Everyone in our family could do a Gammie voice—Lydia's children, my children, Eleanor, Grace. Even my Scottish brother-in-law, Aidan, could do one. "And I like men who like money. And men who like money—"

We both said it together. *"Like me!"*

We laughed. We drank.

"So what do you want to do tomorrow?" I said, moving on. "Anything on your must-see list in Dublin?"

She looked a little sheepish. "Well, actually—"

"What?"

"There's this church, St. Michan's, I've always wanted to see."

"Really? What's there?"

"A couple things, actually. There's this very old pipe organ. They say Handel used it while composing *The Messiah*."

"Yeah?" I had played the pipe organ while a student at Wesleyan, and the idea of seeing the instrument on which Handel played *The Messiah* was definitely appealing.

"Plus, there's this crypt."

"A crypt?"

"Yeah. Apparently there's been a church there since the tenth century. And down in the cellar they have these mummies."

"Mummies," I said. I thought of my old friend King Tutankhamen. I hoped the boy king was doing all right on his own, out in the broad world without me.

"I think the story is, either the air is exceptionally dry there, or else there's all this lime in the basement, or something, because the bodies in the crypt have all turned into mummies. And there's this one you can supposedly go right up to and touch. It's the body of a Crusader."

I began to understand Lydia's interest in the Irish mummies. The Crusader had been alive during the time when all those poems she'd studied had been written. Perhaps he'd heard, with his own ears, someone reciting *The Pearl.*

My wreched wylle in wo ay wrate.
I felle vpon þat floury flat,

[My wretched will in woe was wrought
As I fell on that field with flowers fraught.]

"Sure," I said. "Let's go check out the mummies. Why not?"

She raised her glass and we *ching*ed. "To the Crusader mummy," I said.

"They say you can shake his hand."

"What?"

"His mummified hand is hanging out of his coffin. And if you want to you can shake it."

"Why would you do that?"

She smiled. "It's supposed to be good luck," she said.

I finished my pint. "And they don't know who he was?"

"No," she said. "He was just some guy from the Middle Ages who wound up a mummy."

"Maybe he was your Pearl Poet," I said. "The guy who wrote *Sir Gawain* and those other poems—what are they called?"

"*Patience.* And *Cleanness,*" she said, wistfully, and I could hear in her voice, even as she spoke, the echo of my father's. *Ah. The ancient world.*

"I always hated that poem," I said.

"What?" she said, appalled. "*Sir Gawain?*"

"No, the other one," I said. "*The Pearl.*"

She sipped her pint and sighed. A faraway look snuck into her eyes.

"It's an acquired taste," she said.

"This guy loses his daughter, or his lover, or his sister, or whoever she is? And he stands around in the cemetery, grief-stricken for her.

Then he has a dream and he sees her in heaven, and he tells her his heart is broken, and what does she do? She *yells* at him."

Lydia nodded happily. "She does."

"She tells him, basically, that he's a jerk for being sad. That his constant grief is just a form of self-centeredness. And that if he wants to be happy he'd better just surrender to God, accept that he's a pathetic worm and that God has some sort of master plan and He'll just kill off whoever He pleases. I mean—isn't that pretty much it?"

"I don't know if I'd put it that way exactly," she said. "But you can't judge the Middle Ages using a modern consciousness. They saw the world differently."

"They thought we should all be miserable?"

"They thought that it's not God's job to make us happy. That's a modern conceit. In the Middle Ages, suffering was considered part of what humans do."

"Well," I said. "That's fucked up."

"Is it?" she said.

"I don't know," I said. "I mean, I do think people in the world are too self-centered, too narcissistic. But at the same time, I don't think we're here to suffer. I can't see that people crying their eyes out until they're insane is part of God's plan."

She was looking at me intently, waiting for me to go on.

"Like, if you were blind, and you could have an operation to restore your sight, you would have it, right? You wouldn't just stumble around in the dark and call it part of God's plan. Would you?"

She looked disappointed in me. "You're not a Crusader," she said.

I opened my mouth, then shut it. She was right. I *wasn't* a Crusader.

"What was it you wanted to tell me?" she said.

"When?"

"Before, when you said *listen*?" She touched my arm. "You know you can tell me anything."

Was that true? In my experience, when people say *You can tell me anything*, what they really mean is, *You can tell me anything, except that you're a woman.*

"Jim," she said. "Tell me."

I looked into her eyes and saw something. She knows, I thought. She knows. She's always known. Who knows me better than Lydia? She'd been the one person—other than my mother—who'd been with me all along, the girl who'd stood by the front door when my mother brought me home from the hospital in 1958, and asked, reasonably enough, "Who is this baby? Why is he here?"

"What?" said Lydia. "What is it?"

From the corner, the boys ended their song of emigration.

And now to conclude and to finish my ditty
If ever friendless Irishman chances my way
With the best in the house I will treat him with fine welcome
At home on the green fields of Amer-i-kay.

"Nothing," I said to my sister. "Forget it."

As it turned out, I would not accompany my sister to the crypt on the next, or on any other morning. I recalled, even before my head hit the pillow that night, that I had to be up at dawn to load all my Colby students into the tour bus that would take us all off to the Boyne Valley in County Meath to see Newgrange, a megalithic passage tomb built in 3200 B.C. Grace and our children, meanwhile, would head back to Cork by train.

By midday, the Boylans would be scattered, one by one, all across the wide green map of Ireland.

As a result, my sister was alone as she took her last walk through Dublin.

I wasn't there so I can't tell you what she saw, or what she did. But I can imagine her waking up in her hotel, having her black pudding and sausage for breakfast, a cup of strong coffee, and then heading out onto the street, looking across the open space of St. Stephen's Green. It would have been deserted that Sunday morning, as the citizens of Dublin slept late, or read the *Irish Times* in their living rooms, or put on their good clothes for Mass.

I don't know which route she took, but I'm certain she would have set out on foot, rather than hail a cab. Lydia would have liked the feel of the air on that bracing March morning, the wind blowing through her shoulder-length blond hair, her silk scarf around her neck, her ankle-length wool coat with only its bottom button buttoned. I would think she'd have walked north from the Shelbourne Hotel along Kildare Street, following it until she reached Trinity College.

Almost surely she walked through Trinity, past the Berkeley Library and the New Square, enjoying the sight of a few young scholars stumbling either out of or into the Old Library at that hour, professors riding their bicycles wearing their ridiculous academic robes. She'd have passed through the college gates and emerged on Pearse Street probably, then followed it on to D'Olier Street and the River Liffey.

Then she'd have walked west along the Liffey, along Aston Quay, past the O'Connell Bridge, watching the dank Liffey lap along the stones. She'd have kept the river on her right as the quays changed their names, from Aston to Wellington, from Wellington to Essex and Merchants, until at last she came to the Father Matthew Bridge and made her crossing.

Once she'd reached the far side of the Liffey, it would only have taken another few minutes to walk past the squat, elegant dome of the Four Courts, past Arran Quay and Hammond Lane, to find St. Michan's. Still, she'd have been out of breath when she arrived, her cheeks pink with the cold morning air, and perhaps embarrassed, for a moment, that she'd come all this way to see a dead man.

She'd have felt self-conscious, too, to realize that a church service, naturally enough, was in progress, it being Sunday morning. The voice of the priest would have echoed in that great open space. Perhaps the old organ, with its keys chipped and worn, was at that moment being played by someone not so unlike me, someone who wondered, occasionally, how she was going to survive.

Not wishing to disturb the service, she'd have gone around to the crypt entrance and slowly walked down its narrow stone steps. The stench of the place would have stunned her as she descended—the stark, raw, dusty smell of human decay. At the bottom of the stairs she'd have found the dark tunnel that leads to the mummies, a long passageway with bars on the left and right, through which she'd have seen the hundreds of ancient coffins, strewn like jackstraws. In one chamber, to her left, one pleading, outstretched arm emerged from a casket. From another, a pair of legs. The bodies of a pair of children, their arms around each other, emerged from a third. Perhaps, for just that moment, she was reminded of the two of us, falling asleep in each other's arms while watching *Sing Along with Mitch* on TV when we were kids. *Follow the bouncing ball.*

At last she'd have come to a dimly lit chamber with three open coffins.

By now Lydia would have felt her heart beating in her breast, feeling alone and bewildered in the heart of that alien place. Over her head, through the thick stone ceiling, she might have heard the distant sound of the priest giving the sermon, or the men and women of St. Michan's, raising their voices in a song of praise.

The coffin on the left held the body of a nun covered in brownish white dust, her skin transformed to parchment by the dry air and time. Her body curled to the left, and the remains of a wimple were still visible, decaying around her neck. On the right was another woman, her mouth open, staring up to heaven. And in the middle casket was a huge man, more than six feet tall, his head turned slightly to the right. He was missing his right hand and both feet.

Lydia would surely have been tempted to leave the crypt at this point, to run out of the place screaming and get herself back on the next boat to Scotland and the safety of Loch Ness. But she'd have pushed onward by the thought of her Crusader, by her scholarship in medieval poetry, by—who knows?—even the memory of my father and his love of the ancient world.

She walked around the three central caskets and their grisly contents until she came to the back wall. And there she found all that was left of her Crusader.

Delyt me drof in ye and ere,
My mane mynde to maddyng malte;
Quen I se my frely, I wolde be þere,

[Delight drove o'er me thru eye and ear;
My mortal mind in madness melted.
When I saw my fair one, I would be there.]

As she stood there, looking down upon him, she'd have noticed something else. The mummy's body had been cut in half.

At that moment, over in County Meath, I was walking with my students and our guide into the heart of the tomb at Newgrange. From the outside it looked like a round green hill, ringed at the top by a high wall of white quartz. Large stones on the exterior of the tomb were covered with spiral designs, like whirlpools or gusts of wind.

We walked through a high doorway that led deep into the mountain. The walls were decorated with more spirals. "No one knows what they mean," our guide explained. "But some people think they are meant to be a rendering of the shape of the human soul."

We followed that passage sixty feet into the dark until we reached a cruciform chamber. Then we all paused, my students and I, and looked back in the direction from which we'd come.

"Here," said our guide, "on the day of the winter solstice, a shaft of the rising sun travels through the passages and fills this whole dark chamber with light. It was in this way that the ancient people of Ireland found hope in the darkness, and gave thanks to their god."

There in the heart of the tomb, I thought of my sister and our conversation of the night before. I thought about Grace, and my children, making their journey westward on the train, back toward Cork and our little home near the college.

What *is* it God wants from us, I wondered, and why is it all such a brain-numbing mystery? Did the Pearl Poet have it right, after all? Are we really here to suffer, as part of a plan beyond our understanding? Or, rather, are we here to find our peace, as best we can, during the short time we have?

Back in the crypt of St. Michan's, Lydia was mustering her courage, trying to figure out how to do the difficult thing before her, this ritual that might bring her good luck. From far away came the sound of organ music, the echo of human voices. Slowly, gingerly, she walked toward the tomb.

Her Crusader lay there, his mouth slightly open, as if in surprise. Lydia reached out, tenderly, her heart filling with pity. Then she put her living hand in his.

At my sister's touch, the dead man's eyes flashed open.

Whoa-ho, he said. *For a moment I thought we'd lost you.*

The Radiot

"Ghost One to Ghost Two, do you read me?"

Wendy, the ghostbuster, handed me a walkie-talkie. "You talk to him, Jenny," she said. She was behind the wheel of her car, wearing a T-shirt that read TOTALLY BATTY.

"Ghost One, this is Ghost Two," I said. "Come in."

"Roger, Ghost Two," said Hawk's voice, crackling through the tiny transmitter. Hawk was Wendy's boyfriend and the leader of our investigation. "We are approaching our destination."

It was the summer of 2006, seven years after my sister and the mummy had joined hands.

We were now only minutes away from this guy Benny's house, just beyond the part of town Philadelphians call the Great Northeast. Earlier the ghostbuster group had assembled at the Essene Café, near the Delaware River, and discussed the case. Benny, in fact, was a ghostbuster his own self; he'd participated in some of the meetings until his medical issues got in the way. Unfortunately, he'd caught the Sleeping Sickness that was going around. You'd be talking to Benny and all of a sudden he'd just nod off.

"Why doesn't somebody give him some Red Bull?" Wendy had asked, back at the café. I thought it was a good question.

Hawk just shook his head gravely. "A can of Red Bull?" he said. "That could *kill* him."

This wasn't my first meet-up with the ghostbusters, but it was one of the more interesting ones. Part of the reason was that Hawk, the group's leader, had come, and Hawk was a dynamic personality. There'd been other newcomers as well—an African American woman named Sharmay, with a crackling sense of humor, and a mysterious dark-haired woman named Trina. Trina, as it turned out, was a shaman, or "a near-shaman," as she put it. She was able to hear all sorts of invisible voices, to discern the unheard whisperings of dwarf planets and the like.

"There is a world beyond our own," she'd said in the café, as she drank green tea.

"I tell you what," said Sharmay. "That's a *relief*. Can you imagine, this was it? De-*pressing*."

A guy named Leonard had been sitting next to me, checking out the huge pile of ghost-hunting equipment. He was a small, nervous man, like a character in a Woody Allen film.

"Where do you live?" he asked me.

"Maine," I said. "But my mom lives in Somerset."

"Me," he said. "I live in Fishtown."

He picked up the thermal scanner and pointed it at me.

"Ninety-eight point six," he said, and sighed. "You're normal, Jenny."

I thought this was a generous thing to say.

I took the thermal scanner and pointed it at Leonard. It read 87.5.

"You're cold, Leonard," I said.

"What else is new," he said sadly. "I'm always cold." He scratched himself. "I think it's 'cause of my psoriasis. My skin can't hold in heat."

At the end of the meeting, Hawk turned to the other paranormal investigators and asked if there were any questions. There was a long pause.

Finally, Leonard put his hand up.

"Yes, Leonard?"

Leonard scratched himself restlessly. "How do you learn—" he asked tremulously. "How do you learn not to be afraid?"

We all looked at one another—Hawk and Wendy, Sharmay and Trina and I. Nobody knew what to tell him.

We pulled up in front of a tract house in Pennsylvania's Levittown.

"This is Ghost One to Ghost Two," said Hawk through the walkie-talkie. We could see him sitting in the car ten feet in front of us.

"Roger, Ghost One," I said.

"We have reached our twenty."

I looked at Benny's house. It didn't look haunted. "What's the story on this place again?" I asked Wendy.

"The washing machine went nuts," said Wendy sadly. "The blade for its fan went spinning across the room, imbedded itself in the wall."

"You sure they need us?" I said. "Sounds like they should call Maytag."

We met Hawk, Leonard, Sharmay, and Trina on the sidewalk. They were unloading their equipment. "Okay," said Hawk. "We'll split into two teams. Jenny, Wendy, and Sharmay on the one squad; Trina, Leonard, and me on the other."

"This is a *dark* house," said Trina. She began to do something with her left hand that she would continue for the next hour or two, a swishing movement, similar to a person moving water around in a bathtub.

"Well, maybe they need to turn some *lights* on," said Sharmay.

"I don't mean its illumination," said Trina. "I mean its heart."

"Here we go," Wendy muttered to me, and rolled her eyes. I got the sense that Wendy didn't have much use for Trina.

"I've got the video," said Leonard, carrying the camera like a newsman. A big pair of headphones was clamped down over his ears.

"Let me talk to Benny," said Hawk. He was wearing a black baseball cap with the word SALEM and a pentacle on it. He had intelligent black eyes, a rakish smile. I could see why Wendy found him attractive. "Like I said, he's not in the best of health. We don't want to tire him out."

Benny, a burly man in his forties, welcomed us in. He didn't seem all that sleepy. His wife sat on the couch, next to her two children. They were about the same age as mine.

On one wall was a vast saltwater aquarium. It contained a sea anemone and two huge parrot fish. Against the back wall were hundreds of tiny dots. These turned out to be baby starfish.

"Ooohhh," said Trina, standing in front of the tank. She was still waving her hand around. "What a beautiful aquarium."

"Make sure everybody keeps their fingers away," said Benny. "That anemone is pretty fierce. Look." He dropped some bacon bits into the tank and the anemone folded its fingers around them.

"A sea cucumber eatin' baco-bits," said Sharmay. "Now I seen everything."

"It'll do that to your fingers, you give it half a chance," said Benny.

"No," said Trina, waving her hand through the air. "It won't do that to us. It's not angry at us. It only has anemone consciousness."

Wendy sighed.

"The anemone of my anemone," I said, "is my friend."

Trina gave me a hard look, as if she were just seeing me for the first time. "*What*?" she said.

"A tank like that's a lot of work," said Leonard. "I used to have a tank like that."

"The starfish," said Trina, her attention back on the tank. "There are so many of them!"

"One time, the ghost pulled all the hoses out of the filter," said Benny. "Threw them all over the floor. God, what a mess." He seemed depressed about it.

"You all heard about the washing machine, I guess," added Benny's wife.

"We heard about it," said Sharmay. "You got a flyin' propeller or something?"

"That's what finally convinced me we had an issue," said Mrs. Benny. "Before that, I just thought this was more of Benny's bullshit."

The kids sat on the couch. They were trying to watch *The Simpsons* on a large flat-screen TV, but it was hard to see the picture with all these strangers in the house.

I sat down next to them. "So—do you believe in ghosts?"

The girl looked at me as if I'd asked a very obvious question. "Living here?" she said. "You have to."

We busted ghosts into the evening. The results were mixed. For the first two hours our electromagnetic field recorders and thermal scanners remained largely silent, except for one or two paralyzing moments when they all went off at once and the members of our team looked around in horrified anticipation of disgruntled protoplasm. Fortunately—or unfortunately—our devices soon fell silent again, leaving us all to carry on, ghostless.

Just before midnight, Trina began to moan, as if she were in pain. She was standing by the fish tank, her dousing sticks swinging wildly.

Everyone converged on her. The lights on my ghostbusting device began to blink red. An alarm on Sharmay's thermal scanner went off. The temperature read 42 degrees.

"Uh-oh," said Sharmay. "We got company."

"What is it, Trina?" said Hawk. "Talk to me."

"It's huuuge," Trina moaned.

"I don't see anything," said Sharmay.

"It's enormous!" said Trina. She staggered, as if a great weight had suddenly been placed upon her.

"What is?" said Sharmay.

"I'm getting an image of somebody choking," said Trina.

We all looked around. None of us were choking. The tips of Trina's dousing rods were swinging like propellers. "Did someone choke you?" she asked. "Is that how you died? You were strangled?"

Yes.

"Wait," said Trina. "Who are *you*?"

The alarm in Hawk's hand went off.

"THERE'S TWO OF THEM NOW," said Trina.

"Two of *what*?" asked Sharmay. "I don't see a *thing*."

"NOW THERE'S THREE. FOUR!"

Trina raised the copper divining rods over her head, as if she'd been skewered by an invisible sword. I saw a flash of light.

"*Yaaaggghhhh*!" said Trina. She dropped the rods, which clattered onto the floor.

"Lights," said Hawk. "Somebody turn on the lights."

Trina staggered, as if she'd been hit by lightning.

"The rods got too hot to hold," she said. "There was a whole bunch of entities behind me, and then I got a shock. They all pulsed through me."

"What was there?" said Hawk. "What did you feel?"

"Anger. I've never felt anything like that." As she spoke, I reached down and felt the dousing rods. They were red-hot. "They'd all been murdered. Strangled!"

"Well," said Sharmay. "No wonder their washing machine's gone nuts."

Leonard, to my surprise, was smiling from ear to ear. "That was *awesome*!" he said. "That was the best possession I ever saw!"

Benny, who'd been lying on the couch all this time, opened his eyes and looked around, astonished. "Hey," he said. "What'd I miss?"

As the others dismantled the equipment, and Benny talked to Trina about the aquarium, I chatted with Leonard on the couch. He said that he'd been studying astral projection.

"I've heard of that, but I don't know what it is," I said.

Leonard seemed a little surprised that a college professor wouldn't know about astral projection, but he explained it to me. It's a process, he said, by which you send your spirit wandering around while the rest of you stays put.

"Some people think that's what ghosts are," he said. "It's just people who've projected themselves out into space and time."

"Do you really think that's possible?"

He looked thoughtful. "I hope so," he said. "I went online and got the plans for this thing, it's called the Radiot. It's like, you build this door, out in a field somewhere, and then you wire it up to these transistors and a car battery. You have to leave it for a little while so the charge can build up. Then you can walk through it, and project yourself." He rubbed his chin thoughtfully. "It's the source of all time travel."

I resisted my first impulse, which was to say that I thought this idea sounded totally *radiotic*, but it was hard. The only reason I was able to hold my tongue was that Leonard seemed so wholly genuine about his desire to travel in time, and I knew what it was like for people to mock you for an idea that they could not imagine and which for you was all-encompassing. Maybe, I thought, transsexuals and time travelers are just two different examples of the same basic problem.

"What would you do if it works?" I said. "Is there a special time in history you'd like to visit?" I was presuming he'd say he wanted to check out Pickett's Charge, or the Crucifixion, or something.

"Well," he said thoughtfully. "There was this one girl. I knew her a long time ago. I just wanted her to know the truth."

"What truth did you want her to know?" I asked.

He looked at me as if the answer were obvious. "That I'm not really a bad person," he said.

"Why would anyone think you're a bad person, Leonard? Honestly."

"I'm a coward," he said matter-of-factly. "You know what else I've been doing? Is writing letters. Lots and lots of letters. To give to myself."

"What do you mean, to give yourself? Why would you give yourself a letter?"

He smiled. "I don't mean *this* me," he said. "I mean that *other* me. The one *beyond*."

Some people might have found it hard to keep up with this conversation, but Leonard was making more sense to me than ever.

"Yeah. See, what I want to do is throw a letter on my bed. Give it to myself at age fifteen, or twenty. To warn myself about things that are coming. So I can prepare for the future."

"Do you think that will work?" I said.

"Of course it would work," he said. "But the thing is, when I do it, I'll never know, because once I change things, I'll never know what it was I was supposed to be looking out for. It's like, if I changed the past, this future—the one where I'm writing the letters—won't exist anymore."

"Do you have any memory of having received any letters from yourself yet?"

"No," said Leonard. "But maybe that's how I know it's working. I finished building it, in the future."

This was like a line from "It's a Long Way to Tipperary": *Paddy wrote a letter to his Irish Molly-o, saying if you don't receive this won't you write and tell me so?*

All around us now, the other ghostbusters were packing up. Benny's wife had put the kids to bed. Hawk and Wendy were standing outside in the moonlight, having a quiet talk.

"I'd also like to write a letter to my sister," Leonard said quietly. Trina and Benny were still across the room, staring at the tiny starfish.

"What happened to your sister?"

"She got murdered," he said.

Benny's wife came out of her bedroom with a big pile of laundry and opened up the lid of her washing machine.

"Oh Leonard," I said. "Really? I'm sorry."

He opened his empty hands. "She got killed in a bar. I would tell her not to go into that bar, to be careful. That's what I'd tell her. Stay away from happy times."

I thought about this. From down the hallway came the sound of water rushing into the washer.

"It's a terrible thing, to lose a sister," said Leonard. "I think about her all the time. What she'd be doing now."

Outside on the sidewalk, Hawk and Wendy leaned in for a kiss. The divining rods that Trina had dropped were still on the floor in front of Leonard and me.

"What did you mean?" I asked Leonard. "When you said, stay away from happy times? Why should she stay away from happy times?"

He nodded gently. "That was the name of the bar," he said. "Where they killed her. Happy Times."

If Lydia had hoped to gain good luck by shaking hands with the mummified Crusader, she was surely disappointed in the months that followed. The most likely explanation for this, of course, is that the legend was all blarney, that a pickled old corpse in the cellar of a Dublin church is about as likely to bring a person good fortune as, say, a copper dowsing rod is likely to enable a person to have a conversation with the invisible.

Or maybe it was just that the wrong sister had sought the Crusader's blessing.

At first it had seemed no special luck would be necessary. As I moved, in 2000, from the potato-blighted land of men to the new green country of women—through a round of therapists, endocrinologists, social workers, and surgeons—I found myself, to my amazement, receiving one unexpected blessing after another. Chief among these was my wife, Grace, who decided after some consideration that her life was better with me in it than without, and so, to everyone's amazement, we moved on into the unknown territory before us together. My mother, too, reacted to my news by putting her arms around me and announcing that love would prevail. My children, around whom my transition was perhaps most gradual, announced one day that they were going to call me by a new name, Maddy, their combination of *Mommy* and *Daddy*. The president of my college said that the institution would stand by me and that he was "proud of my courage." My friends, my students, and even the members of my rock and roll band all rolled with it. My good friend Russo, who had started out calling my female self "mannered, studied, and implausible," wound up saying I was "the best-looking woman in Colby's English department." When I thanked him for his generosity, he looked a little surprised.

"I didn't mean it as a compliment," he said.

Was the fact that everything had worked out far better than anyone had believed possible the result simply of my having been extremely lucky with my family, my work, and my friends? Or were there other explanations? Had the culture, possibly, become slightly more forgiving of its ugly ducklings, over time? Was it possible that even transgendered people, by the year 2000, had finally begun to be recognized not as "gross," as Germaine Greer had once so compassionately called us, but as humans with a unique tragedy, deserving of kindness?

Was it, even, not such a big deal? Was my friend Zero's initial reaction—"Well, you live long enough, you see just about everything"—or my sister-in-law, Katie's—"Oh I'm so glad it's only that you're a woman. I was afraid it was something serious"—really so atypical? As Russo was to ask, sometime later, "What makes imagining the worst so easy? Is it really so much more plausible? Or, frightened children that we are, do we imagine the worst as a kind of totemic magic, in hopes of fending it off in reality?"

There were plenty of people, nonetheless, who found the news of my transition bewildering, or impossible, or too strange to bear. I tried as best I could to be sympathetic; people know so little about this condition that they can scarcely be blamed for believing things about it that are fundamentally untrue. It is an unfortunate fact that transgendered people generally have to take responsibility for educating the people around them about their nature, in a way that is unnecessary for most people who emerge as gay or lesbian, or, say, Flemish. And so it fell to me to be patient, to respond to the wide variety of perplexed responses with patience, even when people said things to me like *You ask me? When you were a child you must have been mole-assed.*

There was one reaction I had no response for, though, and it was the one belonging to my sister.

It would have been better, she suggested, *if you had died.*

She didn't mean this figuratively, either. In years to come, she would proceed on in the world as if a rock had fallen on my head from a great height or as if I had plunged, like Amelia Earhart, into the sea.

In the future, Lydia said plaintively, she would be grateful if there would be no more contact between her children and mine, or between herself and Grace.

When she came home to visit my mother, she preferred that my name not be spoken aloud.

Books that I had written had to be taken off the shelf during her visits. My photographs had to be hidden away, removed from the walls and stuffed into drawers.

In some ways, her reaction was not all that different from the one she'd had when our father had driven us over to the Coffin House for the first time, the voices on the radio singing, *Shadow of a shade!* and we looked up, the three of us, at our brand-new haunted mansion.

No. Wait, she'd said. *You're kidding.*

And so, after all these years, when I entered the doors of the Coffin House, it was I who had become, at long last, a ghost, and she a ghost to me.

I knew full well that in asking for her love, I was asking for no small thing. It's inevitable, perhaps, that she'd be unable to see my emergence as the gift of a sister, and instead only see it as the loss of a brother, someone she had loved so dearly. That's her right, of course; there is surely no law that says everyone has to learn about the brain structure of transsexuals, or be comfortable with gender variance, or accept that people can go through tremendous changes even in the middle of their lives.

But being transformed into a corpse struck me as excessive.

My mother and I both hoped that time would soften my sister's stance toward me, but two years went by, then three, then seven. Once her decision was made, she never spoke to me again. She has still, as of this writing, never looked upon my face.

I don't know. Maybe harsh judgment is what I deserved—for being a source of shame, for being so *mental*, for destabilizing the sweet new world she had invented for herself in Loch Ness. Maybe, above all, she resented the fact that I'd never come to her, in all those years and years, with the sorrow that was in my heart; for hiding myself so completely from the one person, other than my parents, who had loved me longer than anyone. And so, instead of protecting her, I'd instead returned her to the day in her late childhood when she'd run down a country road holding a currycomb, rendered mute by the cruelty of the world, and all its random injustice.

From time to time I would think of the time I had gone down to the apartment on Jane Street and found my sister in tears. *Oh, I hurt*, she'd said. *I hurt.*

It's okay, Liddie, I'd said. *You won't always hurt.*

But I hurt now.

I held her in my arms. *I know it.*

Wendy drove west along the Schuylkill Expressway. "What do you do for a living, Wendy?" I asked. "Besides hunt ghosts, I mean?"

"Me?" She laughed. "I work in the lingerie department at Strawbridge's."

"Really?" I said. "Have you been doing that a long time?"

"Oh, forever," she said. "Sometimes I think if I see another panty table I'll scream."

"Is that good work?" I asked.

"Oh sure," said Wendy. "Nice people. Except if someone comes in sweaty, oh I hate that. Somebody wants you to do a bra fitting and they've just come from the gym? I think that's rude."

We drove through Delaware County. "Wendy?" I asked in a wistful voice. "What do you think ghosts are, anyway?"

"Well, there's five different kinds of ghosts," said Wendy. "And each is something different."

I sighed. "What are the five kinds?" I asked, although it wasn't this that I wanted to know.

"Well, first off, you have your intelligent spirits. Those are the most interesting ones to encounter, I think, because they can teach us things. Then you have your residual spirits, or repeaters. They just keep doing the same thing over and over again. Then there's poltergeists. The best way to tell a poltergeist is if you can hear them."

"I thought poltergeists were mischievous," I said. "That they were known for causing trouble."

"Some are like that. Others just want to stomp around."

"Are there others?"

"Oh, well there's a new class of spirit. They just added it. Shadow people."

"Shadow people," I said.

"Actually, there are three different kinds of shadow people. Class A is a full figure. Class B is fuzzy. And Class C is just globules."

I nodded. This was probably the kind of ghost I was to Lydia now, a shadow person. Somewhere between full figure and fuzzy.

"Okay," I said. "And the fifth kind of ghost?"

It took her a moment to remember the fifth type. "Malevolent," she said.

"Malevolent," I said. "Those sound like good ones to avoid."

"If you can," she said wistfully. "But you don't always get the choice in life, to meet the ghosts you want."

We drove on without speaking for a while.

"What do you think they want from us—the undead?"

"Want?" she said.

"Yeah. I mean, are they trying to scare us? Or do they want to give us a message? Or are they just some reflection?"

Wendy shrugged. "What does *anybody* want, Jenny?" she said. "To be loved."

I thought about this. "Seriously?" I said.

"Sure. Why should that change, just because you're dead?"

We passed another sign for Hersheypark and Pennsylvania Dutch Wonderland. I remembered going to Chocolate World in Hershey with the guys in the weeks before my sister's wedding. *Totally excellent version of the peanut vendor song, man.* It had been almost thirty years since I'd seen some of those boys.

"Sorry," I sniffed, as the tears rolled down my cheek. Wendy handed me a Kleenex.

"It's okay, Jenny. It's upsetting, sometimes," she said. "Trying to make your peace with the dead."

I laughed. "It's not the dead that haunt me. I'm fine with the dead. It's the living I can't make peace with."

Wendy sighed. "You said it."

"Hey," I said, as we passed the King of Prussia Mall. "There's a Strawbridge's. We could pull over and have a busman's holiday. Go buy some lingerie. Get a bra fitting."

Wendy looked me up and down. "I could tell you what size you are without a tape measure," she said.

"Really?"

"Thirty-six C," she said. "Am I right?"

"Yes," I said, a little embarrassed.

"You work in a lingerie department long enough," she said, "you get a kind of sixth sense."

As we drove toward home, I thought again of Leonard, his Radiot, and of our two lost sisters.

Maybe, I thought, Leonard and I weren't so different after all. What was it he'd wanted people to know about him? That in spite of it all, he wasn't really a bad person?

I don't mean this *me,* he'd said. *I mean that* other *me. The one* beyond.

Reunion

In June 2006, I parked my mother's car in front of the Haverford School. A sign read WELCOME ALUMNI CLASS OF 1976—30TH REUNION. I wondered whether it was worth pointing out to someone that some of the *alumni* were now *alumnae*. Since I'd been a student there, they'd built something called the Walk of Virtues. Chiseled into a set of marble arches were the words: RESPECT. HUMILITY. JUSTICE. And so on.

The old quad was filled with guys just shy of fifty, wearing Dockers and plaid pants and tasseled loafers.

"Dude," said a guy with long hair, a beard, and a baseball cap, coming up to me with a cockeyed smile. Then he looked a little self-conscious. "I mean—uh—"

"Doober?" I said. He nodded.

"How've you been?" I said. Doober was drinking a gin and tonic, looking on at our classmates.

"I was kind of hoping this place was some hallucination. But—*denied*!"

"Where do you live now?" I said. Last I'd heard, he'd been out west on a dude ranch.

"Oregon," he said. "Me and my wife, and our daughter."

"You have a daughter?" I said. His eyes twinkled with pride.

"Yeah," he said. "Named her Sparkle."

I nodded. I'd heard worse names than Sparkle. "So," I said. "Guess you heard about the sex change."

He nodded. "Out of control," he noted.

A few years before this, I'd called the school and suggested they might want to remove me from its alumni rolls. The very nice woman who took the call asked why, and I'd replied, "Well, I'm transgendered and everything. I'm assuming the school doesn't want me stinking up the house?"

She didn't miss a beat. "Why, Jennifer Boylan," she said. "What makes you think you're the only transgendered alumna?"

I paused. "There are others?"

"Yes," she said thoughtfully. "Since 1960, I think there have been three."

Doing the math in my head quickly, that came out to something close to one in every five hundred boys graduating had emerged as transgendered. Which, according to at least one set of statistics I'd read, wasn't so far off the national average.

"Well," I said self-consciously. "If you all don't mind having me around. It'd be kind of nice, to stay in touch with everybody."

"Oh, I'm so glad," the woman said. "Believe me, Jenny. We've seen worse things than you."

After a little while Doober and I sneaked away from the Class of 1976 cash bar and walked through the hallways of the Upper School, gin and tonics in hand. The place was eerily unchanged, the old corridors still filled with the smell of pencil shavings and sweat, the eagle on the top of the American flag in Chopper's classroom still covered with the same old dust. We peeked into the empty cafeteria, looked out the windows of the old study hall. I remembered throwing a paper airplane out of one of the study hall's high windows one spring afternoon, and watching that airplane sail forever on an invisible updraft.

On a wall near the headmaster's office was an oil painting of my former nemesis, the lame Mr. Flinch, who'd been dead for nearly twenty years.

"You know, he was right about me," I said. "I *didn't* have any gumption."

"Yeah, well," said Doober. "Fuck him. You got plenty a gumption. You ask me, you're the fuckin gumption *poster* child. What the fuck does he know about it? Nothing."

We walked down the hallway of the Upper School. It was odd to be walking around there with a gin and tonic and a vagina. There was a time I could have gotten detention for this.

"This is all like some crazy dream," I said. "I keep thinking I'm going to wake up."

"It was like some dream the *first* time," Doober noted. "You know what they say. About how history repeats itself? First time as tragedy, second time as some big ol' pile of *bull*shit."

We paused before the doorway of the biology lab. Once, there'd been giant slide rules on the wall, a tattered chart of the periodic table. We'd all had to write reports about the elements, back in the day. Me, I wound up with mercury.

"I guess I owe you an apology," I said.

"You don't owe me nothing."

"No, I do. That last time we talked? The summer my sister was getting married. I'm sorry if I was mean. You know. About your glue."

Doober looked dumbfounded. "Glue?" he said, flabbergasted. "What are you *talking* about?"

"You said you wanted to sell me some—what did you call it—? Vita-Meata-Vegamin?"

"What?" he said. "You mean like, from the *Lucy* show?"

I felt my cheeks redden. "That was what you called it. You said you had some—"

My old friend shook his head, worried for my sanity. "That never happened," he said.

I pictured myself lying on my back in my old bedroom, talking to Doober on the phone as the thunderstorm approached. Sausage gave me that look.

"Well," I said. "Just because it never happened, doesn't mean I can't remember it."

"You know what would be excellent," said Doober. "If you could find your kid self, and like, tie him up, have some sick conversation."

"What would you tell your kid self?" I asked him.

"Me?" said Doober. "I wouldn't tell him anything. What the fuck do I know?"

"You wouldn't warn yourself about the future?"

Doober looked confused. "*Warn* myself?" he said. "About what?"

It was possible, I thought, that Doober and I had two entirely different conceptions of time.

I looked down the hallway, imagined the bell ringing, all the schoolboys pouring out of their classrooms, thundering toward their lockers. Nixon was president again. There I was, last out of English class, already late for whatever came next. *Hey kid. Wait a second. I have to tell you something.*

Young James paused for a moment. He thought he'd heard something, but he wasn't sure what. The startled, willowy creature looked over in our direction, with his television-tube glasses, and his long hair, and his tie.

But there was no one there.

"Looocy," said Doober somberly. "You got some 'splainin' to do."

"Can I ask you a question?" I said. "Seriously?"

He shrugged. It was all the same to him whether I asked him a question or not.

"Do you believe in ghosts?"

He nodded. "I do," he said, but now he was speaking in the voice of the Cowardly Lion. "I do, I do, I do believe in spooks. I do."

I bypassed the ensuing all-school banquet and met some women friends for a late dinner at a place in Bryn Mawr. Unlike me, they'd gone to our sister school. Moments after my arrival, a beautiful, elegant woman put her arm around me.

"I'm sorry—" I said, lamely. I couldn't remember having known anyone this fabulous.

"Jenny—" she said. "It's me. Sarah Towers?"

Sarah's features morphed into those of the girl I had known. We sat and talked and drank glasses of pinot grigio. All the women wanted to know about my children, about Grace. It was very powerful, being welcomed into their circle.

"You know, you began it," said Sarah, over dessert.

"What?"

"My long history of getting dumped."

"I'm sorry," I said. "I never meant to—" I was stunned to find my throat closing up over an injustice I had committed over thirty years ago. "I'm sorry if I hurt you," I said, and the tears rolled down. Jeez, I thought. Here we go again with the waterworks.

To make the situation even more pathetic, Sarah's eyes brimmed over at this same moment. "It's okay, Jenny," she said. "I think there are some things I understand now."

"Still," I said. "It was fun, wasn't it? Remember that party at the Wedgwoods'? Sitting out in that field?"

"You showed me the Northern Crown," she said. "The constellation."

"I can't believe you remember that."

"I remember lots of stuff," she said. "Mostly I remember how much fun we had. What did we have—a month together, maybe two? But it was sweet. I feel so lucky we had that."

"I feel lucky, too," I said. Everyone looked over as Sarah and I, two middle-aged women, held hands at the table and wept like idiots.

"You know what else I remember?" said Sarah. "Rolling around on your bedroom floor. And that sandwich you made me, with the Velveeta."

"When I was young," I said wistfully, "I was good with cheese."

"Oh Jenny," said Sarah Towers. "I'm sure you're still good with cheese."

I blushed. It was a nice thing for her to say.

Sarah looked thoughtful. "Hey, can I ask you a question? Did you ever get a weird feeling in that house?"

"A weird feeling?"

"Yeah. I know I used to, sometimes."

I nodded. "Yeah," I said. "Sometimes I felt that, too."

Later I talked to another old friend from Shipley, Tori d'Angelo, who turned out to be married to Chuck Yeager, the famous test pilot. He was in his eighties. Apparently Tori and General Yeager had been in the news recently. Lots of people had an opinion about their marriage. I knew what that was like. There were those who had an opinion about mine as well.

"As if it's any of their business," said Tori. "As if anybody who's not in the couple has any right to pass judgment."

"You know what I'm trying to imagine," I said to Tori. "What it must be like, to be Mrs. Chuck Yeager. I mean, when the two of you are out driving together, do you go, like, Honey, slow down! You're doing Mach Three, and it's a Mach Two zone!" Then I imitated Chuck Yeager's face and cheeks being distorted by the incredible G-forces. "Honey!" I said, in my best Chuck Yeager voice. "I'm only going Mach Two and a half! It's like, every time we're in the experimental test rocket, all you do is nag, nag, nag!"

I laughed, unable to believe how funny I was. Sarah looked at me thoughtfully.

"What?" I said.

"Do you think you'd have your same sense of humor, if you'd been a woman from the start?"

I shrugged. "I don't know. Maybe not. Maybe the humor is what I needed to survive."

"I didn't think she was all that funny before," said Tori a little self-consciously. "Actually. When you were a boy? Your jokes always seemed so panicked, or something."

"Maybe," said Sarah, "*this* is your original sense of humor? And what you had before was the replica?"

I knew what she was getting at, but it made my head hurt. It reminded me of something James Thurber once said at a party, in Paris, when a woman told him how much funnier his work was in

French. "I know," said Thurber. "It does tend to lose something in the original."

I got back to the Coffin House late that night, parked the car in the driveway, and walked quietly through the back door. I turned off the light switch, the same one that had fried me with blue electricity back in 1972. My mother was spending the night with a friend down at the Jersey Shore, so for the first time in years, the old house was all mine. It rang with the silence of late night.

I walked, half lost in thought, from room to room, thinking about the faces I had seen that evening, all those old friends changed by time. It was nice to have seen them all at last without disguise.

I went into the living room. There was the old piano, my father's chair next to it. There was still a barely visible stain on the top of it, from his Vitalis.

My sister had visited my mother just the week before, so all the photographs of me in the living room had been removed and stuffed into hidey-holes. Mom hadn't had time to bring me back out of storage yet.

I let my hands fall upon the keys of the old piano.

Good-bye to this house and all its memories
Little sister remember try to look ahead

I'd arrived for the reunion in advance of my family, but the next day, I was joined in the Coffin House by Grace and our children, who'd driven down from Maine with the dog, Ranger, a one-year-old black Labrador. The boys spent much of the day running around the yard with Ranger or playing a game with the neighbors called Sardines, which is kind of like hide-and-seek in reverse. They ran up and down the creaking stairs, swam with the dog in their grandmother's pool, lay on the floor of what had once been my sister's bedroom watching SpongeBob on television. My mother spent a lot of time sitting in her rocking chair, watching her grandchildren chase each other around.

We'd brought down lobsters and corn from Maine, and we had a big feast out on my mother's deck, rolling our corn in the butter dish. Mom and Grace and I drank our white wine and watched the twilight advance.

"I call it the happy house," my mother said, with a contented sigh.

"You should know you don't have to live here forever, though," said Grace. "It's a big house for one woman to run all by herself. If you ever want someplace a little more manageable, all you have to do is say so, and Jenny and I will help you."

"I think about that sometimes," my mother said wistfully. "But then I just put it out of my mind."

From inside the house we could hear the voices of children.

That night, I got into bed and turned on the television. From the screen came the sound of people screaming. The members of the press had been warned not to use their flashbulbs on King Kong, but they didn't listen. He'd yanked on his chains, tore them right out of the wall. Now he was running amok. I shook my head. Always the same story.

"What's going on?" said my son Luke, rushing into the room.

"It's *King Kong*," I said.

"Wow," said Luke. "It's some really old version."

"It's the original," I said haughtily.

"Boy," said Luke. "Does that look fake."

Paddy and Ranger rushed into the room and climbed up on the bed. "Look," said Luke. "It's King Kong. Climbing the Empire State Building."

"Boys," said Grace, out in the hallway. "It's time to brush your teeth."

"Grace," I said. She leaned her head in the door, and there we were, the two boys and dog and me, watching TV. She sighed. "What's this?"

"*King Kong*," I said.

They were after him with the biplanes now.

"Poor monkey," I said.

"Poor monkey?" said Grace, climbing into bed next to me. "Poor *Fay Wray*, you mean. She's the one I feel sorry for."

"I feel sorry for everybody," I said.

"Ssshh," said the boys.

We sat there, the four of us, under the covers, watching the end of the movie. The dog lay happily on his side. My boys looked sleepy, too, their eyelids slowly drooping.

Well, the airplanes got him, said a member of the press.

No, it wasn't the planes. It was beauty killed the beast.

Grace started in on the *New York Times* crossword puzzle. The boys stared at the television a little longer, but they fell asleep pretty soon. I lay propped up on pillows in my adolescent bedroom and looked at the old familiar walls.

Through the open window came the distant sound of a freight train passing through my hometown.

"Jenny," Grace said softly.

I turned toward her. There she was, the woman with whom I'd first slept in this room twenty years before. I remembered waking up in this room on Christmas morning after we got engaged, the point of her diamond ring stabbing me in the chest.

"What?" I said.

She looked at me, at the boys asleep on our knees, at the dog barking softly in his Labrador dreams. There we were in a big dog pile.

"Jennifer Finney Boylan," she whispered. "We are the luckiest people in the world."

Maybe, I thought, it was a moment such as this that Paddy had in mind, when he advocated the virtues of super-stickiness.

The next day, we took the boys to the National Constitution Center in Philadelphia, while Ranger stayed back at the Coffin House with my mother. We all sat there in the amphitheater getting all teary-eyed about the Interstate Commerce Act. Afterward, we went to the cafeteria, where Luke ate pizza and Paddy slurped a bowl of spaghetti.

Paddy had just completed a report on the Statue of Liberty that spring, and as we ate our lunch, he provided us with some little-known facts about it.

"The Statue of Liberty," Patrick said quietly, "is made of green cheese."

"Really?" said his brother.

"No," said Patrick. "Not really."

"Who gave the statue to us?" Grace asked.

"Czechoslovakia," said Patrick. "We traded it for a cow and some magic beans."

"Really?" said his brother.

"No," said Patrick. "Not really."

"Excuse me," said a woman in a floppy hat. "Are you Jenny Boylan?"

"Yes," I said. We all looked up, embarrassed.

"I saw you on television. Is this your family?"

"This is us."

She looked at my children suspiciously, searching for signs of derangement. Patrick and Luke, on cue, distorted their faces so that they looked like zombies.

"What brings you all to Philadelphia?"

"I'm *from* here."

"The Statue of Liberty," said Patrick, "is equipped with rockets at the bottom. So if it is ever attacked, the whole thing can launch into space."

The woman with the hat looked surprised. "Really?" she said.

Grace smiled proudly. "You hang around our family," she said. "You learn all kinds of stuff."

That night, after the boys were in bed, I climbed the stairs to the third floor to check on them. As I listened to their sleeping breath from the dark doorway of the Brown Study, I wondered if Dorothy Cummin's mother had stood here almost a hundred years ago, watching her child.

I looked around the other rooms on the third floor, the doors all closed now—my own old bedroom and the Haunted Room and the Gammie Room. The door to the Monkey Bathroom stood half open, and the full-length mirror on the door reflected the dim light of the house.

I walked with my wineglass into the Gammie Room, where my sister now slept when she came over from Scotland, and stood by the door for a moment. On one wall was a drawing of Matt the Mutt. A string of pearls hung down over the mirror. A bookcase was full of her books; her hairbrush rested on the bureau. The room was so full of her spirit that I felt I could almost touch her. My heart ached for the sister I had lost.

My mother had told me to be patient, so I tried to be patient. I would wait for her, for as long as it might take. If the message I wanted to send my sister, using Leonard's Radiot, was that I was not really a bad person, then the opposite might be true as well. Maybe someday she would put her living hand in my mummified one, and then I would know her fully, even as I am fully known.

It was something to hope for, anyhow.

I reached out to put my glass of wine down on her bureau. The stem of the glass caught against the side of a knob on a drawer, though, and the glass fell out of my hand and shattered on the floor.

I stood there, looking at the mess I'd made, the shards of glass in every direction. Then I walked across the hall to the Haunted Room, where there was a broom and dustpan in the closet. I walked back to my sister's room and began to sweep up the glass. There seemed like a lot of it.

And then electricity sizzled on the back of my neck. It had been a long time since I'd felt it in this house, but sure. It was still familiar.

I looked up, and *there she was*, just as in days long past. Floating in the mirror was the translucent old woman in the white clothes. I hadn't seen her reflected there for years and years, but here she was once more, looking at me with that surprised expression I remembered from my childhood. *Why, Jenny Boylan. What are you doing here?*

Except that, as I stared at her, I realized that it was no ghost. After all this time, I was only looking at my own reflection.

Against all odds, I had become solid.

Was it possible, I thought, as I looked at the woman in the mirror, that it was some future version of myself I'd seen here when I was a child? From the very beginning, had I only been haunting *myself*?

It sounds like something I would do.

It was Scrooge, of course, who looked at Marley's ghost and declared that there was "more gravy than grave" about him. As for me, I have begun to suspect that far more hearts are haunted than houses.

Maybe you don't really even need an electromagnetic field recorder, or a thermal scanner, or a voice-activated tape recorder to investigate the paranormal. You only need a mirror.

I looked at the reflection before me of the middle-aged woman with the long hair, the white nightgown. *What?* I asked her. *What do you want?*

She smiled, and it occurred to me that at long last I understood what the woman in the mirror had been trying to tell me all along.

Don't be afraid, Jenny, she said. *It's only me.*

"Oh look," said Babs Hunt, standing in the third-floor hallway. "It's Jesus's bathroom!"

Our family had always maintained contact with the Hunts, who had lived in the Coffin House before us. The weekend of my reunion, I'd invited Babs, the daughter of the Hunt clan, to come over and have a look at the place where she'd grown up. It was a Sunday morning, and my mother was at church. Babs is about ten years older than I, a ruddy-faced woman with laughing eyes. She'd told me that she hadn't seen any ghosts here, but it was hard to take her at her word. Every room seemed to hold another story for her, another vision of something that was no longer there. The most deeply moving moment had been when we walked into the basement, and she pointed to a nook behind the stairs.

"There," she'd said. "That's where I would hide, during hide-and-seek. Right there."

I had never even thought about the space behind the basement stairs, but then I'd never been a six-year-old girl here, either. I looked at the dark, dusty place and imagined Babs hiding there, fifty years ago. For a moment I saw them—Babs, and her brothers St. George and Bill and Al. Al Hunt, who was called "Hoops," had gone on to become the

Washington editor of the *Wall Street Journal*. I could hear the laughter of the Hunt children as they ran through the house. St. George, the youngest, slowly counted up to ten. *Olly olly oxen free*.

I'd interviewed all four Hunt children when I started writing this book, and the variety of their experiences, growing up in the Coffin House, was astonishing. Al Hunt, the journalist, said he'd never felt anything untoward about the place. "That was totally off my radar," he said. The middle son, Bill—the boy whose laboratory had been down in the basement—was now a doctor out in Pennsylvania Dutch country. He hadn't seen any ghosts, either, although he had plenty of stories, one of which completely changed one of the tales I'd told in *She's Not There*. (I'd written about the night a drunken Vietnam vet in a Santa Claus suit showed up one Christmas; after all these years, Bill Hunt was now ready to admit that the Santa had been himself, and that his whole family at that moment had been in a car parked out in the driveway. He'd come up with this ruse just so he could find out what the hell we'd done to their house, a curiosity I find completely understandable.)

As for St. George, he was a veterinarian now, and he said he'd seen *plenty* of specters over the years, especially in the haunted closet of the Brown Study.

"One time," he explained, "those ghosts convinced me to jump out the window while I was asleep. My father came upstairs to find me with one leg out the window."

Would he spend a single night alone in the house now? I asked. Now that he was all grown up?

"Not for a million dollars," he replied, a little embarrassed. "Not for any price."

Babs Hunt and I walked into the Monkey Bathroom. "Oh my goodness," she said. "It's Jesus's window." She showed me the window that overlooked the front yard, the same yard where first Babs and later Lydia had their wedding receptions. "This is where Jesus used to sit and look out at the world, a world he knew he could never be a part of."

I'd stood at this same window myself when I was a teenager, wearing my hippie skirt, staring down at the front lawn.

"Why was the monkey named Jesus?"

"Because," said Babs, "people used to open the door and see him swinging around the shower curtain. And yell, 'Jesus!' "

I nodded.

"Poor little Jesus," said Babs wistfully. She pointed to the basin. "And look, here's the sink where Jesus had his baby."

"He had a baby? Your monkey?"

"Poor little Jesus," said Babs. "She wasn't much of a father."

There were no good words in the language to respond to this sentence.

"What happened to Jesus's baby?" I asked. "Did he raise his monkey baby?"

Babs sighed. "The baby didn't make it."

"Man," I said. "Jesus really had it rough, didn't he?"

"About the only time Jesus ever had any fun," said Babs, "was when we let him out of the bathroom on his birthday. Made him banana cream pie."

"Really?" I said. "What day was Jesus's birthday?"

Babs looked at me as if I'd asked her a question for which she'd long been prepared.

"Why, Jenny," she said. "Christmas, of course."

Adagio

Forced into the position of having to kiss Lois Lane beneath the mistletoe at a Daily Planet *Christmas party in 1963, Clark Kent mischievously decides to shock the daylights out of Lois by giving her a super-kiss, in the manner of Superman, instead of the mild-mannered kiss she would be likely to expect from Clark Kent. Indeed, when Kent finally releases Lois from his embrace . . . , Lois is glassy-eyed and on the verge of swooning.*

"Holy Toledo, Clark," exclaims someone at the party, "—where'd you learn to kiss like that?"

"Yes," stammers Lois, plainly impressed, "for a while I thought you were—er—someone else! Where'd you pick up this technique?"

"Maybe it's sort of a hidden talent!" replies Kent. "After all, you don't know everything about me!"

—The Superman Encyclopedia

The night was over at the Astrid Hotel. Big Head Chester and Nick were loading the amplifiers into the truck; Erica was gently lowering her cymbals into their cases. Out in the ballroom, the bouncer swept the floor. A waitress wiped down the counters with a rag.

Near the front of the room was a table with two empty chairs. On top was a pair of empty glasses. There were prunes in them.

I joined Shell over at the bar, where she was counting out the money. It had been a good night for Blue Stranger, my mano-a-girlo with Brandy notwithstanding.

"Hey," she said, handing me eighty-five dollars. "Here's your cut."

"Thanks," I said, and took the cash. "Tonight was fun."

"I guess." From the parking lot came the sounds of people shouting. Shell rolled her eyes and sighed.

"You getting tired of this scene?" I asked. It wasn't exactly a wild guess.

Shell looked tired. "What I get tired of, is this. The takedown. If I could just teleport from the bar back to my bed at super-speed, that'd be perfect."

I sipped my Diet Coke. "My son says that super-strength slows down super-speed."

Shell blinked. "What?"

"Super-strength. Your muscles make you less aerodynamic, or something."

"Well, I'm no expert," she said. "But I think that's why they call it *super*-speed. When you're that fast, the aerodynamics don't matter."

"My point exactly," I said. "But try explaining that to a ten-year-old."

Shell smiled. Her sons were grown—one in college, the other in the Air Force.

"Try explaining it to any guy," said Shell.

"Still," I said wistfully. "It'd be nice to have superpowers, wouldn't it?"

Shell looked at me and raised an eyebrow. "Jenny?" she said. "In case you didn't know it, you already *have* superpowers."

"You think?"

"What was the deal with you tonight? You and Brandy?"

I felt the blood rushing to my face. "You *know* about that?" I said.

"Jenny," she said. "Everyone knows about that." She grinned happily. "I tell you what: this evening I think you had the power of super-skankiness."

"I don't know," I said. "I can't explain it."

"See, that's the thing, Jenny," she said. "You have superpowers, and you don't even know what they are."

"I don't have superpowers," I said, with a bitterness that surprised me. "Believe me."

Shell just shook her head. "You don't even know," she said. "That's the amazing thing. It's like you just landed here from Krypton, and you think everybody's just like you, with your super-smell and your X-ray vision."

A car pulled into the Astrid's lot. Police beacons flashed through the window.

"Uh-oh," I said.

"What's happening?" Shell called out to the waitress.

"Fight in the parking lot," she said.

"Who's fighting?"

"A bunch of drunks," said the waitress.

I sat back down. "Why does everybody always have to murder each other?" I said. "It seems like that's all anybody does, is sob their fucking eyes out."

We sat there for a while sipping our drinks. The waitress looked out the window a little longer, then went back to wiping the counters, stacking the chairs on top of the tables.

"Hey," said Shell. "Are you all right? Seriously?"

"Of course I'm all right. Why wouldn't I be all right?"

"When I came upstairs before. When you said you'd seen that girl. I've never seen you look like that before."

"Like what?"

Shell didn't blink. "Like you were going to jump out the window."

I opened my mouth, then shut it. I sipped some Diet Coke. The red beacon of the cop car was still flashing outside.

"I'm not going to jump out any window," I said.

"Promise?"

"Please. Shelly. It's me."

"I know who it is."

We sat at the bar in silence. The bartender was washing glasses in the sink.

"I was just thinking about my family up there. There's something about this place that reminds me of the house I grew up in."

Shell took this in. Then she began again, in a different place. "You ever regret it?"

"Regret what?"

"You know, the whole switcheroo."

I smiled. "Are you kidding?" I said.

"You ever want to go back?"

"I don't *think* so."

"So why the long face?"

"What long face?"

Shell looked thoughtful. "I don't know, Jenny. About ninety percent of the time, you seem like the happiest person I know. And then, every once in a while, I'll catch you looking out a window like that. I don't get it. How come you're so sad, if you're happy?"

I shrugged. "Happy, sad," I said. "Same thing."

"I'm serious."

"I don't know, Shell," I said. I mulled it over. "I get tired sometimes, of being different."

Shell nodded. A fat tear welled up and spilled over my eyelashes. Fuck, I thought. Here we go again.

"Sorry," I said.

"It's all right, Jenny," she said.

I wiped my eyes. "It's like, I went through this whole amazing change, and at last I feel content, at last I feel whole. But what about that kid I used to be? What about all those memories? That's the one thing they can't give you in surgery: a new history."

Shell rubbed my shoulder again. "Maybe that's your superpower," she said.

"What, super–self pity? Super-narcissism?"

"Super-gender," she said. "Super-memory."

I shook my head. Another big tear dripped down my face. "Super-memory slows down your super-gender."

Shell rolled her eyes. "Poor you," she said.

"Poor you?" I said. "That's what you have for me, is *poor you?*"

"Sorry. But honestly. You know how many people wish they could see the world the way you see it? I mean, that's the thing about you, Jenny. It's like you have this gift. I'd love to be a man sometimes, to see what it would be like. So forgive me if I can't feel too sorry for you when you start complaining about your X-ray vision."

"You think it's fun, looking through walls?" I said. "Seeing through clothes? Seeing everybody naked?"

Shell's husband Nick—by any measure, an extremely good-looking man—came through the door. "Good evening, ladies," he said.

Shell looked at me. "I don't know," she said. "I think it might be kind of interesting, once in a while."

I headed to the women's room one last time before embarking on the long ride home. I looked at myself in the mirror. My eyes were red.

As I exited the lavatory, I found myself back in the hotel's broken-down foyer. Before me were the long stairs leading toward the deserted upper stories. The fire door at the top was slightly ajar.

I paused, feeling a strange tingling on my skin. It was like the frisson of electricity I used to feel in the Coffin House, moments before I saw the ghost.

For a long moment I stood frozen at the bottom of the staircase, looking up into the darkness. Then, once again, I climbed the steps, one hand trailing on the banister.

Hello?

The upstairs looked the same as it had earlier—a long corridor with many doors, most of them open. I peeked into the grandest of the Astrid's old bedrooms and looked out its ornate window. I'd stood here before. Out in the cold night I saw the dark water of the river snaking southward through the Kennebec Valley.

Out in the parking lot, Shell and Nick were kissing next to the box truck that contained all our sound equipment. Their steaming breath gathered around them in clouds.

From here, it looked so simple: the world of men and women.

As I looked out on the night, I remembered Grace Finney sitting there at the foot of the South College steps, so many years ago, reading up for her exam on dialectics. *You mean, like, Scientology?*

That's Dianetics. Dialectics is the philosophy of opposites.

How do you make a philosophy out of opposites?

By paying attention, she'd said. *By finding your balance between the extremes.*

In the nearly thirty years since that first, sophomoric conversation, Grace and I had traveled a long road together. I wondered if she had any idea, back then, how much her own happiness would depend on finding peace in the gray areas between men and women.

Since she'd become a social worker she'd done a fair amount of work with a newfangled treatment called dialectical behavior therapy, in which she tried to get her clients to accept the complexity of the world, to come to terms with all of life's unsettling ambiguities.

I remembered a T-shirt I'd seen someone wearing at a conference once: THERE ARE ONLY TWO KINDS OF PEOPLE: THOSE WHO REJECT THE BINARY, AND THOSE WHO DON'T.

It was that division of experience into binaries and extremes that haunted me even now, made it so hard to connect my male history with the reality of my female present.

Interestingly, Grace had turned out to be better at integration than I was. She didn't recognize a tragic divide between her former life as Jim's wife and her present one as Jenny's partner. She didn't see herself as an Ex, had less than zero interest in that. She only saw herself as Grace.

But don't you get sad? I'd asked her. *When you see other couples embracing each other? Don't you miss what we've lost?*

Yes, she said. *I am sad sometimes. But I don't live there, in that sadness, because it would be paralyzing. Remember how I used to say that everything contains its opposite? Our history contains that other couple, that husband and wife, but it also contains us as we are now. So I'm grateful for what we have together, for all the good things in our lives. And that's where I live, and that's what I focus on.*

Why can't I learn what you've learned? I asked Grace, my desperation clearly audible. *How do I learn to connect the present and the past, to be one person instead of two?*

Explain to me how you're two people, she said.

I'm Jennifer Boylan. And I'm the Former James Boylan. I'm an X-Man!

Jenny, she said. *That's one person, not two.*

I know, I said. *But what if my heart doesn't know it?*

She sighed. *You remind me of my clients with posttraumatic stress,* she said. *The problem with posttraumatic stress is that people separate themselves from the trauma. They're haunted by it, and then they're stuck reliving it over and over again.*

Exactly.

Part of the reason people get haunted is because they can't make sense of their pasts. I think that's the deal with Lydia, actually. It's not that she'd have anything against you, if she ever actually met you. She just can't make a bridge between the person she grew up with, and the person you are now.

So what's the answer?

Well, what you do with people in therapy is try to get them to tell their stories, to weave the narrative of their lives backward and forward, with one thread that puts your experience into a context that includes a past, and a present, and a future.

I thought this over for a while.

So you're saying I should tell stories? I couldn't believe it. Maybe I might yet be saved by the transformative powers of blarney.

Yes, Jenny, said Grace. *You can do that.*

Well, I know I can tell stories, I said softly. *But sometimes I think it doesn't make any difference. Stories disappear after I tell them.*

It's not enough to tell your stories, Jenny, said Grace. *You have to listen to them, too.*

I stood in the window of an empty room of the Astrid Hotel, watching the silhouette of the embracing lovers.

All at once, I kicked the wall of the crappy old bedroom in the crappy old Astrid Hotel. *Goddammit,* I said. *Goddammit all to hell.*

I looked at the place where my shoe had dented the wainscoting.

There were lots of other scuff marks on it, even a couple of holes. Apparently, in the place where I was now, people kicked the wall all the time.

I laid myself down on the bare mattress in the bedroom. On the ceiling were brown water stains shaped like dragons. The flashers of the cop car out in the parking lot turned the ceiling red, then blue, then red again.

Softly, stealthily, a set of footsteps came down the hall and paused outside my room. My heart began to pound.

I looked toward the empty corridor.

"Hello?" I said. "Is anybody there?"

I was behind the wheel of a minivan filled with sound equipment.

It was a short drive from the Astrid to the long bridge that crosses the Kennebec. To my left, I could see the lazy river, chunks of ice floating in it. In the middle of the river, every five hundred yards or so, was a tiny island of rock, a vestigial link to the log drives. Back in the day, those little islands used to help break up logjams when the river was filled with timber.

That last log drive on the Kennebec was 1976, the same year I graduated high school and headed off to Wesleyan University, with its bell tower and its bats.

I turned on Maine Public Radio. They were playing the third movement of Beethoven's Ninth, the "Adagio molto e cantabile."

To my right were the furious, icy waters of Carrabec Falls. An iron railroad bridge was suspended over the water.

Above the railroad bridge was a sky filled with stars. I remembered Eamon O'Flynn as I picked out the constellations: the Archer, the Scorpion.

If I'd considered it, this alone should have been enough to tip me off that something was afoot, since of course Sagittarius and Scorpio are summer constellations, visible only during July and August, and here they were visible in January. But at the time I didn't give this much thought. I just assumed that, once again, I had somehow gotten lucky with the heavens.

When I reached the far side of the river, I paused for a moment. I looked at the clock on the dashboard. It was two-thirty in the morning.

Then I turned the car north, toward the waterfall.

Hey Professor. Now what?

I turned off the main highway and followed a dirt road, covered with snow, into the woods. There were no other tire tracks on it.

Fresh snow clung to the pines. Two stone columns stood on either side of the road. On one was posted the sign: NO TRESPASSING. AUTHORIZED PERSONNEL ONLY.

I'm not trespassing, I thought. I'm just trying to learn something.

A crazy hydroelectric plant occupied the near bank of the Kennebec. As I pulled into the empty parking lot, I saw a few spotlights trained on its oddly shaped structures—a set of turbines, an iron scaffolding covered with snow. The iron bridge I'd seen from the road was suspended above the falls. It looked a lot more rickety up close.

I turned off my engine and heard the roar of the waterfall. The sound was shocking, as loud as an airplane taking off. I zipped up my coat, put my gloves on. I didn't remember it being this cold back at the hotel.

Then I headed through the dark woods toward the river. It was a longer walk than I expected.

I've never seen you look like that before, Shell had said.

Like what?

Like you were going to jump out the window.

I'm not going to jump out any window.

I walked out onto the bridge. The mist from the falls hung in the air. My lungs filled with oxygen, with the piercing smell of cold water and pine pitch.

Suddenly, my foot sank deep into the bridge's rotted timbers. I grabbed on to one of the iron support columns at my side, and pulled my foot back up. I heard the rushing waters below.

The moon came out from behind a small cloud, bathing all that snow with soft luminescence. I could see other holes in the bridge now as well. Some of them went all the way through.

I took a few more steps to the midpoint of the river and paused there, looking down at the Kennebec. The water rushed along in a wild flume. I wondered how the log drivers, back in the day, got the logs over the falls. I imagined those men standing midriver, spearing the logs with their medieval-looking peavies and cant hooks.

On the hill just beyond the far bank, I could see the roof of the Astrid Hotel, still illuminated by floodlights. I imagined its ghost walking down the hallway where I'd stood earlier, one hand trailing along the banister as she went downstairs and then across the wide front porch.

I wondered what made her think her family might be here, in this drifting cloud of mist. My own family was many miles from here, back in our home, asleep in their warm beds.

I took another step toward the edge. The rotted old timbers groaned again. Beneath my feet the boards bent and warped, like wet balsa. If she jumped up and down a couple times, a person could probably go right through, if she wanted.

My footprints led from the middle of the bridge, back through the woods toward the parking lot.

Was he in Sherlock Holmes, the fellow whose
Tracks pointed back, when he reversed his shoes?

I looked down at the rocks in the falls again, and wondered upon which one of these that girl was found. Upon which one would they find me, if it turned out that my fate, in the end, was no different from hers?

Dim lights flickered on the near shore. There was the sound of many pairs of boots scraping against frozen mud.

I squinted into the night and took a step back. My foot sank into, but did not punch through, the rotted boards.

They came forward in a long line, one after the other. Gammie and

Hilda Watson were first. They didn't look like cadavers, not at first, anyhow. "You," Gammie said, pointing one long, bony finger at me.

What about me?

"You're a spoiled brat."

I nodded. She had that right.

Hilda Watson looked startled and amazed. I didn't blame her. "Whoop, whoop," she said. I was wearing her wedding ring. "Whoop?"

A young Aunt Nora was right behind Hilda. She had a kittygirl in one arm, which she was sewing with a clew of crimson thread. I hardly recognized her at first. She was wearing a kimono.

Aren't you cold in that?

"Cold?" She hardly remembered what I was talking about. "Cold?"

My uncle Sean had a jelly doughnut in each hand. There was sugar on his cheeks. "I told you now was the all-one-heart time," he said, and took a big bite out of the doughnut. Jelly squirted out one end. "Would you listen?" He looked fed up with me, with all my heartache and malarkey. "Miss College Professor. Miss Big Shot."

I'm listening, I said.

"You think?" he said, and kept on walking with his doughnut toward the far shore.

On and on they came, in a long line, crossing from one side of the bridge to the other—Faith Bartelsby, Mrs. Muhammad, even my friend John Moynihan from Wesleyan, who'd died of liver failure down in Florida. He'd always wanted to be a pirate, and now he was one, with a hook for a hand and a talking parrot.

"Ahoy matey," he said, as he passed.

"Pieces of eight," said his parrot. "Pieces of eight."

Wait, Moynihan. Don't you want that map? I pulled it out of my pocket. There was a big X in the center, surrounded by the unknown lands. *Here be dragons*.

Moynihan was shocked by my stupidity. "I don't need a map," he said.

Which was more than we could say about some people.

As he walked away from me, I heard his voice rising in the dark night. *Cause celluloid heroes never feel any pain,* he sang, *And celluloid heroes never really die.*

I watched them walk through the mist, the haunted and the dead, as I stood there midriver. I stood there for a long time. There were more of them than I'd thought.

The last man in line was eating spiced wafers, right out of the box. He was wearing his London Fog coat. Warmth radiated out of him, like a fire in a cold room.

"Jenny," he said. It was nice to hear him say my name.

Hey old man.

He looked me up and down. "You've been busy, haven't you."

I have.

"I've been busy, too." He held out the box of spiced wafers. "You want one?"

I'm good.

He raised a baton, held it in midair for a moment. "On three," he said. "One, two—"

Dad.

"The 'Adagio molto e cantabile'. First I'll give you Nine. Then I'll give you Seven." His eyes danced with wonder. He counted out the time again and waved his baton through the air.

I can't hear the music.

He looked at me with pity. "Ah," he said. "But you will."

I could tell that he wanted to say more, but he wasn't sure what would help. Even now he was shy.

"Okay." He reached forward and shook my hand awkwardly. "Well, good luck, old man," he said.

Wait. Dad. What about Lydia? What am I going to do about her?

He turned back. There was blood on his collar, as if he'd cut himself shaving. "She hurts, Jenny."

But can't you tell her I love her? Can't you do that?

He blew a smoke ring through the mist. "She knows you love her," he said.

Then he walked away again, following the others through the vapor.

As I watched him go, again I smelled the sharp scent of the river—the oxygen in my lungs, the raw pitch of pine needles.

I heard someone singing something. *If you're looking for a moral to this song, fifty million little monkeys can't be wrong.*

He wasn't much more than a boy, really. The wind blew the hem of his long black coat around. He had long blond hair, glasses shaped like television tubes.

He paused at the midpoint, and took me in. I felt embarrassed and frightened.

"What," he said.

I don't know. I'd think you'd be pretty mad at me.

"Why would I be mad at you?" he said. "I think this is great. Boy, look at you! Hot tomatoes!"

Stop that.

Between the folds of his coat I could just make out the ridiculous shirt he was wearing. It bore the image of a cartoon moose. I ACT DIFFERENT, it said. BECAUSE I AM DIFFERENT.

"It is a gift, Jenny," he said. "You, of all people, ought to know that by now."

Yeah, well. Sometimes I don't want a gift. Sometimes I want to be like everybody else.

"Well, I'm sorry about that." He shrugged. "But maybe you don't get to choose your gift. You only get to choose what to do with it."

I opened my mouth, then shut it. Stupid kid.

So you're not mad. About my doing away with you.

He laughed. "Do I look done away with to you?"

Not this second.

"Remember what he told you?"

Who?

"Chopper. When Dad got sick. You asked him if there was heaven."

Yeah. When he said he'd count my writing as sports.

"What did he tell you?"

My voice was a whisper. *He said of course there's heaven.*

The kid nodded.

You think he's right?

We looked at the river, the moon reflecting off the cold water.

Then his face beamed with his deranged, comic hopefulness. I remembered the kid's ridiculous buoyancy, his preposterous faith that somehow, in spite of everything, it would all work out. Looking at him now, in this unreal place, it occurred to me that nothing in my life so far had really proved him wrong.

"Jenny," he said. "How could there *not* be heaven?"

He turned his back and headed toward the far bank, winding his way through the freezing mist. I stood at my end of the bridge and watched him go. I could just make him out as he turned toward me one last time. He took his hands out of his pockets, and he held his open palms out to the side.

For just that moment, the halves of his long black coat fluttered in the winter wind, like wings.

"Jenny," said Shell. She was sitting by the side of the bed in the room of the Astrid Hotel. Nick was standing in the door.

"Oh," I said, sitting up. "I must have—"

"Time to go home, missy," said Nick.

I stood up. "I'm so embarrassed. I just came up here for a second, to look around. I thought I heard something."

"What was it you thought you heard?" said Nick.

We walked out into the hall. Outside, the big neon sign of the hotel clicked off.

I could hardly speak. "Some kid," I said.

An hour later, I parked the car in the garage. I decided to leave all my rock and roll gear where it was for the night. I'd unpack in the morning. Softly I crept into the house and hung up my coat. It was nearly four in the morning.

I was exhausted, but I didn't feel like going to bed. So I got a glass of milk out of the refrigerator, sat down in the living room, and drank it. There were embers in the fireplace, evidence that Grace, as always, had kept a fire burning in my absence. I could picture her sitting on this same couch hours before, reading a book to the boys before tucking them in their beds. On the wall was a collage of photographs—of Grace and me on our wedding day, of my older son playing the tuba, my younger son scoring a goal in soccer. There was one of me as a guy in college, performing in one of Moynihan's movies, dressed up like a wandering minstrel. There was another picture from this fall, of the four of us standing in an orchard, our arms around one another.

I put the glass in the sink and turned out the lights. For a moment I paused in the doorway of Paddy's room, and looked at the chaos of it all—the LEGOs on the floor, the half-finished chess game on his desk. I could just see my son's sleeping face upon his pillow. His eyes fluttered behind his eyelids as he dreamed the dreams of boys: of soccer goals and Labradors, of the powers of time travel and super-stickiness, and of love.

I walked up the stairs and quietly put on my nightie, then slipped softly into the big bed in which Grace lay sleeping. The black Lab, Ranger, was stretched out next to her on the bed, and the dog lifted his head and groaned as I softly slid beneath the covers.

Grace opened one eye, then smiled sleepily. She reached out for me, and for a long moment we held each other, beneath the warm blankets of our bed.

"You're back," she said.

Acknowledgments

I am grateful to everyone who has helped me on my way.

To Deb Futter and Kris Dahl, who stood by me as I wrangled this story, again and again, and to Amelia Zalcman, for her legal counsel.

To Oprah Winfrey, Anna Quindlen, Janet Maslin, Katie Couric, Larry King, Susan Spencer, Jennifer Pozner, and David Brancaccio, for speaking or writing generously about my work.

To the members of Blue Stranger—Jack "Big Head" Hennessee, Erica Spaulding, and Tom and Laura "LaRoux" Hudson—who have endured bar fights, girls with navel rings, and drinks with prunes in them, all in order to protect my honor.

To my friends Kenneth Zolot, Peter Frumpkin, and Richard Russo, for their genius and humor, and to Timothy Kreider, who autographed his first book of cartoons for me with the words, "For Jenny Boylan, the first person I ever knew who published a book. That was when I realized how easy it must be."

To Will Forte, at *Saturday Night Live*, for doing me better than I do myself.

To my great teachers: Edward Albee, John Barth, Stephen Dixon, Franklin D. Reeve, Edward Hallowell, Todd Pierson, Steve Dahl, and Robert Ulysses "Chopper" Jameson; and to the great students of Colby College in Maine, whom I have *chopped*, now and again, my own self.

To the authors of the online Superman Encyclopedia, whose site, http://theages.superman.ws/Encyclopaedia, provided the epigraph for the final chapter.

To Shelly, at Batty About Ghosts; and to all the members of the Philadelphia Paranormal Investigators Society, as well as to James

Randi, of the Randi Educational Foundation, for helping me learn more about the invisible; to the members of the Hunt family—Albert, Bill, Babs, and St. George—for enduring my endless questions about the house we share.

And most of all, to my family—my mother and sister, my spouse Deirdre Grace, and my radiant sons, for their boundless love.

About the Author

Jennifer Finney Boylan is the author of ten books, including the novels *The Planets* and *Getting In*, as well as the short-story collection *Remind Me to Murder You Later*. She has published a number of young adult titles under a pseudonym. In 2003, her memoir *She's Not There* became the first best-selling work by a transgendered American and won a Lambda Literary Foundation prize. Jenny has spoken widely around the country about gender issues and writing, and has appeared frequently on television and radio programs, including *The Oprah Winfrey Show*, *Larry King Live*, CBS News' *48 Hours*, and the *Today* show. In 2007 she played herself on several episodes of ABC's *All My Children*.

She lives in rural Maine with her two sons and her spouse, Deirdre Grace. Since 1988 she has been Professor of English at Colby College, in Waterville.

Readers are invited to visit JenniferBoylan.net, which contains additional material related to this title.